Sunrise in Jerusalem

Sunrise in Jerusalem

by

JACOB TSUR

Translated from the French

by

VIOLET M. MACDONALD

South Brunswick and New York:
A. S. Barnes and Company

New York: The Herzl Press

© Plon, Paris, 1967

First American edition published 1973 by
A. S. Barnes and Company, Inc.,
Cranbury, New Jersey 08512, and
The Herzl Press

Library of Congress Catalogue Card Number: 72–9068

ISBN 0–498–01308–1

Printed in the United States of America

To the memory of my parents,
who died at daybreak

'And our eyes shall see
Thy return to Zion in Thy compassion'

Glossary

Aliya   ('the Ascent') A wave of immigration, of which the first began in 1882, the second took place in the first years of the twentieth century, up to 1914, the third (that of the author) from 1920 to 1923, the fourth from 1924 to 1926. A fifth, that of the refugees from Germany, lasted from 1935 to 1939.

Emek, the The Valley of Jezreel, a great centre of agricultural settlement in the twenties.

Haluts   (pl. *halutsim*) Pioneer immigrant intending to work on the land or as manual labourer in the towns.

Kibbutz   A collective village.

Olim   Those who came on *Aliya*, new immigrants.

Moshav   A smallholders' settlement, composed of individual farms.

Yishuv   The Jewish community of Palestine before the State.

9

Foreword to the American Edition

WHEN this book was published, first in the Hebrew original, then in its French version, some reviewers defined it as an autobiography. This was not my intention. Although it describes my childhood and youth, its purpose is to evoke the atmosphere of a long-forgotten period in Jewish life, too distant to be part of our present, too close to rank as history. It is the story of simple, long-suffering people who had the courage and the tenacity to lead a desperate struggle for survival in the midst of stormy European upheavals and to start a new life on the faraway shores of a new country.

It is the saga of a Jewish family like so many others, trapped in Tsarist Russia at the beginning of the century, caught up in the turmoil of World War I, in the revolution and civil wars, wandering about the Russian steppes, braving dangers and breaking frontiers to make their way to a fabled land, where a handful of dreamers were doggedly engaged in building up a new Jewish homeland.

I tried, in these pages, to describe the reality of the Land of Israel half a century ago, as seen through the eyes of an eager and naive adolescent whose childhood has been spent among the drifting snows of a strange and hostile world, and for whom Jerusalem, then a sleepy little town, forever remained the pivot of his life, the beloved city in which his existence was anchored from the moment he threw a first glance on her rocks and stony walls.

The little joys and sorrows of a handful of pioneers in the Mandatory Palestine of the twenties could hardly foretell the coming struggles and accomplishments of the Jewish State to come. It was then just a provincial, half-forgotten corner in a world torn between two wars, which I sought to describe in the chapters devoted to my student years in Florence and Paris. But it is there in those modest beginnings that one will find the roots of many great achievements of later years.

The real heroes of this tale are my father and mother, who died on the threshold of an era they had dreamed of and were not destined to see. Both of them died young, before they could enjoy the full emergence of the new world of their visions. But they knew that they had inculcated in their children a love for their native tongue, a deep attachment to their past, and a pride in their Jewish identity that could never desert them.

Sunrise in Jerusalem is a tale of long forgotten days of yesterday warmed by the first rays of a rising morrow.

Jerusalem, 1972.   JACOB TSUR

Contents

The Snows of a Childhood

For many years the events preceding my life in Jerusalem, when we were being hustled from town to town, from village to village in war and revolution, remained hidden away in some secret corner of my mind. But one does not easily rid oneself of one's earliest memories. Even the hot wind of Jerusalem cannot wipe out the imprint of snows of exile, of a stove warming the long winter evenings, of childish games within the four walls of a soot-grimed yard, of a fur cap thrust down to one's eyes, of felt soles squeaking on the ice.

Such fragile links with a far-off, hostile world might well have been effaced forever on that autumn day of 1921, when our train issued from the Judean hills and the walls of Jerusalem came into sight. Above the gateway of the old Turkish station we saw the mysterious name 'El-Kuds El-Sheriff' writ large in Arabic and Latin characters. An ancient cab was waiting at the entrance, and the driver—a ringleted Jew—leaned over to help the Arab porter to shove passengers and luggage inside. The horse started off at a trot, over stones, through muddy puddles, waste land and rock-strewn fields, into the shady lanes of Zikhron-Moshé. A few days later I was seated on a school form among boys and girls born here, along with their parents, listening to their conversation, being initiated into the problems of a little world peopled with stern teachers and impudent pupils, entering the labyrinth of Bible lessons, becoming involved in a network of exams, good and bad marks, and the games and jokes of children raised like any other children in the world.

In the forty years that followed there occurred enough events —riots, war and the holocaust of the Jews of Europe, foreign missions, the struggle for independence and the proclamation of the State—to fill a ponderous volume of history and efface all memory of the past.

But a few years ago, on a visit to the new Russia, chance took me to Kiev, the capital of the Ukraine. It looked no different to me from the many other towns I had seen in the course of my travels: fine and spacious, with new buildings erected over wartime ruins, and gardens beside the Dnieper, gleaming with the gold of its cupolas and the whiteness of its ancient churches.

I wandered about, trying in vain to revive the feeling of the past. Everything was different and baffling: new houses, the air of a spring day, the scent of lilac, Ukrainian shop signs. Through street after street I ended by reaching the quarter where we had lived during the Revolution. The street had changed its name, but not its appearance—a narrow lane ending in a cul-de-sac, with a wide, steep flight of steps running up the hill. I found the house at the end of the lane, at the foot of the steps. A plate bore the number forty. There was the same arched doorway, the same yard with pointed cobbles, the same walls covered with an apparently timeless soot. Here were the recesses in the yard, overgrown with moss, that we looked out on from the window of our apartment on the third floor, the window that was frosted over all that winter of misfortune.

This was where our adventure had begun. It was midwinter in the year 1920. Civil war was raging in the Ukraine and the streets of Kiev were covered with snow.

Blizzard

I WAS then thirteen, and half my brief existence had been spent in moving from one place to another. Almost as far back as I can remember I was always seeing my family packing, strapping up luggage, tying up baskets, collecting things together and starting off. War was raging on all the Russian fronts and thousands of Jews were wandering from town to town like hunted animals seeking safety.

My earliest memories of all, however, were of a peaceful, happy home in pre-war Warsaw. A room all warmth and light, a nursemaid in a white head-dress in charge of our walks in the Saxon Gardens and the Jerusalem Alley; family meals round a solid oak table, with Mother dispensing our food. A little girl with copper-coloured curls asleep in a corner, and a baby grizzling in its cradle while a circle of aunts with high-braced busts and wasp waists lean over it to coax a smile. Guests turning up of an evening to share some special delicacy of Mother's cooking, or a homely dish of steaming potatoes with a bit of herring. A world in which fear was unknown, and nothing worse could startle us than the barking of a dog in the yard or a ring at the doorbell late at night.

When the spring sunshine got the better of the clouds, my father laid up his winter coat with the fur lining, my mother fetched a blue coat and a broad-brimmed hat out of the wardrobe, and the whole family migrated to its summer quarters in the country, in a green village at the heart of a pine forest. Parents and children made the journey in a little suburban train, and the luggage followed slowly in a cart drawn by two overworked horses. The driver unloaded our luggage, the village warden with the big moustache turned the key in the lock and opened the door of our log-cabin. As he threw back the shutters the scent of pine cones and hay invaded the damp rooms.

Somewhere far off there was the little village of Sopotskin, with a white Russian church, and an old synagogue in a cleft of the hill. Its streets were peopled with Jews, village Jews, in different coats from those of the townspeople, and high boots like those of the local peasants. Here my grandmother lived, and I sometimes spent a week's holiday in her home.

Uncles and aunts, neighbours and friends forgathered in her wooden house. Grandmother was there, in her ritual wig that enhanced her importance as she throned it in her easy chair. A smell of frozen apples hung about the passage. As soon as the sun broke through, my uncle would take me by the hand and carry me off to the green hills, through the cornfields, between the haystacks and the harvest sheaves.

Everything breathed of peace and quiet in the world we lived in then.

We children talked Russian; it was the language of the governing power, and its use was customary among the respectable families of that day. But my parents talked Yiddish to each other—a language the secret of which, by dint of curiosity, we had succeeded in penetrating. I read Hebrew when I was quite small, even before I could read Russian, for although very few people thought of using it conversationally at that time, Hebrew was the language of our thoughts. My father, a journalist of repute, wrote his articles in it, and the house was full of Hebrew books. The shelves of the bookcase in the drawing-room were loaded with bundles of yellowing newspapers, old numbers of the *Hatsefira*, the Hebrew daily published in Warsaw, alongside the gilt-edged volumes of Brockhaus-Efron's *Russian Encyclopedia*.

Before I had learnt to read and write Russian, I could decipher the announcement that sprawled in large Hebrew type under the title of the newspaper: 'Our readers may renew their subscription for the year 1913.' In the Friday number, at the bottom of the page, appeared an article by my father that I was unable to understand but was very proud of. Everybody knew that the name 'Sefog' ('the sponge') was my father's pseudonym, and I knew that these articles were written of an evening, by the light of the gas lamp adorned with a silk shade. I was often awakened in the night by the telephone bell, to see my father, in his long white nightshirt, talking endlessly into the receiver. Next day he would tell us that the editor had hauled him out of bed, as usual, because he needed another fifty lines of copy to complete

20

the number, and that he had dictated an article, extempore, of fifty lines, no more, no less.

My parents' friends were nearly all writers. As far as we were concerned, they fell into two categories: those who were friends with us children and brought us goodies, and those who joined the grown-ups straight away. One of our immediate neighbours was a young journalist who edited my own newspaper, the *Children's Hatsefira*. Years later, turning the pages of a bound collection in the Jewish Library in Kiev, I found a letter bearing my own signature, addressed to the editor, together with the editor's reply, in the most serious terms, to the venerable subscriber of six, urging him to continue honouring the paper with his compositions.

Outbursts of barking in our neighbourhood heralded the arrival of Zalman Schneour, then a passionate young poet with a fine presence and a black beard. He could imitate doggy language to perfection, and all the dogs of the quarter followed him on his way upstairs, to our huge delight. In the evening, after we had been put to bed, Mother would lay a white cloth on the table, and our old Polish servant Elisabeth would prepare the samovar and put a saucepan full of potatoes on the fire, grumbling all the while at her young masters for wasting their money on entertaining all and sundry when they hadn't the wherewithal to buy their children shoes. We were often wakened in the middle of the night by the bursts of laughter and the Hasidic songs coming from the dining-room. All these grown-ups were very young— most of them in their twenties, and my parents on the threshold of the thirties—gay and full of faith in the future.

It was at this time that the first kindergartens were started in Warsaw, in which modern Hebrew was taught—a great innovation in those days. I too became one of the pupils of the bearded pedagogues who, tossing their shocks of hair, dragged us along in a wild round to the rhythm of Hebrew songs. The roundelays of the Palestinian kindergartens had not spread yet beyond the new schools in Jaffa and Jerusalem, but we chanted fervently 'Round, around, go, children, go!' At first I didn't understand the meaning of the words, but I soon became familiar with the language, and later on, when I had learnt to read it, I became absorbed in the adventures of my Hebrew children's books and Andersen's

Fairy Tales, which David Frishman, one of the masters of Hebrew literature, had just translated into biblical prose.

After the wander-years of a *Yeshiva* student and an apprentice journalist, my father appeared to have reached a haven of peace. His situation was firmly established on the *Hatsefira*, the only Hebrew daily to appear in Russia at that time. His reputation had spread among all the towns and villages with a Jewish population, and his feuilletons were read with interest by lettered subscribers. The editor-in-chief, Nahum Sokolow, was often away, touring Europe or attending Zionist meetings, so that the editing of the paper rested virtually on my father's shoulders. One year before the World War he published an historical monograph which brought him a great reputation among readers of Hebrew.

He was often asked to write for Jewish newspapers in America, which paid high fees. His door was always open to passing guests, and we were often turned out of our beds for the sake of some young author or student we were harbouring in secret. From time to time my father attended a Zionist Congress, and stopped for a few days on his way back in the Swiss mountains or on the Italian coast by way of a holiday. Our family album was then enriched by new photographs of elegant gentlemen in straw hats, with bathing drawers reaching below the knee, and ladies bathing in full dress, with long stockings, a silk parasol, and a shawl round their shoulders.

Many years later, in the Warsaw of the morrow of the Second World War, I wandered about the ruined city looking among the rubble for the house in which I had spent my early childhood. I found it damaged but still standing, in the midst of the debris. Closing my eyes, I tried to reconstruct it in imagination, but at the back of my memory I could only see the little balcony at the rear of the building. I found this in actual fact, as if hanging by an invisible thread, half collapsed, half supported by a twisted girder. I stood for a long while looking at it, and at the broken window through which the cold wind of winter's end was blowing—petrified remains of the calm, carefree life of my parents' house in the days of my early childhood.

Those peaceful days came to an end on a lovely, luminous summer morning in the forest near Warsaw, in our little *datcha* surrounded by pine-trees. On that July morning, when the peasant brought us the Yiddish newspaper, I saw the grown-ups turn pale, and heard them talking in whispers. I had no idea what had happened, but a dim foreboding told me that misfortune was knocking at the door. The sun was shining its brightest, and we had not yet come to the end of our holiday, but our luggage was hurriedly packed and piled on the shandrydan to be taken to Warsaw. We were rigged out in town clothes, and forced our way through a crowd as frightened and bewildered as ourselves to a compartment in the train. Arrived at our destination, we looked in vain for the cab drivers usually waiting there for customers, brandishing their whips or reaching up to remove the nosebags from their horses' heads. My parents were in such a hurry to get home that they took a motor-car, a luxury exclusively reserved in those days for the rich and for bold innovators. This first ride in a car made such an impression on me that the memory of it is bound up even today with the declaration of World War I.

This was the start of our wandering years. Grandmother, who lived close to the German frontier, buried her treasures—copper saucepans, silver spoons, sabbath candlesticks—packed her pillows and eiderdown, and came to join us in Warsaw. Her daughters, who were spending their holidays in the village, soon appeared in the family house. A few weeks later the front drew nearer to us, and an aircraft was even seen circling slowly above the city. An order issued by the authorities in St Petersburg forbade the publication in future of any foreign-language newspaper. The *Hatsefira* shared the common fate and closed its doors. In spite of the local strategists' predictions that the war would not last long, weeks and months went by, our savings were dwindling visibly, and the enemy was drawing near the city. Some of our friends tried to persuade us not to leave Warsaw but to wait for the German occupation, but my mother would have none of it. She decided to seek the interior of Russia while the road was still open. Nobody knew what awaited us there, but the prospect of battles at the gates of Warsaw was more frightening than the uncertainty of the unknown.

Portmanteaus were brought down from the attic, clothes packed, furniture was sent to a repository, and the whole family started off for Pinsk, where a faithful friend was awaiting us and had begged us to seek refuge in his house.

Henceforth we were to undergo the common fate of thousands of Jewish families. We had joined the herd of the refugees. Once we had crossed the threshold of our house in Warsaw our last anchor was gone, and our ship was to be tossed to and fro at the whim of the waves, on a raging sea of war and social upheavals.

II

I remember very little of the few months we spent in Pinsk. As I think of that old Jewish town, I recall the mud in the streets, the narrow duckboard sidewalks, the rain pouring down the double windows, and the icy passage with a packing-case full of crockery in one corner, and in another the muddy galoshes of the neighbours who had come in from wading through the narrow lanes. It was in this town, the first stage of our long travels, that I reached school age, and to my parents' delight they discovered a well-known Hebrew school there. The teaching was carried on entirely in Hebrew. The founder of the school was an old teacher who was to meet his death at the end of the war in a pogrom perpetrated by the new Polish rulers of the country. I spent long hours there, listening to the marvellous legends the master told us, reading stories of the Bible and joining in my schoolfellows' games in the little courtyard. There we talked a juicy Lithuanian Yiddish, which soon took the place of Russian as the language spoken in the family.

I have no idea what we were now living on. The little money brought from Warsaw had soon melted away, and there was little hope of living by one's pen in a provincial town; but we had good friends there and anyway our expenses were very light.

Our stay, however, was being prolonged beyond all expectation. We soon heard no more of the Warsaw optimists' predictions. Autumn was over, winter was already invading the Pripet Marshes, and the war was not coming to an end. While the Russian newspapers were announcing the victories of the Tsar's armies in East Prussia, the Germans were advancing, and taking fortress after fortress. Warsaw was falling into their hands, and who could be sure the front would not reach our city of refuge?

My father's friends were all for his remaining in Pinsk. Even if the town was taken by the Germans, they said, we hadn't much to fear; all we risked was sharing the fate of other Jews in town. But he had always been used to working; idleness was a burden to him, and the idea of depending on his friends was repugnant to him. He decided to go to Moscow, where it was said that tens of thousands of Jewish refugees from the frontier regions had settled. In the metropolis life was strenuous and work would not be lacking. As soon as he had secured a livelihood he would rent an apartment and get us to join him. He wrote letter after letter to his friends there, and ended by starting off alone for Moscow.

Mother got letters from him every week, but news was scarce. He wrote of meeting old friends, and gave detailed accounts of promises made him, of dazzling plans. But the next letter would announce that everything had fallen through, all his hopes were crumbling.

With my father away, Mother felt obliged to take a hand in our education, and one day I heard her say to one of our friends, 'I've decided that from now on we shall talk Hebrew at home.' He was a learned Jew, versed in the sacred tongue, but he burst out laughing.

'What an idea!' he said. 'How will they talk to the other children? Nobody will understand them. Besides, you're not used to talking Hebrew yourself, so how can you teach your children?'

'That's all right, I shall learn it,' she declared. 'After all, my eldest has started school, the little girl goes to the kindergarten, and the baby prattles in baby language. Since we came to Pinsk they've changed from Russian to Yiddish, and who knows where else we shall drift to in this endless war! We must have the support of our own language, wherever we may be. My husband would laugh at my poor Hebrew, but as he isn't here I must try.'

The experiment was so successful that I don't remember the transition period. When we arrived in Moscow we were chattering fluently in Hebrew, to my father's astonishment and delight. Hebrew reigned at home. Mother kept strict watch on this, though she had more difficulty in adapting herself than we had. Her vocabulary was restricted, and we chaffed her when she used a wrong word or made a mistake in grammar. But she went on undauntedly studying, reading, questioning, and remained faithful to the end to the decision she had taken.

After some months my father succeeded in finding a job, and we joined him in Moscow, to live on his modest salary in the big sugar business owned by Hillel Zlatopolski, a Zionist and successful industrialist. The restrictive laws against Jews were still in force in spite of the war. Officially we were forbidden to live in Moscow. To avoid being expelled, my father had himself registered as a 'dependant' of the 'first-class merchant Zlatopolski', and my grandmother as a 'dependant' of himself. This chain of protection served us for a few months—possibly a tip to the doorkeeper had something to do with it—but the Tsar's police ended by getting wind of the trick. A police officer called on my parents and gave them notice to quit the city within twenty-four hours. Arguments and entreaties were of no avail; we were forced once again to pack up and go.

We chose Bogorodsk as our refuge, a little township in the neighbourhood of Moscow to which the interdict did not extend. The place had become an asylum for expelled Jews tied to Moscow by their employment. They lived with their families in the peasant cottages once rented by the tradespeople of Moscow as their summer quarters. Ours stood on the river bank, with a big apple orchard on the hillside behind it, which we children raided in the early morning for the red, sweet-scented apples. A fair was held once a week in the central square, and the town would become then a hubbub of creaking wheels, peasant women crying their wares, horses neighing and blacksmiths hammering, while people crowded round the stalls to buy knives and scythes, and textiles of every colour.

Shoshana Persits, daughter of the Muscovite millionaire, and an active fighter for Hebrew culture, had decided to turn Bogorodsk, a little Russian Orthodox town, into a centre of Jewish education. She imported a learned Rabbi from Lithuania to found a *yeshiva* for the young exiles who had been forced to give up their religious schooling in the frontier regions. She hired a big house, which soon resounded to the chanting of Talmud students, to the puzzled astonishment of the peasants. On the days when my father returned earlier than usual from Moscow, he would often visit the *yeshiva* himself, attend a lecture and listen to the rapt singsong of the pupils, and when I went with him I was struck by his radiant expression as he listened nostalgically to the teaching he had received in his youth. The studious atmosphere of this spiritual centre affected the company of refugees driven to the heart of Russia by the tempest of war. Even my schoolfellows and I, young as we were, fell under the spell. The *yeshiva* students appealed to our imagination, and on the sabbath day the synagogue resounded to our chanted prayers and childish laughter.

But even Bogorodsk was to be no more than a stage of our journey. My father's employer, who was pleased with his work, suggested that he should become his representative at Omsk, in Siberia. There, he said, he would be able to live in peace, no longer as a modestly salaried employee but as an independent agent, buying and reselling the truckloads of sugar sent from Russia to the towns of Siberia. My parents held council in their room. The war did not look like ending, Jewish papers were still banned throughout the country, and this semi-illicit residence in Moscow had no sense in it. Moreover my father's salary was insufficient, and we were finding it hard to make ends meet. My mother, who had little confidence in my father's aptitude for commerce, hesitated for a long while, but the tempting proposal was finally accepted.

So one day we found ourselves crowded into a compartment of the Trans-Siberian, rolling leisurely eastwards across the frozen steppes of the immense Russian plain. The journey took a week. We spent the day with our noses glued to the frosted windows, and slept at night on the wooden seats of our third-class compartment, buying food from the peasants and filling our teapots with boiling water at the wayside stations. Of that long journey I recall the unforgettable vision of the splendour of the Urals— snow-clad peaks, waterfalls prisoned in ice, spotless snow sparkling with all the colours of the rainbow in the cold sunshine—the long nights of a milky darkness in the heated carriage, and a somnolence rhythmed by the jolts of the locomotive slowly forging its way through infinite space.

III

We spent two years in Siberia. My parents rented a big two-storied house in Omsk, with plenty of room for us all—Grandmother, two aunts, our parents and us children. Soon afterwards we were joined by a young teacher of Hebrew, specially engaged by my father to keep us conversant with our native tongue. We made friends with some Siberian Jews, descendants of the soldiers of Tsar Nicholas I, strapping lads in fine fettle, barely educated but faithful to Jewish customs and tradition. Summoned to read the Tora aloud in the synagogue, they put on their spectacles to decipher laboriously the small print in their prayerbooks. They radiated friendliness and practised a touching Jewish hospitality. Treasures of meat and poultry lay buried under a carpet of snow in their vast courtyards, and in the long winter evenings they gathered round their white-hot stove to eat *pilmeni*—a Siberian kind of pancake stuffed with meat—warming their hearts with Russian songs of the steppe and tossing off a lot of little glasses of vodka.

It was time for me to start on my Russian schooling. After passing the entrance exams I proudly donned the uniform worn by a *gymnasium* student: blue blouse, leather belt, long trousers, and a coat with shining brass buttons that covered the tops of my boots. In summer I wore the regulation cap, in winter, a tall fur hat. As the only Jew in my class, I was obliged to attend Christian prayers every morning, under the eye of the bearded priest, and I remember to this day the discomfort I felt during this religious service, and the way my fellow-students looked at me when I failed to cross myself or kneel down as they did. I was ten years old, but I had never before been outside my family circle, with its warmth and its Jewish intimacy. It was here that I experienced for the first time the feeling of being on the fringe of the Russian ethos, which haunted me until the end of our stay in that country.

Seen from this remote Siberian town, the war seemed somewhat unreal. Terrible disasters were convulsing the vast Russian territory; soldiers were falling at the front, the German armies were pushing further into the country, while here life went on, calm, peaceful, contented and sleepy. My father's business was prospering and we had no lack of money, but we were beginning to find our isolation oppressive, for news of our family, dispersed more or less all over Russia, reached us only very irregularly. Besides which, the harsh climate was affecting my mother's health. She had developed a cough, which was gradually growing worse. Earlier, in Moscow, during an exhausting journey to save her young brother from military service, she had contracted pneumonia, and had never really recovered. Now she woke us in the night by her coughing fits, though by day she seemed quite well, laughing, listening to our childish chatter, and devoting herself to her endless household tasks. Optimistic as usual, my father thought her trouble was due entirely to the rigours of the Siberian winter, but the doctor told him it was definitely the onset of tuberculosis. Father at once suggested giving up his business and returning further south to look for work in a milder climate, but Mother was resolutely opposed to the idea: war was raging, the big cities were overpopulated with refugees, and there was really nowhere to go. On damp days of thaw she stayed in bed, coughing, but as soon as she felt better she got up, and her warm, bright looks lighted up our little world once more.

My father came back from the town one morning at an unusual time. Before shaking the snow off his greatcoat, he called out to my mother, who was in the kitchen: 'Something's going on in Petrograd. They don't yet know what's up, but a telegraphed order has reached the station, signed by a new Minister of Transport, a notorious politician of the Left and a member of the Socialist-Revolutionary Party.' It was in this roundabout way that we heard of the Revolution of February 1917.

As often happens, this historic event remained graven on my childish memory chiefly in connection with a minor incident that shook my confidence in the written word. Until then I had believed implicitly in the absolute truth of everything printed in books and newspapers, even the bombastic dialogues in the *Valley of the Cedars* and the extraordinary tales of the *Memoirs of the House of David*. I was subscribing at that time to a weekly paper for children called *The World of Adventure*, and I was so proud of having a paper all to myself that I used to give the family a detailed report, at mealtimes, of all I had read in the latest number: the Russian generals' brilliant deeds, the heroism of our soldiers who were routing the German and Austrian battalions. Like all my schoolfellows, I was sure of the victory of our valiant troops, and filled with admiration for the brilliant Commander-in-Chief of the Russian armies, the Grand Duke Nicholas Nicholaievitch, and even more for the Tsar and the Imperial Family, whom we looked upon as the incarnation of the noblest virtues.

Before the news of the Revolution reached us, my paper had published the Tsar's photograph on the front page with the caption: 'The Saviour of the Fatherland', and a detailed eulogy of the courage of the Emperor of all the Russias and his great military gifts. Nicholas II had assumed supreme command of the armies, and victory was henceforth assured. But the next number, which reached Omsk not long after, had its front page adorned with the bearded countenance of Rodzianko, President of the Duma, and the same caption: 'The Saviour of the Fatherland'. The leading article, long and detailed, made it clear that the Tsar had been on the point of leading his people to its doom, and that the glorious Russian army would have been defeated by the enemy (which God forbid!) if it had not been for the President of the Duma, who had relieved the Tsar of his command and freed the Russian fatherland from the yoke of a narrow-minded tyrant.

This was my first lesson in the relativity of political glory.

Those first post-revolution days in Omsk left me memories of effervescence and enthusiasm, streets decorated with red flags, processions of workmen, political exiles moving in a body past our window. The revolutionary committees sat through the night, and the leaders of the Jewish community assembled to deliberate, decide and act. On what subjects, I never knew; but they had a comforting conviction that the days of oppression were over and we need no longer live in fear of hearing the police knocking at the door. As the new régime was in dire need of specialists, my father was given an honorary appointment as editor of the gazette published by the Local Workers' Committee (*Ispolcom*). Although he was not used to writing in Russian, he threw himself into the task with delight, as if returning to his first love.

With the first audible cracking of the thawing ice in the river, cheering news reached us from Moscow of an expansion of activity unknown since before the war. Jewish public life had revived after the Revolution. We learnt with intense emotion that a fund of several millions had been created by a new Maecenas, A. J. Stybel, a merchant who had made a fortune in oil, to encourage Hebrew literature, and that there were even plans for publishing a daily paper in Hebrew. Mother, who had become stronger with the first rays of sunshine, immediately urged our return to Moscow, but this time the objections came from my father. His business was prospering, we were better off than we had been for years, our bank account was healthy, why give all that up? He was visibly torn between his present tranquil existence and a longing to return to his profession, his circle of writers and the stormy sessions of the Zionist conferences. I heard murmured conversations going on in my parents' room until the small hours of the morning, my father talking, talking endlessly, as if trying to convince himself.

These tergiversations might have continued for a long while if the hand of destiny had not forced a decision. One day, my father came home pale and distraught, threw himself on his bed, buried his head in the pillow, and appeared to be sobbing. Mother, who was lying down after a violent fit of coughing, hurried to his bedside. We were sent out of the house, and it was not till some time later that the mystery was revealed to us. My father had lost the whole of his capital. A trusted friend who had been his business partner, and had actually initiated him in the secrets of the trade, had ordered a trainload of sugar. My father, in his innocence, had registered the consignment in the name of the buyer, without demanding a receipt or a bill of exchange from him. When the merchandise reached its destination, his partner had shamelessly denied the specifications of the contract, and my father had lost goods and money. All his savings were swallowed up in this disastrous operation and he was as poor as before.

My mother tossed her head and settled the question out of hand. It was the will of Providence. My father was not born to be a man of business, and you cannot force the hand of Fate. Besides, how long were we to moulder here at the back of beyond? For months past she had been telling him that Moscow was the place for us, it was there that the heart of Jewish life in Russia was beating. We had gone on hesitating and procrastinating, as always happens when one is a slave to money: one loses a clear view of things. Now neither money nor anything else tied us to this town in the wastes of Siberian ice. After all, who could tell where the revolution would lead us? Now that the Russian giant was awake, God alone knew what dirty tricks he might be capable of, and where should we be in greater safety than among our Jewish brethren?

So the luggage was strapped up again, and the whole family packed into the Trans-Siberian, *en route* for Moscow. At one of the stations we passed through, Ekaterinburg in the Urals, we saw a sealed railway carriage over which sentinels were standing guard. Tsar Nicholas's family was on its way from St Petersburg, to its tragic end. The 'Saviour of the Fatherland' had reached the last lap of *his* journey.

IV

In Moscow we settled into a large flat on the top story of a big mansion, not far from the Stanislavsky Arts Theatre, and our home at once became the noisy, jovial rendezvous it had been before the war. Jewish writers and politicians were forgathering in Moscow from every quarter of Russia, together with the flood of refugees and people evicted from the frontiers. My father returned to his beloved desk. He had hardly arrived when he was engaged on the editorial staff of the Hebrew daily *Ha-am* ('The People'), which had taken the place of *Hatsefira*, cut off in Poland under German occupancy. He resumed his old habits, visits to the printing press, board meetings, writing articles at night. Jewish life flourished round the Stybel publishing firm, which David Frishman managed with a firm hand, attracting to it the great poet Saul Tchernikovsky, still wearing his army doctor's gold-braided uniform, and a whole Pleiad of writers—poets, novelists and translators—from Warsaw, and from Vilna, Odessa and other towns and villages of Russia.

Blizzard

The first volume of the literary miscellany *Hatekufa* ('The Period'), the *chef d'œuvre* of the Stybel firm, heralded the dawn of a great era of artistic revival. I delved greedily into the bulky volume myself. I was too young to appreciate its beauties, but I still remember the impression made on me by my first reading of An-sky's play *The Dibbuk*, in Bialik's Hebrew version, a revelation of sublime, mystical poetry.

Endless discussions went on round our table, on literary questions of the day, on the future of Russian Judaism in these revolutionary days, and Zionism and Palestine. People were feverishly excited about the Jewish National Congress soon to be held in Petrograd, and Zionist circles were planning to launch a referendum inviting the Jews of Russia to declare in favour of a Jewish State in Palestine. This project aroused passionate disputes, and our drawing-room was in a turmoil, partisans and adversaries confronting one another with fiery vigour, to the intense delight of us children. Everything had reverted to its old order in our little world.

The Revolution was still in its festive phase: demonstrations, red flags, the *Marseillaise*, harangues at street corners. I had been entered at a distant secondary school, and every day on my way home I joined a crowd of interested loafers listening greedily to fiery speeches that all sounded the same to me. To a boy of eleven all these slogans and exhortations were part of the pattern of red flags waving in the wind and revolutionary songs chanted in the street. News from the front was bad. The Germans were still advancing, and our troops were still fighting valiantly—and beating a retreat. In my mind's eye the army was personified by my uncle, my mother's brother, who had been mobilized and sent to the front in spite of her efforts, and reported missing soon after. I saw him fighting heroically on all the fronts mentioned in the newspapers, brandishing a red standard and repelling the assaults of the Teutonic hordes. But my hero's face became gradually blurred, merging into that of the hero everybody was acclaiming as the saviour of the Revolution. Kerensky, the Prime Minister and Minister for War, was the idol of the masses, and the girls we knew were bewitched by his eloquence, his imposing presence and his determined features.

After school I proudly donned my scout's uniform with its

light-blue tie, and ran off to a meeting of the 'Young Maccabee' troop, in the yard of a Hebrew school in an alley near the Grand Synagogue. I was still at wolf-cub age, but my boy scout friends predicted a great future for me because I knew Baden Powell's manual by heart and could recite all the signalling rules and rules of conduct, besides being an expert in knots. The headmaster of the neighbouring Hebrew school used to come sometimes to talk to us about Jewish history, and the scoutmasters preached fidelity to the Jewish people, the Hebrew language and Palestine. Among my friends of that time were the sons of Yehiel Tshlenov, the great leader of Russian Zionism, who had died in London a few months earlier. When the Zionist Organization staged a demonstration to commemorate the Balfour Declaration in the 'Hall of the Nobles'—from which Jews had been excluded in the days of the Tsar—Tshlenov's children, seated beside their mother, who was dressed in black, attracted the attention of the whole audience. This was, I fancy, the last Zionist gathering in Moscow before the October régime put an end to all public meetings, planning assemblies, festivals and celebrations.

I witnessed the October Revolution from behind the wall of our courtyard, but my recollections are very confused. To the boy I was then, the 'ten days that shook the world' appeared as a succession of bizarre, unrelated incidents upsetting the quiet tenor of my home life.

I remember certain brief happenings, apparently detached from any context: gates closing, streets emptying suddenly, bullets whistling above deserted pavements, machine-guns barking in flurries at the corner of a square. One day the windows rattled to the exploding shells of field guns firing on a detachment of cadets entrenched in a neighbouring block of flats. The firing ceased, and armed soldiers invaded the streets, some in uniform, some with only an arm-badge on their sleeve; they advanced shyly, looking round them as if they had just lighted on the wonders of the world.

The arm-chair strategists who visited our home didn't take the new régime seriously; they were convinced it would soon collapse, and the revolts breaking out more or less everywhere appeared to justify them. The German armies were making their way towards the east; Denikin was threatening the south; the Czechoslovak legionaries were seizing town after town along the Trans-Siberian railway; General Yudenitch threatened Petrograd, and the Ukraine was proclaiming its secession from Russia and putting a hetman at its head.

The Bolshevist Revolution changed the physiognomy of the city. The old, elegant capital with its clean, bright streets, its shops overflowing with merchandise, appeared suddenly neglected, dirty, deserted. The electricity functioned only by fits and starts, trams came along at lengthening intervals, and endless queues gathered before the shops. Gangs of ruffians, taking advantage of the impotence of the new régime, attacked and robbed those who ventured into the streets after dark. Murders were the order of the day, and anarchists broke into private houses to rifle their contents.

In our case, personal anxiety was added to these collective troubles. Mother's illness had grown worse, and the doctor had warned us that the harsh climate and privations of Moscow would be fatal to her. My father had lost his livelihood once again: the *Ha-am* had ceased publication, and the Stybel publishing firm had been liquidated, its wealthy patrons having vanished one after another in the storm. In the early days the Bolshevist authorities had ignored both Zionists and Hebraists: they had other fish to fry. But the star of the Jewish communists was soon in the ascendant, and woe to those not reckoned as their friends! Simon Diemenstein, one of the heads of the Yevsektsia—the Jewish section of the Party—was a friend of my father's, an old fellow-student at the Slobodka yeshiva. At the beginning of the Revolution we still saw a good deal of him, and thanks to his influence we were saved more than one embarrassment. But his visits became fewer, and he ended by turning his back on his old friends. It was obvious that the climate of Moscow was becoming unhealthy in more ways than one, and we should once again have to pack up and seek shelter elsewhere.

But reigning conditions made the removal of a large family hardly possible, and we should have to make the journey in separate units. So desperate a plan would never have entered our heads but for the serious state of Mother's health. It was finally decided that my father should go alone to Kiev, the capital of the

Ukraine, where there was still a nucleus of Jewish public activity, and he would no doubt find means of supporting us. Mother was to go to Yalta for the sake of the Crimean sunshine, and my nine-year-old sister was to go with her to keep her company. As for me and my younger brother, we were to remain in Moscow, in the care of my grandmother and a young aunt, who, carried away by the wind of the revolution, had become an active communist and had useful contacts with the new authorities.

We tried to persuade ourselves that the separation would not last long, but we were all thoroughly unhappy. My father took the few friends we still had in Moscow into his confidence, gave my grandmother a few thousand roubles, and the family scattered. Alone henceforth in the big, icy flat, we awaited the order to start. But events stole a march on us. Only a few weeks later Kiev fell into the hands of Petliura, and the troops of Wrangel, the White general, occupied the Crimea. So there we were, cut off from our parents, separated by the front lines, while the Civil War raged in the immense Russian plains—a boy of twelve and a child of five, under the protection of an old grandmother with rheumy eyes who hardly spoke the language of the country.

Poverty and famine reigned in Moscow. Our funds were exhausted, and money no longer had any value anyway; it was almost impossible to buy food even at an exorbitant price. My aunt brought home the rations allotted her at the office to which she was attached, and shared the bags of millet and buckwheat meal with us. Sometimes I too brought back from school a half-baked loaf of black bread or a smoked herring. Schoolteachers and pupils were given their rations in class, and one day I saw a mistress I adored creeping furtively towards the barrel to filch a couple of herrings, intending no doubt to take them to her hungry children. The trams had stopped running, and I had to get up early to walk, knapsack on back, and braving the blizzard, to the school where I joined my famished schoolfellows and masters. We were not in a mood to learn, and discipline had gone by the board, the pupils spying on their teachers to make sure they were not getting an extra ration. Old women in battered hats, old men in motheaten fur coats, stood at street corners begging a slice of bread. After a few weeks the newspapers ceased publication for want of paper, and dingy leaflets were

posted on house doors containing propagandist tirades and news
of the front. My father's friends and acquaintances had scattered
to the four winds, some of them after leaving us a little money,
others without giving us a sign. People had become a pack of
hungry wolves. Our last possessions had been sold one after
another in the market near the Sukharov Tower. What would be
the end of it all?

In the evening, after eating my share of the pearl barley gruel
that my grandmother cooked on the portable stove, I used to go
out and wander about the snowy streets. Famine hadn't quenched
the fervour of the Revolutionists. Huge placards were posted on
the walls of State buildings, and futurist statues in plaster sprang
up in the squares, only to disappear almost as speedily. Platforms
were set up at street corners, and crowds of wondering peasants,
hungry townspeople and mere gapers listened to the speakers
pouring their bitter hatred on the sabotating bourgeois, the
Whites and the Counter-Revolutionists, and denouncing Lloyd
George and Clémenceau. It was at one of these impromptu
gatherings that I chanced one day to hear a speech by Trotsky,
the idol of the masses, the inspiration and the head of the Red
Army, a fresh incarnation of the 'Saviour of the Fatherland'.

I often spent the evening at the theatre. Tickets were not sold,
as in the days of the bourgeois régime, but distributed by the
authorities among their entourage. Thanks to my aunt's contacts
in high places, I was often presented with a ticket for the Arts
Theatre, the Maly or the Bolshoi, and in this way I came to know
all the great actors of that day. I remember seeing Chekhov's
Cherry Orchard, Gorki's *Lower Depths* and Maeterlinck's *Blue
Bird*. I would come home with my mind on fire, forgetting for a few
hours the uncertainty of the morrow and the pangs of my
famished belly. It was only in the over-excited atmosphere of
those days that a boy of my age could experience such an
intensity of artistic life.

I was sitting one evening listening with half an ear to my
grandmother bewailing her harsh fate, as I forced myself to
swallow down spoonful after spoonful of the black mess on my
plate, when my aunt came into the flat and told me a great piece
of news. She had just met Hanna Rovina, her friend of the Warsaw days, who had told her that in a few days' time the Habima

Theatre, a Hebrew theatrical company, would be giving its first performance in Moscow. She had invited my aunt to attend it, and on her mentioning me, had honoured me too with a ticket, so we should be going to the first night together.

The miseries of the day were wiped out as if by magic. I shot off my chair and flung my arms round my aunt's neck, beside myself at the thought of seeing a play in my own language, the language I felt was known only to myself and my people. Next day I daydreamed all through lessons, and when the great evening arrived I was there long before the time we had agreed upon, and had to wait ages outside the doors of the theatre.

That evening is registered in my memory as a significant event, as though the performance had been given for my benefit alone. We sat there, my aunt and I, in the little auditorium, on boards arranged in a semicircle and covered with sacking. No stage. The curtain had been lowered right down to the floor. A religious silence reigned. Then I heard the opening words spoken in Hebrew, a natural, sonorous Hebrew, and I followed the performance of the young actors with intensity, laughing and crying in sympathy. I went home happy, over-excited, and was suddenly seized with a desperate longing for my parents, so far away, with whom I should so much have loved to share my happiness.

My school was in a bad way; the masters were disappearing, one after another, government orders were contradictory, lesson-books were lacking and the pupils were behaving as they pleased. My boy scout troop, too, was breaking up. The wave of enthusiasm spreading everywhere was carrying the young people away and turning them into communists. But my education at home had gone deep and had immunized me against all foreign influence. A boy of my own age I sometimes played with in our yard—a Jew, son of a militant socialist turned communist—tried repeatedly to inculcate the elements of the new religion upon me, talking of revolution, the new humanity, and treating the bare idea of a national existence for the Jewish people with crushing disdain. I disputed his views and tried to refute his arguments, insisting on the ideas I had so often heard expressed at home, but he was a better controversialist than I, and I had soon emptied my quiver. I was certain at heart that I was right, but felt incapable of demonstrating it. I stuck to my guns, however, and ended up with the overwhelming argument 'And I shall soon be in Palestine!'

He laughed in my face. 'In Palestine, of course,' he said, 'but before you get there, all of you, your father and you, will be locked up in a Siberian convict prison!'

'I've *been* in Siberia,' I retorted, 'but this time, make no mistake, we're going to Palestine. Stay here, if you like, I want to go home. Here nobody cares what becomes of us, with all this revolution. Stay here, if you like, and much good may it do you!'

I threw him a look of triumph and made off. I knew my retort was not very logical, but it seemed to have gone home. I felt no concern with what was happening round me; what did all these debates matter to me, on the future of a nation that was not mine?

At last the long-awaited news reached us. My father wrote from Kiev that communications had been re-established between Russia and the Ukraine, and we could start. Mother, too, he wrote, had succeeded in leaving Yalta and joining him with my little sister, after eluding attacks by anarchist gangs on the journey. Her health had improved, and they were awaiting us with impatience.

My aunt began haunting the People's Commissariats in quest of the necessary documents. Before you could travel you had to have a warrant stating your official business. How to wangle an official-business warrant for an old woman who could not talk Russian and a boy rising thirteen? Fortunately in the confused state of the country any scrap of paper with a rubber stamp on it worked miracles. My aunt had recourse to her exalted contacts, and one day she came home with a warrant for herself as a delegate of the Party cadres, and one for my grandmother as Superintendent of Agriculture in the villages of the Ukraine; as for me, I was commissioned to buy agricultural machinery in the south. A more grotesque camouflage could hardly be imagined, but the soldiers of the Red Guard were mostly illiterate, and we gambled on the red stamp to carry us through.

Our luggage was strapped up once again, and we went to the Kursk station to wait for the train to Kiev. We had waited for twenty-four hours when at last an engine drew up beside our platform, dragging behind it a string of dilapidated coaches. We scrambled in to secure a corner of a compartment. Our documents were checked by the military every hour. Grandmother and I pretended to be asleep, and my aunt addressed the soldiers in a tone of command. I remember nothing of the journey, which was probably undisturbed by any other incident.

Departure Signal

I

WE WERE reunited at last. But even in Kiev destitution was increasing, and we could foresee no end to our troubles. Fighting was going on in the outskirts; Bolsheviks, Denikin's White guards and Petliura's Ukrainians were clashing savagely round the capital. Kiev had changed hands four or five times in a single year, and each time the conquerors had announced their assumption of power by proclamations and posters, by demonetizing their predecessors' currency, massacring their adversaries and spreading terror among the civilian population. Leaving one's house was to risk one's life. Civilians were arrested in the open street, condemned without delay for real or imaginary misdeeds and executed on the spot for obscure reasons of revenge or settlement of accounts. And before their families had time to inquire as to their fate, the régime had changed and the cannon were thundering again across the Dnieper. Carts dripping blood rolled through the streets with corpses piled pell-mell in them, an arm pointing to the sky or a leg hanging over the backboard. The horrified children watched them go by from behind the locked entrance gates of the houses.

Such was the fate of ordinary citizens; that of the Jews was still worse. When the Whites were in power, the agonized cries of those caught in the pogrom were heard in the yards of the Jewish quarter, and the anti-Semitic press did not conceal its delight. 'This is how we mean to torture them, in the throes of terror.' On my thirteenth birthday, instead of celebrating my *bar-mitsva* amid rejoicings, I lay hidden with my father in a dark attic, while the rioters hammered with iron bars on the locked doors of the house. The women had remained downstairs in our apartment. Rumour had it that the ruffians were only after the men, and there was always a hope that, drunk as they usually were with looting and swilling, they would not get as far as the attics and garrets. We lay together in our corner, listening to the drunkards' shouts and praying for a miracle. When the bandits grew tired of banging at the door and had been driven off by some distant rifle shot, we came down from our hiding-place,

41

pale and trembling, humiliated, ashamed, seething with impotent rage.

But even more than the terrors of those nights, one incident of which my father and I were the object has haunted me ever since. It was at the time when the White general, Denikin, was ruling over the city. Life had almost returned to its normal course; shops were open and the houses were once more lighted by electricity. I was walking beside my father along Kreshchatik Street, the fine chief thoroughfare of Kiev. We were chatting happily when an officer in a glittering uniform stepped up to us, his long sword dangling from his belt. He stood stock still for an instant in front of my father, looking him up and down with contempt, and uttered a single word 'Jid!'

My father turned pale. He said not a word, but took hold of my arm and tried to move round the officer. But the latter had not done with him. 'Dirty Jew!' he ejaculated, and with a violent cuff he sent my father's hat flying into the gutter. He then seized the hilt of his sword as if to draw it, but spat, and went on his way.

I bent down, picked up the hat and handed it to my father without speaking. My cheeks were burning and my eyes were full of tears. My father stood there before me with trembling lips, and his figure seemed to have shrunk. Silently he took me by the arm as if to protect me and to efface the insult from my young mind.

It was usually my mother who took the decisions, and this time she was not long about it. We must get away, she said. She was keeping to her bed, coughing incessantly, her strength sapped by a fresh onslaught of her malady. We were all crowded together in a single room with the casual visitors who sought shelter with us on those perilous nights. The room that had been our living room was now the family hearth; it was there that we took shelter from the intense cold, huddled round the cast-iron stove that glowed red in the corner, exuding drop by drop a sort of brownish tar, while a spiral of smoke escaped through the cracks in the pipe. The spacious apartment had been rented in happier days when the big rooms were lighted by electricity and warmed by central heating. Now the icy rooms were locked and bolted, which for us children produced the aura of an enchanted, deserted castle. From time to time I stole secretly into the library belonging to the owner, who had fled the town, leaving his furniture behind. Wrapped in a long greatcoat I tried with my frozen fingers to turn the pages of the beautifully bound books ranged on the shelves.

My father went out every morning in search of employment, coming back most days empty-handed. A few months earlier a Yiddish newspaper was still being published in the town and my father had gone every day to the office to write articles and help in the make-up of the paper. I was often sent with him, because if a man was arrested, a young boy accompanying him could usually escape and inform the family, so that they could make an attempt to have him released from prison. I enjoyed these visits to the press; I liked the smell of the fresh ink, and seeing the newspapermen bending over the long ribbons of paper bearing print that would be read next day by thousands of people. It reminded me of my early childhood to see my father writing at a rapid pace, dipping his pen in the inkpot without raising his head and covering the sheet of paper with his tiny, regular hand-writing.

But now there was no newspaper and no salary. Like his journalist colleagues, my father tried to make a little money in hazardous speculations, buying and reselling demonetized bank-notes. And when the deal fell through he would come home at nightfall empty-handed, trying to laugh it off for the sake of cheering my mother as she lay in bed; but the despondency was visible behind the smile.

In those rigorous days I too had to contribute to the support of the family. A young boy was not liable to imprisonment like an adult, and I was sent to the market where the peasants gathered to barter goods and food. I was given a tablecloth or a sheet, or a pair of my father's trousers that had survived ship-wreck, and I mingled with a crowd of people as hollow-cheeked and famished as myself. Then I came home with half a sack of flour or a sack of potatoes, and perhaps, if fortune had smiled on me, a pound or two of dried vegetables that we cooked as a sort of gruel. It had a nauseous smell, but a taste not unlike that of real soup. In the evening the whole household gathered round Mother's bed. A bucket of water on the stove sent out spiral curls of steam. This was water drawn straight from the Dnieper or from one of the flooded cellars, for the frozen water-mains had long ago given up the ghost and the kitchen taps existed merely as a matter of form. It was there, during those long evenings, that our plans of escape were worked out.

We all knew there was nothing for it but to leave this part of the world, but Mother's illness made us hesitate. How would she stand the hardships of a long, dangerous journey in the depth of winter? But she kept encouraging us, begging us not to consider her, assuring us she could surmount every danger, if only we could leave Russia. My father, she declared, could not live separated from his normal milieu and his work. He needed his Hebrew newspaper, his circle of writers, the Zionist atmosphere in which he had always lived. And even if we had the luck to survive here, what future had we to look forward to? The Bolsheviks had assumed power and we were at the mercy of the agents of the Yevsektsia, full of blind hatred of everything dear to us, a hatred springing from their inner depths, most of them being apostates, *yeshiva-bachurim* who lost their faith. We could no longer hope for any public life in Russia, so what should we find to do here?

We two children went on learning Hebrew. From time to time young students were quartered with us for a few weeks, and gave us lessons before going further afield. They were not paid in cash, money having anyway no value, but my father gave them, at intervals, a pound of melted butter or half a pound of sugar, a pair of old shoes or a patched shirt from his own wardrobe. Every hour of the day, when a pale ray of sunshine penetrated the blurred windows, found me beside my teacher, reading a chapter of the Prophets or writing a composition in Hebrew in my exercise book.

Sometimes, either for the purpose of collecting his own writings, or to give me something to do, my father sent me to the Jewish library, which had remained open by some miracle, to copy out the articles he had published earlier in the *Hatsefira* and the *Hazman*. These newspapers were bound up in thick, dusty volumes, and as I browsed through them I came upon the burning discussions, the Zionist controversies of other days, in a world that knew little of riots, famine, and corpses lying along the roadside.

II

'Make no mistake,' said Mother between two fits of coughing, 'if we ever escape from here we are not going to stop halfway. We're going straight to Palestine.'

To our childish minds Palestine was a country flooded with sunshine, surrounded by a halo of legend. The more cold and famine prevailed in the town, the more radiant with perfection appeared the Promised Land. A collection of postcards of Palestine found at the bottom of an old travelling-bag had stirred our imagination, and we had rediscovered them more than once with the same delight. Here were pupils of the Herzlia School in Jaffa, in straw hats, boating on the Jordan; Herzl Street in Tel-Aviv: little white cottages surrounded by wooden fences, and a bearded Jew astride a donkey in the heat of the day. Here was the Bezalel School of Art in Jerusalem, built of freestone, with a crenellated façade; and here, a company of pioneers in the heroic days of the foundation of Gedera, rake on shoulder, pitchfork in hand, standing barefoot on a sand dune. Beautiful pictures, enhanced by a far-off, mysterious prestige.

I was deep in a book on the geography of Palestine, written in Russian, which I had found in the library of our apartment, and I was searching the Brockhaus-Efron *Encyclopedia* for articles on Palestine, Jerusalem and the Jews. Great things were happening in the distant fatherland of our dreams, and we felt certain that glorious days awaited us there. Before leaving Moscow for Kiev we had heard of the entry of the British into Jerusalem and the fresh wave of immigration that was spreading over the country. Now slender bulletins were reaching us by mysterious channels, in the shape of crumpled leaflets smuggled out of Odessa—then under the dominion of the Whites—bringing us wonderful news of Palestine. A Jewish government had been set up in Jerusalem, with Chaim Weizmann as President and Louis Brandeis as Prime Minister, Nahum Sokolov Minister for Foreign Affairs, Menahem Ussishkin Minister of Agriculture and Jabotinsky Minister for War. Prefabricated houses had been imported in boatloads, and erected in no time to shelter the thousands of immigrants; new quarters were springing up like mushrooms; long caravans of Jews were travelling on foot to the Holy Land by the steep tracks of the Caucasus, led by a former officer of the Tsar, Joseph Trumpeldor.

Meanwhile our house had become the rallying-point of intending travellers. Gathered round the oil lamp, young men ready to start, refugees who had just reached the town, and families of friends living in Kiev, all came to discuss plans with my father. These endless confabulations had not led to anything so far, but one day chance brought a company of vigorous young men to our house, who had completed their agricultural training at a farm school in Ekaterinburg in the Urals. They had succeeded in crossing all the front lines over the whole expanse of Russia, and had just arrived in the Ukraine, thoroughly determined not to stop till they reached Palestine. They were all young and unmarried except for a couple with a little daughter of two. It might have been simpler for them to pursue their journey as they were, but on arriving in Kiev they had got wind of our preparations and gladly agreed to take on the other families as travelling companions, encumbered though they were with children and old people, to form a single convoy.

As soon as we children were in bed the grown-ups began their murmured palavers in the one room that served as a dormitory for us all. With our eyes shut, but ears on the alert, we caught a shred of the conversation now and then. We heard that in the market town of Rujine, in the province of Kiev, it was possible to make a deal with the local soviet, and to obtain documents certifying that we were all refugees from a little town of Volhynia, not far from the Polish frontier, and were returning home. In Rujine we should be able to hire wagons and drivers to take us to the frontier. Anyhow, as soon as we were within reach of Polish territory, there would be no lack of Jews and peasants to help us across the frontier.

The grown-ups spent several days working out the plans of departure in detail. The students came in and out, the *halutsim* from the Urals brought us fresh news of the front, which was now very close to the town. We obtained our documents from the authorities, grubby papers bearing our names, followed by the magic word *Echelon*, which meant something like 'Convoy of refugees' or 'Transport organized by the Public Authority'.

46

In secret folds in the lining of pelisses and heavy winter coats, tsarist bank-notes were stowed away, with the few precious stones still in the possession of our party. At last one of our intermediaries came to tell us he had succeeded in greasing the palm of the stationmaster, who had promised to facilitate our departure.

From now on everything was transfigured by our fresh hopes. Mother got out of bed and declared she felt perfectly well. The country air would do her good, and we need have no anxiety on her account. Grandmother, who usually hobbled painfully about behind her grandchildren, got busy packing cases, boxes and baskets. What remained of our winter clothing was patched and mended; the shoemaker at the corner of the street consented to repair our down-at-heel shoes in exchange for some old clothes. The leaders of the party held council for the last time in our big room, to settle the final details of the plan. The day of departure was fixed. To avoid arousing suspicion it was decided that each family should travel separately by train as far as the last station before Rujine, where we would assemble for the final preparations.

At daybreak on the great day, muffled up in our heavy coats, we took our luggage on our backs and went to the station to wait for the train. There were six of us: Father, Mother, Grandmother and the three children, the youngest of whom was only six.

It was February, the depth of winter in the Ukraine. Snow covered the steppes; the intense cold struck through our old wadded coats.

III

I remember nothing of that train journey, either because it was accomplished without trouble, or because it became confused with another trip which I took a few months earlier. We were without food at the time. The last tablecloth had been sold in the market, and our cash resources—the twenty- and forty-rouble Kerensky notes cut from a large sheet with a pair of scissors, and those of the Tsar's reign, now the only currency to be accepted—had all been drawn from their hiding-place. We were no longer given so much as a sticky slice of black bread a day, or a ration of sweetish frozen potatoes.

At this moment of distress a friend of earlier days came to see us, a wealthy man who had always been attracted to our circle of writers. He took provisions out of an old newspaper, and made the following proposal to my father. At Karabchyev a hamlet in the neighbourhood of Rujine, he owned a mill, of which the Bolsheviks had not yet taken possession. The accountant who had worked there for years had disappeared one day without warning, as constantly happened at that time. So here was an ideal solution for my father. He could keep accounts in the mill so long as it had not fallen into the hands of the Bolshies. His salary would be paid to his family in Kiev, and when he returned he could bring with him as many sacks of flour as he could carry, besides other foodstuffs that were still to be had in plenty in the country.

As it was usual at that time to let nobody leave his house alone, lest he should be killed on the way, or struck down by exanthematous typhus, and his family none the wiser, it was decided that I should accompany my father. I spent several weeks in that little village, where we lodged with a Jewish family who were also preparing to leave for Palestine. I ate my fill there, not only of bread but of long-forgotten foods and delicacies like fresh cream, eggs, and now and then even a bit of chicken. I spent the long evenings reading, or talking to our hosts' children, in an *isba* lying hidden under a thick blanket of snow. On bright winter mornings I sometimes went along with my father to his office in the old mill; as I watched him, white with flour, bending over his account books, I imagined myself back in the happy days when I saw him writing his articles in the editorial office of his newspaper.

I do not know how long we stayed in the village—perhaps six or eight weeks. We were always haunted by anxiety for the family left behind in the town. The post had long since ceased functioning regularly, and letters were often lost in transit. As the weeks went by without news of our people, we ended, regretfully, by leaving our country paradise, with its stone jars full of cream and its fresh, sweet-smelling bread. We shouldered some sacks of oatmeal and flour and went to the station to return to Kiev.

It was a miserable station, with the wind blowing through its broken windows. Peasants were lounging on the bare floor, with the sacks of flour they were taking to the market in the town, together with some refugee Jews from the neighbouring small townships, hoping like us to find seats in the train. As soon as the smoke of an engine was seen, the whole crowd flung itself on the track, taking the roofs of the coaches by storm, clinging to the footboards, and trying, with a lot of fierce elbowing and shoving, to push the sacks of food into the compartments. My father, who was not very strong, and I, who was shivering with cold, were roughly shouldered aside by the hefty peasants. One train after another went by, and we were left on the platform, leaning on our luggage, our hearts filled with despair.

Two days went by in this way. On the third a goods train came along, one half empty cattle-trucks, the other, open trucks laden with iron bars. Rallying the remains of our strength, we scrambled on to an open truck. At first we felt a sense of relief. After all, we were moving, we were rolling towards our goal, and every hour that went by was bringing us nearer. But time passed, the train crawled slowly along, an icy wind was blowing, and contact with the iron bars was costing us frost-burns. It was becoming a torture. I took off one of my gloves to blow on my hand; it touched an iron bar by accident, and a strip of skin remained stuck to the frozen metal. A tingling shock ran through me, my arms and legs became gradually heavy with a pleasant sense of warmth, spreading to the whole of my body, and I lost consciousness.

I came to in a warm room full of smoke, lying on four chairs, with my father bending over me. We were at Fastov, a railway centre near Kiev, where he had broken our journey when he saw that I was gradually freezing. The town had been sacked and destroyed by Petliura's soldiers. The only one Jewish house which remained intact was full of survivors come out of hiding after the massacre. My father had knocked at the door, with my frozen body in his arms—he had had to leave the precious sacks of food on the train—and after long entreaties they had allowed him a place on the floor and thrown him a blanket so that he could lay me on some chairs till I recovered consciousness.

After this adventure I was looked upon as a seasoned traveller, and when we arrived in Rujine I acted as guide to my family in the country round. Life in the little town went on uneventfully. There was no lack of food, and the peasants of the neighbouring villages, fearing the soviet authorities, had hidden their knives till a more propitious juncture. We lived in the house of a Jewish family, and the owner took charge of all the details of our journey, hiring the carts, settling the price with the peasants who were to accompany us, and procuring us refugee cards. I do not know how it was that the rumour of our departure spread, but our convoy kept increasing. Every train that stopped at the station brought us either a few young men, or families with children, with familiar or unfamiliar faces. One day our house was invaded by the *halutsim* from Ekaterinburg, and the room rang with their jovial voices. Their mere presence raised our spirits, and it was at once decided that they should form the guard of the convoy, while the conduct of operations should be entrusted to my father. Preparations for the journey lasted several days; then one night we heard the whinnying of horses outside our door. A peasant muffled up in a sheepskin jacket, with a long whip in his hand, got down heavily from the front seat of the wagon and piled our baggage up on a layer of straw. Grandmother and Mother were hoisted in first, in their thick coats and woollen shawls; my sister and little brother were installed on the straw, and the men—my father and I—jumped in last. The peasant cracked his whip, the wheels creaked, and the cart began sliding over the snow in the direction of the forest, the meeting-place of the convoy. The carts stood hidden among the fir-trees and the furtive shadows of the travellers were silhouetted on the snow. Last instructions were given in a low voice, and the horses whinnied, emitting a thick cloud of breath. The sight of our caravan emerging from the heart of the forest and starting along the frozen tracks called up to my mind some forgotten chapter of an adventure story read long ago.

Mother could hardly breathe, the frost was getting into her lungs. 'Good luck to all!' she said, drawing the heads of her children close to her and caressing them sadly. My little brother asked to be allowed to run behind the cart with some boys of his own age who were trotting gleefully beside the horses. Then, slowly, the convoy took the road.

Across the Steppes of the Ukraine

THIS Odyssey in a peasant cart, across the steppes of the Ukraine, haunts my memory as a white nightmare. Years later, the recollection of it could still check an uprush of youthful happiness, and bathe me in a sweat of fear, like some vision of horror. And yet it had all begun like a joyous adventure. After those nights in our freezing apartment in Kiev, blackened by the soot from the iron stove and the oil lamps, it had been so glorious to leap out of the *telega* and run across the snowy fields, hide behind the trees along the road and then climb on to the surly-faced driver's seat and borrow his reins and whip. After a long day's journey it had been delightful to assemble again of an evening in a moujik's cottage outside some remote village—we kept away from the large built-up areas for fear of falling into the hands of the authorities—to lie on top of the tiled Russian stove and eat a slice of black bread soaked in hot milk.

But day followed day and the journey went endlessly on. The grown-ups did not conceal their anxiety, and the children had lost heart in the game. We advanced slowly along winding roads. The convoy began to straggle, and when a wheel of one of the carts got broken everybody had to wait for a new one to be brought from a neighbouring village. The nearer we drew to the Polish frontier, the more armed patrols we met with, and the soldiers examined our creased papers while we held our breath, trembling lest they should discover our real destination. There was nearly always something to pay, and the gold coins and tsarist bank-notes had to come out of their secret hiding-places. Even the peasants with whom we sought shelter treated us surlily, pocketing the agreed ransom and then casting looks of hatred at us that expressed their thoughts only too plainly: 'Your hour will come soon, dirty Jews!'

Search the map of Poland as I will, I can never find the name of the stream we were forced to cross on a dark night of February, after delaying for two days in a village near by. It cannot have been an important river, but it separated us from the frontier and there was no way of getting round it, so it assumed the proportions of the Red Sea, and there was no Moses' rod to help us to cross it dry-shod. The scouts we had sent to look for a ford came back with the news that frontier guards were keeping watch on the bridges, and that according to the peasants the thaw had made the ice unsafe. The convoy took the road at nightfall, and a peasant from the village, into whose hand a gold coin was slipped, went with us as guide.

We had left the snow-covered highway, and the horses panted as they drew the heavily laden carts through drifts of soft, powdery snow. An anxious silence had fallen on the company; even the babies, as if infected by our fears, had stifled their whimpering. The axles creaked softly, and at one in the morning the convoy reached the bank overhanging the river.

The shadow of a bridge stood out on our left; camp fires lighted the sentinels' bivouacs. Our driver got down from his seat, and descended the bank to try the ice with his heavy-shod feet to judge if it would bear the weight of the carts. At last he raised his hand by way of signal, and the other drivers, holding their reins short, started driving down on to the frozen river and across to the other side. Not a sound was heard apart from the creaking of the cart-wheels and the panting of the horses, and we appeared to be out of danger. There were already a few carts awaiting ours on the other bank, and the men who had crossed on foot were standing about in little groups waiting for the convoy to start afresh.

Suddenly voices were heard in the direction of the bridge. The guards, awake at last, were waving their lanterns about in the darkness. A burst of gunfire tore through the night air, and bullets whistled over our heads. The peasants, knowing as they did that they would not get off cheaply if they fell into the hands of the guards, whipped up the horses with fury. The last carts rolled noisily down the bank and crashed on to the ice, which cracked under the shock, black water seeping up through it. Trembling, the women and children remained seated on their bundles, expecting from one minute to another to be engulfed by the stream. Dimly, we saw figures approaching.

I never knew what saved us that night. Was it the snow, in

which the soldiers' heavy boots sank deep? Was it the speed at which the peasants outran them by whipping up their horses? Whatever the reason, we were soon out of reach of danger. A few bullets fired at us went wide, and at daybreak we arrived safe and sound at the place from which we were to start on the last lap of our journey to the frontier.

My father was immediately summoned by the bearded peasant acting as spokesman for the drivers, and told that we must pay the whole of the transport charges at once, and in cash—without waiting till the end of the journey as had been agreed. The incident of the river crossing had opened their eyes. Who could say what tomorrow might not have in store for them? They were running the risk of a hurried retreat that would lose them their pay. My father argued, implored, called on his friends for help, but there was nothing doing. 'Give us our money, or we shall turn back straight away.' We were obliged to submit. The heads of families handed over their share in tsarist bank-notes as agreed. The chief then calmed down and consented to smile. He reassured my father, declaring that the frontier was near, all would be well, there was no need to worry. Soon, he said, all the Jews in the convoy would find themselves in Poland.

The place was not an actual village but a sort of large farm, called in Ukrainian a *khutor*, consisting of two or three houses, a cow-shed and a stable. Our little company settled as best it could into the houses and outbuildings, and the children were bedded down on our bundles and some trusses of straw brought down from the loft of the cow-shed. It was weeks since we had eaten our fill; our linen, which we had not changed since we started, was crawling with lice, and even the little children got no proper sleep, scratching themselves till they bled. We were tired to death. But none of us had paid much attention to these miseries; hope had buoyed us up. The frontier was near, offering us safety. Soon, we knew, our torments would be over.

But when we awoke next morning and went out prepared to resume our journey, the courtyard was empty. The drivers had fled with their carts and horses, after flinging our luggage pell-mell on the snow. We were abandoned more than twenty-four miles from the frontier.

II

After all these years that moment is still vivid in my memory. As we stood in that deserted courtyard, like shipwrecked mariners whose bark had been swallowed up by the sea, there seemed nothing left to hope for. The peasants flashed us looks of hatred; even the silver coins slipped into their hands no longer had any effect. They seemed to be saying: 'What's the use, since anyhow all they possess is ours already?'

While the leaders of our company debated the next move, and sent emissaries round the neighbourhood in quest of transport, one of the peasants disappeared from the farm. Several hours went by in anxious waiting. Then, suddenly, there was a sound of galloping horses and cracking whips, and to the terrified crowd of refugees this could only mean one thing: the Cossacks! The Cossacks! There was enough in the name alone to freeze a Jew's heart with terror in the Russia of those days. They were overrunning the townships of the Ukraine in raiding bands. Every army was competing for the services of these hardy horsemen, who sold their swords to the highest bidder, to the Red Army of the Bolsheviks as willingly as to Denikin's White Army or the Ukrainian gangs, so long as their freedom was not restricted. Wherever they went, Jewish blood flowed. They destroyed, pillaged and raped from township to township, under orders or without. The horsemen who now held us at their mercy had a red star on their caps, so they belonged to the Bolshevik army and formed part, no doubt, of a unit of frontier guards.

They dismounted, and rushed towards the houses and outbuildings, driving the refugees out into the yard with whips that did not spare the children. 'Your papers!' they shouted. But when we brought out our crumpled documents they threw them on the ground without deigning to look at them. 'Liars, forgers, counter-revolutionists! You want to get into Poland, do you? We'll show you Poland!' A violent box on the ear flung my father on to the snow. The young men tried to rush to his assistance, but they were driven back by the lashing whips. There was nothing to be done; we were now prisoners of the Red Cossacks.

All at once, from all sides, carts appeared, driven by the local peasants, and for an hour or more the soldiers searched our baggage, pitching into the carts everything of value—furs, blankets and clothing, throwing out the rest on the snowdrifts. The peasants took part in the search, hastily concealing a silver goblet or an embroidered tablecloth in a capacious coat-pocket. The loss of these things mattered no longer to any of us, although they represented the whole of our possessions on earth. Death was spreading its shadow over us all, terror was overtaking even the smallest of the children.

The Cossacks stowed away their loot, regrouped us in the yard, and ordered us into the emptied carts. An armed soldier, gun in hand, seated himself beside each driver. Where were they taking us? 'We're handing you over to the district authorities in Novgorod-Volynsk, you sons of bitches,' said one of the Cossacks indifferently, uttering the insult without heat or anger. They mounted their horses and took the lead of the convoy, with the string of carts trailing behind them. We huddled against one another, shivering with cold and fear.

Night fell, and the convoy travelled blind. We could not even see the soldiers. But after a time we realized that we were entering a thick forest: tall trees mingled their branches above the narrow track. How long this journey lasted I do not know—maybe an hour or more. Our hearts were beating furiously, our lips were dry and our throats congested by a spasm of terror. Suddenly the carts came to a stop, and the report of a rifle broke the silence of the forest. The horses reared. The Cossacks stood before us, pistol in hand. 'Get out, carrion! Pack of bourgeois, get out of the carts!'

The sequel remains to this day like a chapter of some horror tale I had read. Shadows among the trees, babies crying, women uttering cries of terror. The Cossacks sent their whip-lashes whistling through the air, and blood flowed down the white faces of our companions. The soldiers tore the fur coats off the women's shoulders and lined up the men, to feel their clothes for hidden treasures, all that remained to them after the pillage in the farmyard.

I can still see my father, shivering with cold without his overcoat, being led by two soldiers to the commander of the Cossacks.

'You there with the moustache, you're the chief of the smugglers, are you?' My father made no reply, and the officer raised his whip. 'Now we'll show you how to cross a frontier. To Poland, they wanted to go!' Two soldiers dragged my father away by the arms and stood him against a tree. Someone gave the order 'To the wall!' Everybody knew what those two words meant in Russia. Soon we should hear the report of the gun. My mother appeared suddenly out of nowhere and spoke rapidly in a low voice to the commander. He drove her back with the handle of his whip. My own voice broke into a cry. Men and women moved among the trees. Suddenly I saw our friends from the Urals, the handful of good *halutsim*, approaching and mingling in the dark with the ring of soldiers. They surrounded my father, threw him to the ground with a violent blow and dragged him behind them over the snow. When the commander turned his head his victim was no longer there. A few hours earlier the soldiers would have hunted for him, no doubt, but in the darkness of the forest they could hardly have distinguished one man from another. Anyway, the Cossacks were now busy counting their fresh booty—coats, furs, money and diamonds. Some time went by, and the danger seemed averted.

When we got back into the carts I saw that my father had been dressed in a coat belonging to one of our party and his face hidden by a borrowed cap. For the space of a second somebody looked fixedly at him. I held my breath. Would they recognize him? No, the guard turned away. The officer leapt into the saddle. My father was safe.

The convoy took the road again. Were they going to deliver us into the hands of the *Cheka*, the dreaded Security Police, in the district capital? One of our company, familiar with the country, reassured us. We were not driving in that direction. We had passed the turning to Novgorod-Volynsk and were approaching the Polish frontier.

At sunrise we halted in the courtyard of a disused police station near the frontier. We were all pushed into a large room without chairs or tables, and dropped exhausted on the frozen floor. Sunshine struggling through the dirty windows promised a bright, warm spring day. Winter had suddenly come to an end, and the mounds of snow were melting in the yard. In the adjoining room we could hear the voices of the Cossacks, shreds of conversation, abuse and shouts. It was clear that our fate was in the balance. Were they going to deliver us up to the authorities or drive us back from the frontier? As usual, in each group there was a man who knew everything, and our particular oracle told us what he had gathered from the random sentences he had overheard. The Cossacks were discussing the fate of their booty. If they handed us over to the authorities the pillage would be discovered, and they would be forced to return the lot; they might even be punished. It would be much better to set us free.

We had eaten nothing that morning nor the day before, but nobody cared. Towards evening the door opened. Two Cossacks appeared in the doorway and ordered us to get up and follow them. Was it death? They vaulted into the saddle and drove us forward. 'Hurry, gang of Jews, hurry! We haven't time to drag after you!' Summoning the remains of our strength we quickened our pace, carrying the small children in our arms.

The thaw had set in, and the thick mud clung to our boots. Robbed of our warm clothing, we felt the cold striking through to our bones, and yet we were streaming with sweat. We walked as fast as we could, exhausted and afraid. My mother was panting. I had hold of her arm, and could feel her rallying her strength so as not to be left behind. She stumbled, recovered her breath and went on. It was a dark night. A single spot of light shone in the distance, somewhere on the horizon.

The Cossacks reined in their horses. 'Listen, you sheenies! The light you see over there is the Polish frontier post. Trot along to it, and the devil take you! And take care you don't come back to us, or we'll kill you like dogs.'

The human herd struggled along. The twinkling light seemed to draw further away from us the nearer we approached it. The thick mud clinging to our feet made the going harder and harder. We went on and on, and all at once I wanted to drop down where I stood, to lie flat on the ground, fall asleep and stay there—anything to put an end to this interminable march. After what seemed an eternity we could see the outline of a house with lighted windows. A burst of gunfire resounded in our rear. Was this a warning given us by the Cossacks, or had they run into the frontier guard?

Suddenly we heard the trampling of horses close by.

'Who goes there? Halt, or we fire!'

My mother, the only one among us to speak Polish, answered the patrol. 'We're refugees,' she told him. 'We're coming home to Poland.'

'Follow me,' he said, 'we'll check that over yonder.'

In the Polish police station two Jews were seated in a corner near the hot stove. They came from Koretz, a small town near the frontier, sent by the Jewish community there to meet Jewish refugees fleeing from Russia. They were to parley with the frontier guard, offer the authorities their guarantee, and see to it that the Jews were not driven back from the frontier. They immediately came to our help, giving the children milk, spreading blankets on the floor, asking questions and starting conversations with us. My father stood before them unshaven, with tousled hair, lingering terror in the depths of his eyes. 'Koretz? Koretz?' he said. 'Do you perhaps know so-and-so?' He mentioned the name of the correspondent that his paper had had at one time in the town. He told them his own name, and the good Jews of Koretz flung their arms round his neck. 'What! You've come! It's you! What an honour for us!' And it turned out that they were old readers of the *Hatsefira*, and admirers of my father's articles, which they remembered from long before the war.

They consoled us all, as we lay there utterly exhausted on the floor. 'Don't worry,' they said, 'you've nothing more to fear.'

The door of the Polish officer's office closed behind them. We heard the rustling of paper and murmurs of talk. A few minutes later the whole of our caravan set out in the direction of the little town, the lights of which shone in the distance.

Two or three hours later my sister and I were seated in a warm room in the house of the head of the Koretz community, at a table on which were a pot of honey and a big round loaf of bread. My parents and my little brother were asleep in our hosts' beds, and we were waiting for a place to be found for us. I cut slice after slice of the black bread, fresh and sweet-smelling, buttering them and spreading them with honey, devouring them one after another. My little sister was sitting opposite, and

I saw the slices disappearing down her throat too, and her eyes recovering their brilliance.

No meal I have ever eaten since has tasted more delicious than those slices of bread and honey in the little frontier town of Poland.

Beyond the Frontier

I

THE day that dawned after that night of darkness illumined a fairy world. Beyond the border line separating the little *staedtel* from the hut of the frontier guards, now blurred in the mist, foamed the waters of the fabled Sambation, but on this side a sabbath peace reigned in a world whose existence we had forgotten. A quiet, wonderfully real world. A house flooded with the warmth of a white stove, beds with clean sheets, pillows and eiderdowns, a table loaded with delicious food: potatoes baked in the embers, yellow butter running off the point of the knife, thick, steaming soup in an earthenware bowl. Calm in the street. A door opens, a Jew comes out of his house and walks placidly towards his neighbour's, without glancing round him in fear. Polish soldiers and frontier guards enter a shop to buy a packet of cigarettes and exchange a polite word or two with a passer-by. A good Jewish citizen, seated in his armchair after a meal, opens a Yiddish newspaper, just come from Warsaw, and reads aloud to his family the latest news of the debates in the Polish Diet, the Community Council elections, and the events taking place in far-off Jaffa and Jerusalem. Can all this world have been in existence while we were starving in Kiev, barricading ourselves against the rioters and enduring the terrors of our distressful trek to the frontier?

The Jews of the little town had invited us into their houses and were showering kindnesses upon us. We had come from Russia destitute of everything, and the agents of the American Joint Distribution Committee rigged us out from head to foot. I was provided with a long, warm coat of an uncertain colour inclining to mauve. I was also equipped with a suit that must have belonged to a corpulent American Jew—the sleeves were too long, and the trousers were so wide that I had to have a string tied tightly round my waist to prevent them from slipping.

Of an evening the heads of the Council came to the house that was sheltering us, to discuss the next stage of our travels with my father and give him the latest news of other Jewish communities in Poland. My parents listened avidly, begging for news of old friends they had been cut off from for many years. What newspapers were being published? What were the leading Zionists doing? Was it true that so many *halutsim* had left for Palestine? And as far as we were concerned, should we be able to continue our journey? Under what conditions, and who would help us? We were told that the community of Rovno, the chief town of the province, where we had many friends, had been informed of our arrival; the Zionists were at the head of the community there, and the relief committees were helping the parties of refugees that stopped there on their way to the Promised Land.

By order of the frontier authorities we were confined to our residence, as newly arrived immigrants from Soviet territory without identity papers. A bored policeman paraded up and down the street, seeing to it that none of us ventured outside the village. But a few days later our intercessors announced that the commandant of the local garrison had decided to send us to Rovno under police escort, who would hand over our dossier to the provincial authorities. We were packed off, one fine morning, in a cab drawn by a pair of horses, with a uniformed guard beside the driver, and the notables of the village went a little way with us before my parents took leave of them, tears of gratitude in their eyes.

Rovno, the first important town this side of the frontier, was full of refugees dressed in the strange garments distributed by the American philanthropic organizations. From there they scattered to the four winds, either to return to their little native town, to settle in Warsaw or the neighbourhood, or to make for Palestine. The immigration candidates were mostly young people infiltrated from Russia like ourselves, or Polish citizens who had come in from all the surrounding villages for the purpose of their *Aliya* and were besieging the offices of the community and the AJDC to secure their travelling expenses.

All this motley crowd of *halutsim* and large families were lodged in the public buildings and schools of the community. I still have a photograph of one of the groups, taken in a school yard the day before they left, muffled up in their American overcoats, or proudly throwing out their chests in their Russian blouses, tightly held at the waist by a leather belt, their luxuriant hair crowned with a peaked cap.

My mother slept in a room in the town, while the men and children settled down for the night on the school forms and desks. It was Easter time, and the pupils were on holiday. The days were warm now, but we were still cold at night under our blankets. In the evening the *halutsim* met in the class-rooms and launched into endless discussions, rehashing the Zionist ideology and weaving their dreams of establishing *kibbutsim* in Palestine. The children watched them with admiring eyes and were always at their heels. As an adolescent, I was admitted to this grown-up company but not taken very seriously. Most of these young pioneers were seventeen or eighteen years old and entirely independent, whereas I was still tied to my mother's apron-strings, and could only be present as a dumb, admiring disciple.

The young men from Ekaterinburg who had travelled with us from Kiev were the most active of the *halutsim* party. After that night in the forest, when by their daring intervention they had saved my father from certain death, they had assumed an aureole of heroes in my eyes, and I longed to be accepted as a full member of their company. Once in Palestine I would help them to clear the land for their communal fields, and together we would build the village they had talked about all these evenings at the school. Their colony would be the largest and finest in the country. I hoped secretly that they would invite me to join them, and I saw myself bidding my parents goodbye and attaching myself to my new party. But the call never came. At light-hearted moments, when all the young people joined hands to sing Zionist songs or dance a *hora*, I was dragged into the circle with the others, but when the time came for discussions I was left sitting sadly in my corner.

Who would have thought at that time that this ardent group, so greatly admired, would be dissolved and scattered almost as soon as it arrived in Palestine? The young pioneers were unable to realize their dream of founding a village of their own, and tried to find work as agricultural labourers in the old settlements, but they were soon obliged to separate. Some of them got jobs building roads, or hewing stones in the quarries at Jerusalem. Others settled in the towns, and I often came across them here and there. I heard in this way that a handful of them had enlisted in the *Gdud Avoda*—the Labour Battalion, one of the big Labour associations of the time—and when this was dissolved towards the end of the twenties, disappointed at the way things had turned out in the country, they had joined the communists and left the Labour group. In the end they went back to Russia, where all trace of them was lost. It was a great blow to me; I could not bear to think that those heroes of my youth, those *halutsim* so full of ardour and enthusiasm, could have met such a tragic end.

II

Good food, medical care and complete rest put my mother on her feet again. She was still coughing and short of breath, but she had recovered her spirits, and looked forward to the rest of our journey and the sunshine of the Orient that was to restore her finally to health. My father, too, was a new man; he had returned to his natural milieu, from which the war had cut him off. I am not sure what work he had found, but he was getting a salary, and brought enough money home to buy us all clothes, besides house-linen for our future home. He sat on a school form in the evening, covering long sheets of paper with minute black characters, as in the old days. His articles began reappearing in the Warsaw papers; and the *Morgen-Journal* of New York, one of whose Russian correspondents he had been before the war, had resumed contact with him. As soon as the first cheques arrived from the United States we packed and moved to Warsaw.

The months in the capital went by like a dream. We lived in a timber-built house at Otwock, a local holiday resort in the middle of a forest. After the privations we had suffered in Russia this little nook of Jewish life seemed a paradise, and plenty a daily renewed miracle. At dawn a Jew in a black caftan and a little hasidic cap left a basket on our doorstep, full of delicious rolls, butter, cream and eggs. At the sound of his footsteps I leapt out of bed to watch this prodigious proceeding from the doorway, and sometimes, unable to resist the temptation, I stretched out my hand to grasp a roll and nibbled it slowly, to convince myself that it was no illusion.

I often went to the newspaper offices in Warsaw with my father, and the beauty of the city made a great impression on me. It was exciting, too, to be seeing with my own eyes so many of the famous men—Zionist leaders, journalists and authors— all friends of my father's, that I had heard so much about during our years of exile in Russia.

Warsaw was the capital of liberated Poland. Anti-Semitism was rife in the provinces, and Jewish students were being perse- cuted by their colleagues at the universities, but the heads of the Jewish community were convinced that this was no more than a momentary crisis, a sort of children's illness from which the young nation must soon recover. Isaac Grunbaum, at whose house we stayed on our visits to Warsaw, was the proud, indomitable spokesman of the Jewish minority in the Polish Diet. The Zionists, whose ranks were increasing thanks to the expansion of Jewish Palestine, set the tone in most sections of the community press. Owing to the isolation of Russia, cut off by the blank wall of the communist régime, Poland had become the centre of Jewish life in Europe, and the political parties that used to fight one another in Odessa, Kiev and Moscow, had migrated to Warsaw where they were carrying on their quarrels with the same virulence as before.

We were no longer alone in speaking Hebrew. *Tarbut* schools had been started all over the country, and we often met boys and girls among our friends who could express themselves fluently in a Hebrew as pure as our own. Young people from the remotest townships were flocking to the training centres, and the Palestine Office in the capital was always crowded with people preparing for the *Aliya*. Accounts of Palestine in the Yiddish dailies were read with avidity, and my father could now give himself free rein and publish his articles in more than one journal. He wrote feuilletons and literary articles, gave lectures, and his friends urged him not to leave the country, assuring him that he would find plenty of well-paid work in Poland. Some of them shrugged their shoulders and did not conceal their disapproval when my parents told them that they were preparing for *Aliya*. What would they do over there? It would be better to wait a few years in Warsaw and save a little nest-egg, until conditions in Palestine improved. The population there was small at present, and very poor, newcomers found no work, and there could be little hope of making a livelihood. But my father rejected all these attempts at persuasion. 'We haven't made this long trek,' he said, 'to stop halfway.' As for my mother, she did not even argue with them, but went on quietly packing our goods and chattels.

The news from Palestine was certainly not encouraging. Letters from our friends in Jerusalem and Jaffa gave a sombre picture. The Jewish Government referred to in the reports we received from Odessa was no more than a dream. At Passover in 1920 riots broke out in Jerusalem. A month earlier Trumpeldor and his comrades had fallen at Tel-Hai, a small fortified spot on the northern frontier of the country. As the months went by and we neared 1921, Polish Zionists became increasingly pessimistic, and were justified by events. One day we read in the papers that disturbances had broken out in Jaffa, many Jews were killed by Arabs and the British Government had suspended Jewish immigration.

Our stay in Poland was thus prolonged beyond all expectation. A cold wind began blowing again, the autumn rains poured over the roof, and the cold crept through the cracks in the timbers of our *datcha* in Otwock. The school year had begun and we were not attending school. Mother packed and unpacked, Grandmother baked her cakes in preparation for the journey and stowed them away in her red tin. When our departure was delayed yet again she summoned her grandchildren and distributed the goodies between them, lest they should grow mouldy in the meantime. My father went to town every morning to make enquiries at the Palestine Office with no result. Our friends assured us that restrictions would soon be lifted—but meanwhile we were stuck there, half citizens, half refugees, and Palestine seemed further off every day.

At last my father brought us the great news. The permit had been issued, the passport was ready, all that remained was to have the British visa stamped on it. A few more days went by while my mother hurriedly finished our packing. We donned our new clothes, and the 'halutsim train' left for Vienna.

We were delayed in the Austrian capital for another few

weeks along with a large contingent of *olim* and *halutsim* awaiting their entry permit to Palestine. The first days were a time of
enchantment for us youngsters, as we roamed about the great city,
entranced by the marvels of the Prater, and watching the Great
Wheel turning. I was dispatched from the second-class hotel
where we were staying to a café nearby to get a kettleful of
boiling water for a few *kreutzer*, and we drank a vast number of
glasses of tea in our room, with young men still in Russian
student uniform, young pioneers trained for work on the land,
and simple Jews who had joined our convoy in Warsaw. The
most contradictory news reached us, as we went tirelessly to the
Palestine Office only to return more discouraged than ever.
Weeks went by, and the hotel porter began casting suspicious
glances at the miserable emigrants who were still hanging on to
their rooms. We were sick of the beauties of the town. At the
end of such a long, hard trail, were we to be told, on this last
lap, that the gates of Palestine were closed? My father posted
letter after letter to Jerusalem and Warsaw, to the people he
knew in the Zionist Commission. Their replies were brief and
disappointing. Nothing doing. We must be patient.

The delay dragged on, and we were on the verge of despair,
when at last we were sent word from Jerusalem that immigration was authorized again. The hundreds of passengers who had
been held up in Vienna prepared to leave. We joined a party of
halutsim who were to embark on the liner *Helouan*, of the
Lloyd-Triestino Company, bound for Alexandria. A picturesque
crowd gathered at the station: families burdened with children,
parties of young men and girls shouldering knapsacks, officials of
the Palestine Office running hither and thither, distributing railway tickets and rations of food, and helping the passengers to
stow their luggage. At last, to the shrill whistle of the engine,
the trainload got under way.

Once through the Tyrol we entered a southern, sunlit landscape. The ship was waiting for us at Trieste, dazzling white,
rocking gently on the waves of a blue sea. All was new and
strange to our eyes, and each day of the voyage brought us
something fresh: the ship itself, the first we had ever seen, the
bunches of grapes on the wharf at Brindisi, island coasts, and
little fishermen's huts; the shrill cries of the Arab stevedores in

Alexandria, the burning sun of Egypt, the railway journey at night from Alexandria to Kantara, the red fezzes of the Egyptian customs officers and the brown burnouses of the Beduins, the undulating shadows of a camel caravan moving over the desert sandhills.

By midnight we had reached the Suez Canal, and when day broke, a white train of the Palestine Railways was slowly making its way across the sands of Negev and the verdant orange plantations of the coastal plain.

PART TWO

The Rocks of Jerusalem

Daybreak in Galilee

I

AT DAYBREAK on a bright October morning of 1921 the train slowed down and came to a stop in Haifa station. The journey was over. We were at last about to tread the soil of Palestine. Exhausted though we were by the final ordeals of our pilgrimage—going through the disinfection station in Alexandria, waiting at night at Benha junction in the desert wind of Egypt—when the reddening dawn appeared over the desert sands all our sufferings were wiped out. In the morning air we felt a little dizzy from want of sleep, but we stared with wide-open eyes at the marvels around us, and our hearts throbbed at the thought of the unknown awaiting us in this new country where we were now to make our home.

Even at Kantara, on the edge of the desert, it was like a dream come true. There was a notice in Hebrew on the side of the coach, an official was talking politely to the passengers and wishing them *shalom*, the brass badge on his uniform telling us in our own language that he was a ticket-collector. Then came the desert by moonlight, and the palm-trees casting their long, slender shadows over the sands of El-Arish, and, from Rehovoth onwards, Jews filling the compartments, travelling without fear or haste, exchanging quiet remarks about things of no importance. And all that in Hebrew, as a matter of course.

At Haifa we were approached by a young man in khaki shorts and an open-necked shirt, offering politely to help us get our luggage down. The Arab porter in a tarbush took possession of our bags on the platform and smiled at us from under his trimmed moustache, assuring us in his halting Yiddish that *Haifa nishto ganef!* ('In Haifa no thieves!')

Grandmother took the announcement seriously. She had feared that the motley crowd of Arabs and Jews jostling in the market-place were intent on her possessions. Keeping her red-painted tin firmly under her arm, she scrutinized her strange surroundings: the goyim, unlike any she had seen in her little native town, and

71

the Jews—strange bronzed, weather-beaten Jews, walking con-
fidently through the narrow streets lined with houses of yellow
stone, running down the slopes of Mount Carmel.

Everything struck us as new and strange. The roughly paved
streets full of hawkers, and sellers of fruit and vegetables, whose
stalls sagged under the weight of grapes of Hebron, juicy and
transparent. The Arab cabmen on the look-out for passengers
in Hamra Square, the central square of the lower town, and the
lemonade sellers clashing their little brass plates together to draw
attention to their merchandise; Jewish tradesmen standing in the
doorways of their shops, the sleeves of their white shirts rolled up
to the elbow, and children running about, their sandals clatter-
ing on the paving-stones.

Our porter had taken our bags on his back and a big bundle
on his head, and led us by narrow lanes to the flight of stone
steps at the entrance to our first hotel in the land of Israel.

We were lodged in a single room, whose vaulted ceiling gave
it a strange grandeur. We had hardly stowed our luggage in a
corner and spread the mattresses and blankets on the paved floor,
before we were asleep; and we spent the whole day dozing till
sundown. Night fell suddenly, and we were given a little paraffin lamp. At dawn next day the Arab porter reappeared to
carry our luggage to the Turkish station, and put us into a compartment of the little narrow-gauge train for Semakh, whence
we were to reach the Galilean village that was the goal of our
journey.

The engine belched a puff of black smoke and started off at a
leisurely pace, as if taking as much pleasure in contemplating the
landscape as we did. Our fellow passengers treated us amicably;
they were surprised to hear us speak such good Hebrew, and
questioned us at length as to our plans. They pointed out with
pride the biblical sites on our way, pronouncing names that had
had a halo of sanctity about them when we read our Bible round
the sooty stove in Russia. Here was the Carmel range, crowned
with green thickets and looking like the vignette on the bottles
of 'Carmel Oriental' wine. Then the bridge over the Kishon—
how small and insignificant it looked!—the ancient river sung by
the prophetess Deborah. And here was Mount Tabor, and over
there, the hills of Gilboa. Here was the first settlement to be

established in the Emek, the wall of the communal village of Merhavia. The train made a long stop outside some Arab huts built of *pisé*, near Afoula station, and then, as it ran between the slopes of Gilboa and Givat-Hamore, we caught sight of a group of white tents pitched on the hillside near the source of Ein-Harod.

'Those are some young people from the latest *Aliya*,' we were told. 'The place is called Nouris, and they are starting a new settlement there.'

The train, with its panting engine, went slowly on, stopping at small stations, picking up and dropping Beduins with big moustaches. Early in the afternoon it brought us to Semakh. An Arab cabman drove us to the *kibbutz* of Degania, where a lanky youth met us beside the hut that was doing duty as a refectory.

He introduced himself and began unloading our luggage. In the spacious refectory he poured us cups of tea, offered us some dried figs and began firing off questions. What was happening in Russia? And what would become of the *olim* who had remained in Vienna? And what news of the Warsaw Zionists? My father answered him with a beaming face as he sat there, hardly daring to believe himself in Degania, on the shores of the Jordan, talking Hebrew with this young scholar who had turned to farming. While this was going on I went out into the yard with the children, to feast my eyes on the palms and fruit-trees, the plough standing beside a straw-stack, and the cows returning from their pasture.

It was getting late. Our young friend harnessed a couple of mules to his cart, and we seated ourselves on our baggage again, forded the Jordan and landed up at nightfall in the yard of a peasant's house in the old settlement of Kinereth. The settler, a true Jewish peasant, was awaiting us in his doorway with his wife and children. They welcomed us warmly into their little house built of black basalt, and conversation started at once beside the table spread for a meal. The children ran about, playing, while the grown-ups went on endlessly talking. What was life like in Russia? And when would our Polish friends be coming?

Next morning we started off again in a cart and on foot, climbing slowly to the ridge of Mount Kinereth, in the direction of the Valley of Yavniel.

II

Beth-Gan was no more than a little Galilean village with some ten families living in houses built of black basalt, with one two-storied building doing duty as village hall and school, but the name stood for a legend of our childhood.

Among our family photographs of gentlemen with moustaches and stiff collars, and corseted ladies in feather-trimmed hats, there was one of a guard on horseback, gun in hand, an Arab *kefiya* on his head, the very picture of valour. This uncle from Galilee, of whom we were so proud, had left his wealthy parents' house in Lodz in his youth and come to Palestine with the second *Aliya*, where he was allotted the task of mounting guard round the peasants' farms in Yavniel and Sedjera. But when the PICA decided to found new settlements in Galilee, and he could set up on his own account, he returned to his native town to look for a wife. From among the girls of Lodz he chose my mother's sister. A pampered, well-educated young lady, she surprised everybody by following her husband to this wild spot in distant Galilee, and there were countless stories of the trials they had had to go through and the difficulty the young lady of Lodz had found in adapting herself to her new home. Her husband, faithful to the ascetic tradition of *Hashomer*, refused to make concession to comfort in his house, as a derogation from the virtue of proletarian simplicity. She had had some difficulty in persuading him to lay tiles on the mud floor, not before she had been obliged to spend a whole day on a table, terrified by a mouse. Her husband had left the house to plough his field, and found her there when he came back in the evening. Many other tales were told of this couple, as curious incidents of pioneering life in Palestine, but in our eyes, as children, this Galilean farmer fighting brigands and drawing his livelihood from the soil was arrayed in heroic glory.

We imagined him galloping on his noble Arab mare, the folds of his burnous flying, putting to flight the Arabs, fighting the Beduin robbers. Even his name had the sound of glorious deeds. He shed his old *galuth* name of Berele Bilotworsky to become Dov Ben-Galil, the son of Galilee. So Dov Ben-Galil and Beth-Gan stood for all the virtues of pioneer heroism. We looked upon Galilee and its inhabitants as the incarnation of our children's books. Noble Beduins and brave Jewish guards, fearlessly bestriding their horses, riding like the wind from hill crest to hill crest, were the great heroes of our games and dreams, against the background of the village with the magical name of Beth-Gan.

The reality was very different, but the picture of the uncle that was its hero remained untarnished even when we met him in the flesh. Times had changed, and the glorious hour of the Galilean peasant-farmers was over. The *Hagana*, a clandestine military organization, had replaced the *Hashomer* and its heroes, the *kibbutz* had supplanted the individual village. Everything around him was evolving. Some friends had prospered and were now public characters, politicians, popular orators; some of them leaving their farms for the town had soon made a fortune. But he, Dov Ben-Galil, was still weaving the dream of his youth, as far as ever from reality, faithful to the spirit of abnegation of the first pioneers, which never deserted him, but sustained him through poverty and suffering to his last day.

The Beth-Gan we came upon that autumn day had certainly nothing about it of the golden picture of our fancy. Two villages had taken root in the wide, fertile valley, and ours, the smaller of the two, nestled in the shadow of the mountain, with its few houses scattered along the edges of a track rutted by cart-wheels.

Two cypresses stood in front of the house, surrounded by basalt stone, carved with bunches of grapes and pomegranates, relics of some ancient Galilean synagogue. An unfenced terrace led to the living-room, and behind this was a large yard from which arose the smell of the *taboun*, a pit dug in the ground, Arab fashion, used for cooking. Hens were hopping about, cows lay around on their stable litter. At sunrise the master of the house climbed the mountain to his *haccura*, a vineyard on the slope, followed by his Arab day-labourer, who helped on the farm after the fashion of the day and had nothing about him of the noble Arabs of our fairy-tales.

When our cart turned into the village street, the children crowded round it, staring curiously at our unfamiliar faces and listening to our strange Hebrew. Our aunt clapped her hands at the sight of us, and her eyes filled with tears as she embraced the mother and sister she had not seen for so many years. Newcomers were rare at that time, and the Galilean children plied us with questions. 'They've come from Russia!' cried one boy with pride. 'Say, is it true that the Arabs talk Russian in Russia?' queried another.

I felt old among these boys of my own age, born and bred here. I had come from the wide world, I had lived through the nightmares of the war, the Revolution, the riots and our long trek across the Ukraine. I had seen big cities, Warsaw, Moscow, Kiev, Vienna. I had crossed the wide sea. And yet who was I beside these boys whose horizon was bounded by a dusty street, many of whom had never even seen Tiberias, and had never got as far as Semakh and knew the railway only by hearsay. I felt them to be superior to myself because of their self-confidence, their lack of fear, and their feeling of being at home, in their own country. They were a part of the place, whereas I was a stranger from beyond the seas. I knew I should find it very difficult to become one of them. They were the reality of the country, whereas I had only the memory of books and imaginary tales. They were real children, like all the children of the world, but who could give me back the childhood I had been robbed of in the snows of a world gone mad?

That evening all the inhabitants of Ben-Gath came to wish us welcome. Relations between the families of the neighbourhood were usually strained, but the big event of the day wiped out all acrimony for the time being. Friends and enemies sat together in the dark room, dimly lighted by a paraffin lamp that threw their shadows on the walls. As the guests helped themselves to almonds and raisins from a dish, questions and answers followed one another, punctuated by nods, sighs, and sidelong glances at the newcomers—odd-looking people who reminded them of a world they had deserted in early youth. Conversation would have gone on forever if my aunt had not made a move, saying, 'Well, it's growing late; soon we shall be getting up to milk the cows.'

At dawn next day I was tagging at my uncle's heels, following him round the yard, untying the calves' halters and taking them to the meadow. I followed the Arab labourer going to harness the mules, and stroked a donkey's neck—the first donkey I had ever seen. The sun rose higher, and an oppressive heat settled on the valley. The village children were waiting for us outside the ring fence, shouting, laughing, scuffling their bare feet merrily in the dust of the road. They showed us round their little village and invited us to visit their big neighbour, Yavniel. A bearded peasant we met on the way gave us a broad grin from the seat of his cart. 'Well, boy, d'you like our Galilee?' he cried.

Sweat was pouring down my forehead, I was scarlet from the sun. The children took us to the door of the school, summoned the pupils who were playing in the yard and announced, 'Look at this lot, they've come from Russia!' They said it with visible pride, as if proclaiming, 'See what happens to us in our little Beth-Gan, and not in your big Yavniel!'

We were surrounded once more by faces burning with curiosity, until the master, a young man in spectacles, came up and spoke to me as one speaks to grown-ups. He asked me about the Revolution, and told me the history of Yavniel in return, pointing out the Wadi Fidjas, running from there to the valley of the Jordan, and the Golan hills showing blue in the distance beyond the Lake of Tiberias. When the bell rang, masters and pupils returned to their class-rooms, and our little party took the road back to Beth-Gan.

We spent several peaceful, relaxed weeks there. My father wrote constantly to friends in Jerusalem and Jaffa, asking them to find him some work, and at last he was told that he had been appointed Secretary of the Jewish National Council.

The school year was beginning, and it was decided that the two younger ones should remain in Beth-Gan for the time being and attend the school at Yavniel. I was to go to Jerusalem with my father, where he would assume his new duties and I should at last return to my interrupted schooling.

The City of my Youth

I SHALL always remember Jerusalem as I saw it first, with a light rain falling on its roofs, and puddles forming in the thick mud among a welter of rocks. On rainy nights a cold wind swept the waste ground between Jaffa Street and Zikhron-Moshé and the rock-strewn fields of the Bokharan quarter, and in the dark streets the paraffin lamps were no more than faint spots of light with misty haloes.

Then as now Jerusalem spread out over its rocky hills to the west of the Old City, in enclosed settlements isolated from one another by outcrops of stone. The Old City was still the heart of the capital; all distances were measured from the Jaffa Gate, and cabs carried passengers from Meah-Shearim and Zikhron-Moshé as far as the wall of the city, the drive costing a piastre. When the first shaky little motor buses were introduced, in which seats cost only half a piastre, I saw a procession of cabbies manifesting their displeasure. Jews and Arabs, seated in their cabs, they assembled near the Jaffa Gate to protest to the authorities against the loss of their livelihood. Actually only the well-to-do could afford to travel by cab. The common herd went on foot, wading through the mud in winter and ploughing through the dust in summer, keeping well to the middle of the road even after the streets had been lined with narrow sidewalks, and the good citizens of Jerusalem keep this custom to this day.

The New City extended as far as Jaffa Street; beyond this was open country. Little stone fences separated the main street from the wheat and barley fields stretching on the south as far as the convent of Ratisbonne. Past winding alleys one came to the Bezalel School of Art, looked upon at that time as one of the architectural marvels of the city. The site intended for the modern quarters of today was still an area of undulating land bearing a few decrepit trees. It was not till years later that the first street leading to the south of the town was opened up. I was already an old inhabitant, in the last classes of the secondary school, when

One day, passing the corner of Jaffa Street, I caught sight of a party of V.I.P.s, British and Arab, headed by Sir Herbert Samuel, the High Commissioner, and Ragheb bly Nashashibi, the Mayor of Jerusalem, wearing his red tarbush. They were unveiling a stele beside a cutting across the wheatfields, marking the line of a new street that was to bear the name of the King of England, George V. Some time later a second street was cut through not far away, and as the official opening was celebrated soon after the death of Eliezer Ben-Yehuda, even the Arab members of the Municipal Council agreed that his name should be given to the street. After this the business centre of the city moved more and more towards the top of Jaffa Street, in the heart of the Jewish City.

Sheltered from the unrest of modern times, Jerusalem slumbered, still weaving the traditional texture of its communities and its ancient quarters. In the courtyards of the Houses of Warsaw and the Houses of Hungary, children played, side-curls fluttering in the wind, and the voices of zealous pupils rang out from the *yeshivot*, the religious schools of Meah-Shearim. The singsong of the precentors and the devout lamentations of the *hasidim* arose from the synagogues on the sabbath. In the Bokharan tenements carpets were spread over the paved floors of the vast rooms; old men pottered about the streets in multicoloured garments and gold-embroidered skull-caps. In the gloom of Sephardic houses, where the light penetrated only through the wooden slats of little loggias, the family lay on low cushions along the walls, enjoying orange preserves and munching almonds after the repose of the sabbath, as their ancestors had done in Smyrna and Saragossa. Tradition held sway among the Ashkenazim, and even emancipated families that sent their children to the lay schools—consigned to the fires of Hell by the preachers of Meah-Shearim in their sabbath sermons—still breathed the spirit of the dark alleys of the Old City and communal life sheltered by the ancient walls. Elsewhere, brown-skinned Yemenites with straggling beards strolled about; Jews from Georgia and Urfa, Baghdad and Aleppo entrenched themselves in their isolated settlements, and even those who were new to the city appeared to have grown up among the rocks of Jerusalem.

79

Above this mosaic of settlements and suburbs towered the walls of the Old City. Whenever we had time, we went wandering about its alleys, up and down its sloping streets, in the gloom of the vaulted stone passages, buying sweets from the stalls of Bab-Khan-el-Zeith and mingling with the fellaheen driving their donkeys before them through the long, narrow Batrak Street. Near the Wailing Wall beggars out of the abysm of time dozed in the torrid heat, holding out their hands to passers-by and murmuring their beseechings as if actuated by the force of inertia. During the sabbath, the precinct of Rabbi Yehuda-ha-Hassid's synagogue was full of young men from the New City, standing about in little groups, while the girls from the Old City cast furtive glances at them, amid whispers and bursts of laughter. As for the boys of Jerusalem, their chief amusement was to go the round of the walls, striding over the old bastions and the city gates, chasing one another over the ancient stones, climbing up and down the slopes of the yards, and looking across from the Temple Place to the steles of the Mount of Olives, Absalom's tomb and the tomb of Zechariah in the Valley of Jehoshaphat.

Jerusalem was always behind the times compared with Tel-Aviv, which was at the point of progress, even when it was no more than a suburb of Jaffa. When the first houses in Tel-Aviv had been supplied with taps, water in Jerusalem was still being drawn from wells dug under the paved floors, and the noise of the bucket hitting against the stone sides still echoes in the ears of the old-timers. Towards the end of summer, especially in years of drought when the wells ran dry, we were roused from sleep in the early morning by the fellaheen women of the village of Lifta crying 'Mo-ye! Mo-ye!'

Mother would get out of bed, hail a water-carrier, and buy water from her at half a piastre a can, to fill up the barrel from which we should draw our supply for the next few days. Electricity, like main water, made its appearance very late. At sunset the lamplighter, an Arab servant of the municipality, went slowly down the street with a long pole, lighting the pallid lamps one after another, and sending long shadows creeping over the stone fences. There was no café in the town, and *gazoz*, the sweetish lemonade that was to become our national drink, had not yet made its appearance in the kiosks at the cross-roads, when the luckier people of Tel-Aviv had begun indulging in it on broiling hot summer nights. The 'Lux', the incandescent lantern lighting the centre of the Zikhron-Moshé quarter, was the first and largest of our standard lamps; it cast a circle of light round it which attracted the young people, and lively conversations and ideological discussions were carried on there, before the company scattered over the flat rocks of the waste ground leading to the Bokharan quarter.

Radio had not yet come in, and silence reigned at night, except for the monotonous oriental chants issuing from the rusty gramophones in the Arab café near the Jaffa Gate, and an occasional burst of music from the house of a Sephardic notable teaching his daughter to play the piano. But in the early morning, when the sun rose behind Mount Scopus, and the housewives started filling their kerosene stoves, the neighbourhood was stirred from sleep by the cries of the hawkers and itinerant artisans, old Araba from Musrara and the Damascus Gate, carrying their tools with them and announcing their trade in Yiddish, according to ancestral custom.

'*Waissn kesselakh*,' wailed the old tinker, and the cobbler countered him from another street with '*Farrikhtn Shikn!*' adding a translation in Hebrew for the benefit of customers of the new generation! '*Letaken naalaim*.'

The ragman—Jew or Arab was a moot question—with his white beard falling over his chest, joined in the chorus with his 'Ole clo'! Ole shoon!' and the housewives ran down with threadbare cotton frocks, shrunken trousers, down-at-heel shoes, and began a lively battle over the number of piastres the old man would beat them down to before extracting his faded purse from his coat pocket.

In the streets we came upon familiar types lingering on from an earlier age: tramps and beggars, village idiots, bearded and hilarious, clustered in the precincts of the synagogues; bailiffs of the Law Courts in the Russian quarter, kavasses in embroidered coats, sporting silver-headed sticks, who had acted as escorts to the European consuls and were now engaged in heralding the solemn arrival of the First of Zion, the great Sephardic Rabbi of the Land of Israel, Rabbi Yaacov Meïr.

A Sephardic doctor might be seen in Jaffa Street of a morning, mounted on a white horse. His legs were paralysed, but he went on visiting his patients on horseback, even when motor-cars were already on the increase in the streets of Jerusalem.

Mendel Kremer, pot-bellied and puffy-faced, amber chaplet in hand according to Muslim custom, sat on a little stool in the Arab café near the Fast Hotel and the government offices. Everybody knew he was a police spy, and it seemed odd that the authorities should have given a job of that kind to a man whose identity was so well known, and who was so easily recognized at a distance. But like the kavasses and the bailiffs, he was yet another relic of the Turkish régime. He was proud of his function and his relations with the authorities, and liked telling people that the Pasha of Jerusalem had once ordered him to keep an eye on the comings and goings of Theodor Herzl, the creator of Zionism, when he came to the country to meet the Kaiser at the beginning of the century.

When a party of schoolboys set out on one of their traditional walks through the Old City, where there were always fresh wonders to be discovered, they sometimes came upon the 'Messiah', a well-known character of that time. He was a Persian Jew, tall, with a fine presence, a black beard and fiery eyes, wearing a tall black cap, and either riding a white donkey or sitting motionless on the ramparts. He was said to come of a respectable family, and to have studied medicine in his youth. But one day it was revealed to him that Providence had chosen him to save humanity. His wife, an Englishwoman, had followed him from village to village in his native country, ministering to his needs and those of their young son with the little money she earned by giving English lessons. It was also said that he had sent a letter to Kaiser William II, shortly before the outbreak of the Great War, warning him that he was about to drag the world to its ruin, and destroy himself. I never heard him utter a word, but he cast a limpid, penetrating glance on the young men he met on his way, shaking his head sadly as if to say, 'Poor creatures, you have the good fortune to meet the Messiah, but alas! you have lost your faith.'

II

My Uncle Kabak's family had reached Jerusalem a year or two before us, and we stayed with them for the first few weeks. New *olim*, among them teachers, men of letters and public officials, all lived at that time in the modern quarters, either in the little shady streets of Zikhron-Moshe or in the spacious houses of the Bokharan settlement. Like all Jerusalem houses of that time, our uncle's apartment opened on to a little stone-paved patio, while its windows, protected by iron bars, looked out on the sleepy street, and interiors of facing houses had few secrets from their neighbours. At night the big living-room was lighted by a paraffin lamp, and on the sabbath day people strolled along the road in caftans or long white pantaloons, with pointed caps on their heads.

The school year had begun when we arrived. Father consulted his brother-in-law, who was a teacher of literature and biblical studies at the secondary school, and one day I was summoned before the director and the Board to take my entrance exam. I dreaded the ordeal, not having set foot in a school for over three years. However, thanks to my advanced knowledge of Hebrew, I was admitted to the sixth grade, two years before the leaving exam, in spite of my very scanty knowledge of other subjects.

The school was housed in a spacious mansion, built years before by a wealthy Jew of Bokhara. The class-rooms were lofty, with barred windows, and in the middle of the building there was a large vaulted hall in oriental style. The attendance was very small even for those days, hardly more than a hundred pupils, including fourteen or fifteen in my class, mostly girls. The teachers were nearly all Russians or Poles who had come to Palestine before the war, except for the teacher of Arabic, a Sephardi born in Hebron. The usher was a Yemenite, like all school attendants in the country, and his wife fried delicious pancakes in oil, which we eagerly enjoyed during the recess.

Apart from a few recent arrivals like myself, most of the pupils were children of good families of the old orthodox communities, Sephardim, Ashkenazim or Bokharan. I found them all very stand-offish at first. They had all grown up together, and were bound by their common experience and the small, outstanding events of their life—almond harvests in the settlements, for which they were mobilized, fighting the locust invasions, and so on—and like schoolchildren the world over, they treated their new schoolfellow with ironical distrust. I found it difficult, too, to get used to the company of girls, never having attended a mixed school, and their laughter and whispering made me feel awkward. I felt isolated in this little world, different from the others in the way I dressed, in my habits, and the books I had read in foreign languages they did not know. Most of the boys wore trousers reaching below the knee, known as 'three-quarters', and long black stockings, but the sportsmen and the moderns wore khaki shorts with nonchalant elegance. I tried to copy them, but on my first excursion I got blistered knees, and after that, alone of my class, I remained faithful to my long trousers.

However, I soon made my way into the circle, mainly thanks to the headmaster, Shlomo Schiller, who took me under his wing, supervised my work, and smoothed my path with the 'quondams'. The school was very proud of Schiller, a publicist of renown and the outstanding theoretician and ideologue of the Labour movement. His articles on Zionism had fired the imagination of youth in Galicia, where he lived for many years, and of the young *halutsim* of the first *kibbutsim* in Palestine. He had founded the Jerusalem school shortly before the war, and his sole concern now was for school and pupils. Here he reigned over the school by the moral authority of his personality. He seldom resorted even to a harsh reprimand; he had only to look sadly at the culprit and talk in a fatherly tone on the subject that lay nearest his heart: the great responsibility of our generation, destined to shoulder the burden of rebuilding the country, to be the standard-bearers of the movement for its rebirth. He had an ardent, sincere faith in the sacred mission of youth, the prime product of the revival of Palestine, and he inculcated this faith in us. A serious talk was enough to send the pupil back to the class-room deeply repentant, conscious of having sinned against the sacred character of his schooling.

At one time Schiller had taught psychology and history in the upper forms of the school, but in my day he had given up teaching, to devote himself entirely to administration. Now and then, if one of the teachers was obliged to miss a lesson, he would come to the class-room to talk to us, and launch out into his favourite subject, the doctrine of Achad Ha'am, the undisputed master of Zionist philosophy of that day. We were all eager for these lessons. A religious silence reigned in class as he introduced us to a world of unfamiliar, lofty ideas. He made everything seem clear: ideas, problems, and their solutions. I do not know how much of Achad-Ha'am there was in these dissertations, and how much they owed to the imprint of Schiller's own personality, but the impact they made on us was a lasting one.

At the end of a year Schiller left the school, either for reasons of health or because he found his administrative duties burdensome; but even later on, after I had left school, I often went to see him in his little room in the Street of the Abyssinians for a talk about personal and general problems. He had a wonderful talent for making one feel at home, and somehow, when I left him I had the reassuring feeling that I was not falling below his standard for the rising generation.

There were not many Hebrew textbooks at that time, and none at all on certain subjects, so most of our time was spent in taking notes. The teacher seated himself at his desk, took a large black exercise book from his portfolio and began dictating the lesson, while we wrote as fast as we could, without missing a word or stopping to take in the meaning, till the teacher, growing tired, allowed us to ask questions before the bell put an end to the class.

The isolation of the war years had only just come to an end, and the Hebrew educational system, which had not taken shape till 1913, was going through its teething period. Jerusalem publishers had hardly had time to produce any secondary-school books, and those printed in Warsaw reached us with difficulty. Hebrew had become a rich, living language, but the terminology was unsettled, and every teacher set about making his own innovations. A Jerusalem schoolboy was sometimes unable to understand the mathematical terms used by one from Tel-Aviv or Haifa, and even the curriculum differed from one school to another. It was not till I had nearly finished school that the publishers started preparing textbooks, and our note-taking became a thing of the past.

Few of my schoolfellows knew any foreign language; Hebrew was the only tongue in which they were proficient. But Hebrew literature was too scanty to satisfy young readers, especially now that the editions printed earlier in Russia had become exhausted and new ones hardly existed. Never, perhaps, had there been such a thirst for books as among these Jerusalem adolescents. Every new book that came out was read and re-read, and passed from hand to hand, from Flaubert's *Salammbô* to Windelband's *History of Philosophy* in a Hebrew translation. Then came Byron's *Cain*, Tolstoy's *War and Peace* and Maupassant's *Fort comme la Mort*. From time to time we met to read and discuss both translations and new Hebrew novels and poems, scarce as they were.

The National Library was a great help to us in our reading. It was installed in an old house, hidden at the end of a narrow side street, and the librarians, hardly older than ourselves, looked upon us as the élite of their customers. The schoolgirls, even those who were not keen on reading, liked parading through the little vaulted rooms reached by a stone staircase, to ask with an air of importance for some serious book everybody was talking about—the latest translation of Anatole France, the latest novel by my Uncle Kabak, or the *romans à clef* in which people amused themselves by detecting citizens of Jerusalem to be met with in the street.

The school formed a little world apart, but back home the family had to obey the established order of things. When they opened the doors of the home, the boys and girls would find their father seated in his ritual armchair, forbidden to take any interest in matters profane. The comings and goings of daughters were strictly controlled, and paternal surveillance was never relaxed.

It was different in the other secondary school, the 'Seminary', or Training College for elementary schoolteachers. The 'seminarists' were a few years older, having already gone through a period of revolt, many of them recruited from among the new immigrants—*halutsim* from Russia who had left Labour groups to devote themselves to teaching. The Training College admitted only boys, and of course these were attracted by the girls of the 'gymnasium', as our school was called, German fashion. At first this aroused the jealousy of their schoolfellows, who reproached them for going with the 'old ones', but in the end we resigned ourselves to this, the two camps amalgamated, and the Seminary opened before the 'gymnasium' crowd new horizons on the modern world.

Our traditional meeting-place of a summer evening was the 'Lux', the street lamp opposite the Training College. Boys and girls spent hours there, discussing the questions of the day. Later on, when an enterprising caterer opened the first Jerusalem café there, our discussions were enhanced by ice-cream and lemonade. We had not yet got as far as politics, though this was already the rage in our entourage. Like all adolescents in the world, the youth of Jerusalem was concerned with the major problems of life—the value of existence, the significance of life, and so on. But our older colleagues were already more specific: they spoke of the collectivist idea, the new working-class, the Labour Battalion, the *kibbutsim* of the Emek, and the future of Hebrew culture. We listened deferentially to these big fellows expatiating on the grandiose plans for settlement in Upper Galilee and the introduction of modern methods of stockbreeding. Others, bitterly dissatisfied with the current system of education, drew masterly pictures of the schools they intended to start as soon as they had taken their teaching diploma. The girls listened with half an ear to these discussions, not daring to show their boredom; but the seminarists' stock was definitely on the rise.

Life in Jerusalem appeared calm, somewhat dull, compared with the effervescence of Jaffa. In holiday time we were sometimes sent to spend a few days with friends or relations in Tel-Aviv. It was a regular expedition then, either by the train travelling slowly down the hills, or by road in one of the tall Ford taxis that were always stopping for repairs. The pupils at the Tel-Aviv secondary school struck us as freer and jollier than ourselves, in their khaki shorts and white, open-necked shirts. They went about with the gangs of young labourers, assimilating and discussing the ideas they preached. On moonlight nights parties of young people gathered on the seashore, or in the deserted vineyards north of the town.

We always brought home a collection of new songs—

nostalgic Russian airs to which Hebrew words had been fitted, songs of the pioneers and the settlement guards of the generation before us, an Arab chant with its attractive oriental monotony, or an English marching song borrowed from the Jewish battalions of the British Army.

We sang them of an evening in our rock-strewn fields, or the little coppice known as Schneller's, a few straggling, contorted pine-trees planted long ago by a Swiss missionary near the stone fence of an old vineyard called 'Abraham's Vine'. The words were clumsy and naive, the melodies worn out, but we were young, the moon was shining, and who cared for the quality of music anyway?

My Mother's House

I

THE offices of the Jewish National Council were in a cramped Arab apartment in one of the side streets of the Musrara quarter. They occupied two rooms, and the Secretary General's family three. All day long the typewriter clicked, the telephone rang, and strange individuals visiting the offices threw open the door of our apartment, shot a glance at the big table and beat a hasty retreat with apologies. Files piled up in every corner, for the staff had increased, the work had branched out, and it was soon obvious that we should have to move.

Our first real home in Jerusalem was some way from my school and from the quarters where my schoolfellows lived. I often came home of an evening across the empty market-place of Meah-Shearim and the Abyssinian Street. Passing by the walls of the prison in the Russian compound of a stormy winter night I might be startled by the hoarse shouts of the Arab sentinels proving to each other that they were not asleep at their posts.

'Wa-had!'—'One!' from somewhere behind the wall.

'Tne-ine!'—'Two!' from the guard posted at a distant corner.

I quickened my pace, feeling as if the shouts had come, not from a gaoler but from the prisoners themselves, murderers and thieves, attempting somewhere to force the bars and escape along the streets of Musrara to the gates and narrow lanes of the Old City.

On the first day of Mukharem, the Muslim New Year's Day when it was the custom to move house in the East, we settled into a new apartment in the Ahva quarter, a part of the town where ancient and modern neighboured each other—houses in traditional style and modern buildings sacrificing to the 'New Look'. The streets were not asphalted, and in winter the centre of the quarter became one enormous puddle, dubbed the 'Lake of Ahva', in which mothers tried in vain to prevent their offspring from paddling. Our new house was a two-storied one, and we occupied a flat on the upper floor at the top of a stone staircase, consisting of three rooms opening out of one another, and a kitchen with a corrugated iron roof installed in a corner of the balcony.

This time we had settled in for good. The heavy furniture from Warsaw, miraculously preserved in a repository all through our seven years of tribulation in Russia, had arrived, and we bought beds and mattresses for ourselves and for passing guests. Mother had returned to the tradition of her younger days, and our house soon became the rallying-point for friends and acquaintances, veterans of Jerusalem or visitors from Tel-Aviv, and especially for the new, young *olim* who had not yet found anywhere to live.

We soon felt at home in our new surroundings, and easily acquired the *sefardi* accent in Hebrew. We had many friends of earlier days, and people with letters of recommendation began knocking at the door. Anyone known to my father, however slightly, might come for a night, and stay a week, a fortnight, and perhaps longer.

They were mostly young men who, after working for a time in the Emek, or breaking stones for roadmaking, had come to look for a job in the town: young writers without means, relations of our own, or of friends settled in Palestine, all bearing a letter of recommendation to the Secretary General, who must surely be able to help them. They came singly, in couples, in threes, and there was always room for them, for adults in the children's beds, for younger people on a mattress on the floor. Until the day I left home I hardly remember a week going by without my having to give up my bed to a guest. Hospitality was such a habit at that time that even old settled friends from Tel-Aviv never thought of going to a hotel.

After school hours the house rang with the shouts and laughter of our schoolfellows, boys and girls. My sister was attending a girls' school, and my little brother, wearing a skull-cap, went to a religious school near by. My own school friends were captivated by my mother's kindness. She listened to their stories and plied them with good things to eat, besides giving good advice to the girls, who confided their little secret worries to her. Even when she was keeping to her bed, exhausted with coughing, breathing with difficulty, she managed to smile to her young guests, sympathizing and joking with them, and this atmosphere of youth seemed to be doing her good.

She found the steep streets of Jerusalem tiring, but she loved the city with all her heart, and often said, 'If I were the Mayor of Jerusalem, I'd have all the hills levelled to fill up the valleys, so that everybody could walk about there.' There was some question at one time of my father trying for work in Tel-Aviv for the sake of Mother's health, but it would not have been easy, and we should have missed the pleasant atmosphere of Jerusalem, so after a while the idea was abandoned.

Mazal, the little Sephardi maid, came early in the morning to help Grandmother with her housekeeping. When she saw mattresses and blankets scattered all over the floor, she would shake her head in consternation, pressing her hands to her cheeks and exclaiming in her Judeo-Spanish '*Otro dolor!*' as if to say 'Heaven save me from worse troubles!' Then she would tuck up her skirts, roll up the bedding, and start on her daily task of scrubbing the floor.

Our finances remained precarious all through our stay in Jerusalem. My friends looked upon me as a privileged person because of my father's position, but his high-sounding title brought him more worry and trouble than income. The National Council had been inaugurated with great pomp after the occupation of the country by the English, and invested at first with wide powers, especially that of organizing a gendarmerie force—later to become the Transjordan Frontier Force —to organize the communities, municipal councils and Boards of the agricultural settlements. But these brilliant beginnings bore scanty fruit. Very soon, the gendarmerie became a purely Arab unit, and the militiamen who had been so proud of their brass-studded belts no longer got any pay; the Settlement Boards spent their time arguing, all serious political questions were settled by the Zionist Executive, and the National Council soon became an empty shell. The Representative Assembly—the elected parliament of the Palestinian Jews—was summoned, and shattering speeches were delivered, but there was not enough money to keep this local autonomy machine working. A gleam of hope lay in the promise of a constitution that would authorize the Jewish community to levy taxes, but the plan broke down somewhere between London and Jerusalem.

My father travelled round the country trying to collect a little money in the settlements and the towns, coming back more often than not with empty hands. Civil servants' salaries, including his own, had not been paid for months. I do not know how we managed to live, but I remember that when he bought a ticket in the Irish sweepstake, which was very popular at that time, he said to me with bitter irony, 'If I win the first prize I shall lend some of it to the National Council to pay me my salary with.'

The Council was fast disintegrating; its members were lobbying the Zionist Executive in quest of a loan, and when the Zionist Congress sat in Basle or Karlsbad, they addressed petitions to Chaim Weizmann, who was going through a difficult time himself, asking for a financial grant.

My father tried to make ends meet by writing. He was one of the regular correspondents of the *Haaretz*, but his fees were paid very irregularly. He went back to writing articles in Yiddish, which brought him a guaranteed return. Thanks to the cheques from the New York *Morgen Journal* and the Warsaw *Moment*, the grocer could be persuaded to wait for a final settlement of his bills. Anyway, he had little to lose, because most of his customers were clerks and teachers who never saw a shilling.

Poverty was a common condition of the time. A five-pound note was a rarity, and I remember being held up for some days in a village in Galilee because nobody could produce the change for one. The Zionist Executive could not meet its budget, teachers did not get their salaries, customers did not pay their bills, and the circle closed practically moneyless. Public institutions paid in vouchers drawn on *Hamashbir*, the Labour Co-operative Society, which circulated as legal currency. My mother sometimes bought something at the *Hamashbir* that she did not need, simply because it was on sale there at the time, when she had not enough real cash to fill her basket with vegetables. Lack of money was the chief subject of conversation, and, like the weather, a thing to be endured, not cured.

II

One Saturday in winter, on a bright day after the rain, Kadish Yehuda Silman toiled painfully on his short legs up our stairs. He was a teacher at the secondary school, an expert in Hebrew language and literature, famous for his wit as the writer of the popular songs everybody was humming. He sometimes came to see us and crack a few jokes, seizing a chance of correcting the way we children talked, and chaffing us about the foreign words we were still given to using. But this time he refused the chair he was offered and would not even trouble to take off his overcoat.

'I've come to invite you to an excursion,' he said. 'Come and see the site of the new quarter we're going to build in Jerusalem.'

'Who's we?' asked my father with a smile. He was used to imaginative plans of his Jerusalem friends, which usually got no further than the paper they were drawn on.

'Patience, patience!' said Silman. 'This time it's a concrete affair. Teachers and writers are going to build a Garden City for themselves to the west of the town. It'll be a marvel. The society calls itself *Boné-Baït*, but we haven't yet found a name for the new suburb.'

Everybody knew it was Silman who had suggested the name of Tel-Aviv for the modern suburb near Jaffa, so he was sure to find a good one for the new project; but my father could not help laughing. Writers and teachers! How could those dreamers with their heads in the clouds carry out such an enterprise? But it was a fine day; my father put on his coat, and he and I started off, with Silman trotting in front.

Our road led us over rocky ground and muddy pools, hills and valleys, to an Arab limekiln standing by itself on the road to Ein Karem. Our guide pointed to the area on the right and left of the road. 'That's where the suburb is to built,' he said. It was a rock-strewn valley like many others around Jerusalem, exposed to every wind, the hollows in the rocks full of water, brambles flourishing everywhere. Squelching in the mud and leaping from rock to rock, we reached home in time for lunch. Doubt had given way to certainty: the hypothetical suburb would never come into being.

But in little more than a month the framework of the first houses had been erected, and dressed stones were piling up along the road. The quarter was built entirely by Jewish labourers. They were not expert masons, and the wags declared that Arab masons had been engaged to train them at night. But the builders were not deterred, the houses were to be built by Jewish hands. In less than a year Jerusalem found itself in possession of a new quarter on the west, named Beth-Hakerem. The rocks were covered with shrubs, flower-beds had sprung up near the houses, and on the Festival of the Tree the schoolchildren went to Beth-Hakerem for the traditional tree-planting. My school joined the planters, and to this day I can recognize in the shady streets of Beth-Hakerem the tall cypresses that were planted by me during one of those annual ceremonies.

My Uncle Kabak's family settled into one of the new houses, and Beth-Hakerem became the favourite goal of our sabbath walks. Kabak, then in the prime of life, taught literature and the Bible at the secondary school, but devoted himself chiefly to writing, as a novelist first and foremost. Early in the morning, before going to school, he sat at his desk adding chapter after chapter to his latest novel. He was then still tall and robust, with no hint of the malady that was to shatter him physically but purify his creative spirit. His tales were simple and straightforward, with no depth, but fascinating to read. He was a born storyteller, a fervent admirer of the great Russian, French and German masters, whose books I devoured when I went to see him of a Saturday afternoon. He was never tired of re-reading Tolstoy, Turgenev and Chekhov, and he translated the works of Anatole France, Balzac and Flaubert in his free time. A great talker, he enjoyed society and sought out human contacts of every kind. But sometimes in the middle of a conversation he would withdraw into himself, hardly listening, asking a question now and then without heeding the answer. We knew then that he was caught in the meshes of his imagination, and was weaving the invisible tapestry of his characters' adventures.

His wife, Sara-Feiga, was my father's sister. She was a witty, intelligent woman, who had always lamented having to confine herself to housekeeping and the education of her children. If she were a man, she said, she would show people what she was

94

capable of! She would have written books of quite a different calibre! She would have given them useful lessons in politics, for men were only a lot of dreamers, hopelessly naive. She never concealed her opinions, and her witticisms were a terror to her friends. She spared nobody, bantering and lecturing them, but at the end of some fiery discussion she would get up with a sigh and go to the kitchen to cook a meal for her guests.

Her house was a hospitable one. At any hour of the day she might be found entertaining a visitor with amusing tales of her family or her native village, or playing a game of chess with him. She beat all her opponents, to show them what a woman was capable of, and acquired such a mastery of the game that she became one of the champions of Jerusalem.

She was often caustic, and her temper might flare up suddenly, but her loyalty to her friends was proverbial. If one of them was in difficulties she would put on her hat, leave her house and her daughters, and go to town to knock at some door, or cool her heels in the waiting-room of some institution till the matter was righted. She was in difficulties herself all her life, battling with debts, and trying to extract from publishers the royalties they owed her husband, whose books were widely read but brought him no money. But in spite of this she contrived to share her meagre resources with her friends, often borrowing from one to lend to another.

In the evening the big paraffin lamp was lighted in her dining-room, and friends flocked to 'the house with the glow'. I loved sitting in a corner of the room listening to the endless talk of literature and art, and the writers' recollections of days that were done. I met some of my teachers there, the doyen of the party being A. M. Brahyahu, whose lectures on the Talmud bored us so profoundly at school. He would light a cigarette stuck in a long silver holder, and discourse methodically and precisely on some new philosophical theory. Moshé Karmon, young and brilliant, talked in stentorian tones about the latest French novel to fall into his hands, spicing his account of it with a violent diatribe against the leaders of the Jewish community and their wavering administration. Rabbi Binyamin, sticking out his beard, became absorbed in a book on one of the shelves, turning the pages and humming to himself like an old Jew studying a page of the Talmud, and took no part in the conversation except when it turned to some favourite subject of his, such as peace with the Arabs, or matters of faith and religion. He had a Galician accent, and his utterance was as curt and decisive as the aphorisms and comments he published in the papers. Aharoh Reubeni, whose brother Itzhak Ben Zwi was to become the second President of Israel, would come in from the veranda and start a fine-spun discussion of a question of linguistics or the exegesis of the Bible. Besides all these, the company often included residents of the neighbourhood and friends from Tel-Aviv, the poet David Shimon, J. D. Berkovitz, then already a well-known novelist and dramatic author, and Semiatitski, one of the greatest stylists known to literature, who had spent his life correcting other people's prose.

In later days, when that generation was beginning to disappear, I often wondered what it was that gave such vitality to the writers and scholars I had known at close quarters in Beth-Hakerem and Tel-Aviv. They were very different from one another, divided in opinion on many subjects, and certainly not immune from professional jealousy, yet linked by some indefinable, secret bond that had endured since the days of Warsaw, Vilna and Odessa. The telephone was still an unknown luxury, and callers gave no warning of their intentions. Friends passing along the street noticed the light, and looked in to drink a glass of tea or merely to exchange a few words. An author would describe the plan of the book he was writing, a politician frequenting the influential circles of Jerusalem would report the events of the day; and so, from one thing to another the conversation would build up, everyone coming out with what was uppermost in his mind: the founding of a literary review, educational reform, the rebuilding of Jerusalem or the solution of the Arab problem. The latest innovations in Hebrew were discussed, the style of recent translations criticized, the statutes of a pension fund for teachers elaborated. Then, reverting to literature, those men with greying hair would recite the German and Russian lyrics they had studied in their youth, deploring the ignorance and decadence of the younger generation—all this spiced with jokes, anecdotes and recollections of the good old days. They separated late at night, with the comforting sense of belonging to one large family, reunited in Palestine at the end of a long journey, where dark days would not matter now that they could endure them together and not in the bitter loneliness of exile.

When I recall that generation today, I feel it was the last to have that sense of being a homogeneous group, indulging in friendship for its own sake. They went through their spiritual experiences together, with nothing to distract them—neither cinema nor radio, nor public duties. Even when they became involved in passionate literary controversies they practised a tolerance rarely met with nowadays. Their scale of values was definite and unequivocal, and they never departed from it. Their friendship knew no compromise. This may have been the effect of a long stormy period in their lifetime, or revolutionary stresses may have implanted in them, even in Russia, a constant readiness to help one another, to give themselves unreservedly, even if the friend in need was a political opponent. My mother and her friends often told of how they had risked their lives during the Revolution to release from prison a *bundist* friend, a bitter adversary of Zionism; and even in Jerusalem we gave hospitality for long periods to writers who had fought against the Zionist movement and the use of Hebrew, and had now fled from communist persecution.

To their last day these people remained bound together by an unshakeable loyalty. My parents, both of whom died before they were fifty, were the first to vanish from this company; the others survived for a shorter or longer time. Only a few are still among us, and they are old, very old.

Many years went by before the light of the house of Kabak was extinguished. Before his death the novelist went through a crisis that illumined his soul and raised his inspiration to heights never reached before. Even by the twenties he had written his historical novel on Shelomo Molkho, the seventeenth-century Jewish mystic, which differed in style and profoundness of ideas from anything he had produced before. I was in Paris at the time, working in the editorial office of the *Haolam*, and the proofs of his book reached me chapter by chapter. I was astonished at this capacity for renewal manifesting itself suddenly in a writer I had known from my childhood. A few years later, when I was back in Jerusalem again, my aunt, in grief, came one day to tell us that Kabak had been seized with an apoplectic fit and his right side was paralysed. He remained in this state for some weeks, unable to move, fighting death with all his strength and suffering unspeakable pain, till at last he recovered. But a change had come over him after those nights of endurance, as if he had stood for a long while face to face with the angel of death before coming back among the living.

His zest for life had disappeared, and with it the rather superficial lightness of spirit that had characterized him. The mildness and delicacy of his face had acquired a new relief. While he had lain there on his bed of pain, the faith of his childhood had returned to him, and from an inveterate agnostic he had become a pious Jew. He bound the phylacteries round his left arm with an awkward hand, and spent a long time in prayer. He never became a proselytizer, but was careful henceforth to neglect no ritual ordinance. My aunt had now to keep to a strictly *kosher* cuisine, which was not to her liking. She gently teased her husband for having become devout in his old age, but even she was well aware that he had gone through a terrible ordeal, and that he was henceforth under the shadow of death. He smiled kindly at her, replying with some harmless joke, and at the close of day retired to his corner to say his evening prayer.

It was now, on his recovery, that he wrote his greatest work, *The Narrow Path*, a profoundly Jewish version of the life of Jesus. His friends did not conceal their astonishment that he, of all men, a Jew who had returned to the tradition of his ancestors in the twilight of his life, should devote the best of his talent to narrating the life of Jesus Christ. They did not realize that his Jesus, the Pharisee of Galilee, fleeing the horrors of his time and taking refuge in a faith purified by the spirit, was the incarnation of the supreme faith, the nostalgic attachment to the ancestral tradition, that Kabak himself had experienced late in the day, with all the intensity of his purified soul.

Days without Glamour

IN SPITE of the idealizing halo that clings to those years of my youth, I remember the period chiefly as a succession of days without glamour. The exaltation of the first months of the third *Aliya*, the wave of hope aroused by the Balfour Declaration, and the liberation of the country from the Ottoman yoke, the fluttering flags of the Jewish Battalion, were all things of the past. The dreams of national sovereignty born of the Messianic aspirations of the Jews of Europe had, alas, not materialized. The British Mandatory authorities were definitely a foreign Power. The ideas of the British officials were not inspired by the Bible, and the creation of a Jewish State was the least of their concerns. The visa appended to our passports at the British Consulate in Warsaw had borne the specific declaration: 'Object of journey: Zionist'. But in the opinion of the Palestinian government in Jerusalem, Zionism was no longer a title of nobility. On the contrary, it was plain to the executors of British policy that as the majority of the population were Arabs, it was the opinions and aspirations of the latter that must always prevail.

Herbert Samuel, the first High Commissioner of Palestine, resided in the German Hospital building of Augusta-Victoria on Mount Scopus. We all knew he was a Jew and a Zionist, and when he entered the synagogue in the Old City for the first time, he read aloud from the chapter for the week '... and a stranger shall not sit upon his throne'. When he appeared at official ceremonies and solemn assemblies, the splendour of the great empire he represented irradiated him as he stood there before us in his cork helmet, his tall figure encased in a close-fitting white uniform, with a host of aides-de-camp and secretaries busy around him. His assumption of office had put an end to the vexations of the occupation, the Arab agitation against the Jews was carried on less openly, and everything had led us to believe that we were entering upon a period of moderation and tranquillity. Laws and decrees, down to the smallest administrative measures, were all weighed and calculated with jealous care so that no one should have occasion to feel offended or to protest, but to the officials surrounding him the reaction of the Arabs always carried more weight than that of the Jews. At every opportunity the Arabs opposed a peremptory 'No', and the Jews recriminated, drew up petitions, invoked precedents, sent telegrams of protest—in short, the advent of the Messiah was indefinitely postponed.

During my first months in Jerusalem I dreamed of meeting the first 'Governor of Judea' face to face. I had gone with my parents to the opening of some exhibition or other in the Bezalel Museum, when I saw Herbert Samuel coming in, followed by his aides-de-camp. The room was full of people and I was on the outside of the crowd. Pushing my way through, I approached the High Commissioner and stood in contemplation of the supernatural being who held the fate of us all in his hands. One of his aides-de-camp whispered something in the ear of an Arab police officer, who nodded, came up to me, and said something in English that I did not understand. He pointed to the door and I went out into the passage, but changed my mind and came in again by another door. Standing there, motionless, lost in admiring contemplation, I suddenly felt myself being pushed unceremoniously towards the forecourt of the building. It was some time before I realized that the tall, sunburnt lad I then was had appeared suspect to the High Commissioner's guards, as a possible terrorist. The incident left me with an aftertaste of humiliation and put an end to my attempts at approaching the Great Ones of the kingdom.

The officials of the Mandatory Government were at a loss to understand why England should have accepted the thankless task of founding a Jewish National Home. To our minds every Englishman was inevitably an enemy. It was common knowledge that we had no friend left in the Government since the resignation of Wyndham Deedes. Jerusalem had a special grudge against the governor of the city, Ronald Storrs, whose disastrous part in the events of Easter 1920 was not forgotten. When he rode along the street on his Arab mare nobody responded to his smiles, and even the polite formulas he uttered laboriously in Hebrew could not break down the wall of hostility surrounding him.

Jewish high politics were carried on by the Zionist Executive. Menahem Ussishkin reigned over the offices of the former Hughes Hotel, and he was seen tripping down Jaffa Street every day, determination in his tall frame, and the heavy stick he carried harmonizing with the character of 'man of iron' he had acquired by his Zionist activities in Russia. He had settled in Palestine only a few years earlier, but he might have been carved out of the stones of Jerusalem. When he defended his position before the British authorities, he did it with intransigent vigour, as though he had behind him a whole united, powerful nation. When attending meetings of official Jewish institutions and local conferences, he seldom spoke, restricting himself to a few brief remarks in his own particular Hebrew, and the audience split into two rival camps—those who were passionately in his favour, and those who considered him the cause of all the failures of the Zionist movement. But nobody ever succeeded in disturbing his composure.

Delegations from the Jewish community were often seen proceeding in dignified array from the premises of the Zionist Executive to the Government House, to protest against discrimination with regard to the Hebrew tongue, the exclusion of Jewish labour from public works, and demand that promises should be kept. In our own administrative centres lively debates were going on, discussing the empty Treasury, the *kibbutsim* deprived of supplies, and teachers threatening to strike because their salaries had not been paid for many months.

All eyes were fixed on London. The Jews of Jerusalem weighed every word uttered by British Members of Parliament during their debates on the Palestinian question. Our newspapers reported the speeches of our friends and adversaries, followed by endless commentaries, and the hostile utterances, here at home, of Mussa Kazem Pasha, the recognized leader of anti-Zionism in the country, who was greatly assisted by Miss Newton, an Arabophile Englishwoman, from her house on Mount Carmel. The Commission on Mandates of the League of Nations had its headquarters in Geneva, where reports and summaries were sent, and missions went to defend the cause of the Jewish population of the country.

Among the important events of that period I remember the

brief but stormy visit of Lord Northcliffe, king of the British press at that time, who launched a violent attack on Zionism and on the Balfour Declaration. His indictment caused the utmost consternation; it was feared then that a mere breath might overthrow the frail edifice of the National Home, and that the hostile attitude of the papers controlled by Lord Northcliffe might have an unfavourable influence on the authorities in London, whom we believed, in our innocence, to be unaware of the shady intrigues of the British officials in Palestine.

Lord Northcliffe received a delegation of religious extremists, disciples of Rabbi Sonnenfeld, who had come to protest against Zionism and demand the abolition of the Balfour Declaration. Their leader was a Dutch Jew, Jacob de Haan, a perverted, libertine poet, who had earlier been a Zionist and a freethinker, but since his settlement in Israel had become exaggeratedly orthodox and anti-Zionist. He had allied himself with the residents of the Meah-Shearim quarter, and went wandering about the streets of Jerusalem, clad in a long caftan, his beard waving in the wind, persistently refusing to talk anything but Arabic.

One day we heard the community beadle coming along the street, tapping on the windows and chanting in a monotonous singsong the customary invitation to a funeral: '*Yidn, geyt tzu der Levaye*' ('Jews, attend the funeral').

As usual, windows opened, and a greybeard behind the bars enquired 'Who's dead?'

The beadle turned a mournful face towards the window and announced the astonishing news: 'Rabbi Yaacov-Israel de Haan, at the Wallach Hospital.'

A few hours later we heard that he had been shot by an unknown assailant. This was the first act of political terrorism among the Jewish population of Palestine, and for a long while the mystery surrounding it, the motives for it and the identity of the assassin were excitedly debated in the little and closed Jewish society of Jerusalem.

My schoolfellows never tired of describing the events that had disturbed the city a year or two earlier, at the time of the 1920 uprisings, when a few young members of the *Hagana* had saved the Old City, Jabotinsky and his friends had been thrown into prison, and Rabbi Kook, violating the sanctity of the sabbath, had appended his signature to the petition demanding their release. Boys dilated on the prowess of their grown-up brothers, and some of them embroidered accounts of the part they had played themselves in the defence of Jerusalem. The oldest of the pupils told us in secret that they still belonged to the *Hagana*; some had handled real fire-arms and even fired real bullets. We listened to these stories half in disbelief, and the events themselves seemed as remote as if they had occurred on another planet. Things had calmed down since then, and one could walk in safety about the surrounding country, drink a cup of coffee in an Arab tavern, venture as far as Bethlehem or Hebron, or even go on foot of a summer night to King Solomon's Pools to taste the icy water of the Artas springs.

II

But though times were peaceful and achievements modest, discussions flourished apace in our little community. Parties attacked one another with vehemence, orators grew fiery, and in the lamplight the evening sessions lasted well into the night. The Representative Assembly, which held its sessions intermittently at the Zion Cinema, was the chief mouthpiece of political opinion, supported by representatives of all the communities in the country. The subjects then so hotly debated gradually lost their significance and fell into oblivion, but at that time our very destiny seemed to depend on them. And who knows—perhaps it really did, and the struggle was not in vain.

It was a time of transition. The old population was fighting with the energy of despair against the flood of new ideas introduced by the latest immigrants. A young, fresh breeze was blowing from the open sea, bringing with it the spirit of progress and social justice, entirely alien to the confined atmosphere within the walls of the Old City and to those who had grown old there before their time. Even if the debates of the Representative Assembly were ineffective, and the bodies they elected had little authority, they blazed a trail for the years to come.

I remember the violent battles waged on the subject of women's right to vote. It is difficult nowadays to imagine a subject of that kind threatening to disrupt the young Jewish society, but the orthodox Jews, especially the Jerusalem fanatics, declared they would leave the Representative Assembly and the official institutions of the community if equal civic rights were granted to women. More than once the deputies of the religious parties left a session in the middle of the night, and mediators and conciliators had to be sent to bring them back to the Chamber, or devise a compromise.

Relations between Ashkenazim and Sephardim were not always idyllic either. Sephardic delegates too more than once boycotted the Assembly, the sessions of the National Council and the Council of the Community of Jerusalem.

At that time the numerical importance of the native Sephardim was substantial, and during the last years of the Turkish régime some of them had acquired considerable influence. Now a change was making itself felt. The new immigrants flocking to the country in their thousands, with political fighters in their ranks, were importing new concepts of progress and democracy. The position of the Sephardim (nicknamed *los Señores*) was endangered. Public men of Sephardic origin criticized the activities of the Zionist Executive, whose members were newcomers ignorant of the customs of the country. They accused them of having antagonized the Arab leaders, whose mentality they did not understand, and with whom they shared no common language. They did not even know how to attract the favour of the British officials. The Sephardim mounted the platform at the Assembly to air their grievances, and when they were outvoted they left the Chamber in a temper, only to be reconciled soon afterwards.

Another burning subject of dispute was the attitude of the orange planters, who were stoutly defending their right to employ Arab labour, while the Labour parties were fighting for exclusively Jewish labour. The planters declared they could not keep up their farms if they had to pay the wages demanded by the Jewish labourers, apart from the necessity of remaining on good-neighbourly terms with the Arab fellaheen. The opposite point of view was harangued upon from the platform by young workers who were straight from the orange groves of Petah-Tikva and Hedera, bringing with them echoes of fierce discussions in the tents of the pioneers.

I sat in a corner of the great turbulent Chamber, excitedly scanning the tanned faces and black manes of the members of the *Hashomer* and the other heroic pioneers of Galilee who had been the heroes of my childhood. I listened to them hurling harsh words at the veteran pioneers of Guedera and the peasants of Richon-le-Sion, whose chronicles I had read in my father's library; but I was less concerned with the subject of the debate than with the intoxicating feeling that I was in the presence of these legendary figures.

In the sessions of the Assembly the workers joined forces against both orthodox and planters, but their conferences and their newspapers revealed sharp differences between the two socialist parties. On his arrival in Palestine, my father had joined one of these parties, but he was less concerned to defend his own doctrine than to reconcile the adversaries, so anxious was he to safeguard the tottering edifice of the National Council, entrusted to his care.

III

For the first few years after the war, Jerusalem remained the centre of the public life of the little nation in formation. It was the seat of government and of the Zionist Executive, our main link with the Jewish Diaspora. Later, with the growth of Tel-Aviv and the influx of fresh immigrants to that town and to the neighbouring settlements, the centre of gravity shifted from the Judean hills to the coastal plain. At the beginning of the twenties, however, most of the men at the head of affairs still lived in Jerusalem, and the Hebrew newspapers were printed there—two small-size dailies appearing about midday, reaching Tel-Aviv in the evening, and Haifa and other distant parts of the country next day.

In an open shop in Jaffa Street workmen in long caftans stood working the hand-presses of a little daily called *Haarets*, which gave faithful expression to the modern views of the newcomers. It was moderate, discreet and a bit boring. Well-known journalists, some of them teachers of my school, wrote articles for it, and the editor kept an eye on the purity of the language, which was literary, and somewhat pompous. The journal reproduced the polemics of the rival Labour parties and described the difficulties of the new immigrants and the plans for agricultural settlements. Its attitude towards the British authorities was very critical, but as far as home questions were concerned it followed the line of the Zionist Executive and was looked upon as the mouthpiece of the Zionist leaders.

The *Haarets's* rival was the *Doar Hayom*, the Hebrew equivalent of the London *Daily Mail*. Its finances were not in much better shape than those of the *Haarets*, but its editor aimed high, and dreamed of becoming king of the Palestinian press. Itamar Ben-Avi, with a wild mop of black hair, transformed the appearance of the paper by the introduction of sensational headlines, in emulation of Lord Northcliffe, whose innovations he admired. He never let a day pass without publishing some sensational news, and in times of flat calm he inflated minor events to head his pages with. A circle of admirers gravitated round him, composed of native-born farmers' sons and writers of Sephardic origin, most of them opposed to the inflow of 'Russian' ideas into the country. He attacked everybody of importance, and was forever having a dig at the British officials, raising the standard of revolt against the Zionist Executive and denouncing its 'Muscovite' methods of government. A fertile publicist, whose idiom was a bizarre mixture of French and self-invented terms, he treated his readers to a flood of neologisms, some of which have actually served to enrich modern Hebrew.

His paper found most readers in the old quarters of Jerusalem, as an entertainment after the sabbath meal, though the better educated among them were furious at the attacks it contained, and ridiculed the author's neologisms as extravagant and artificial.

Eliezer Ben-Yehuda, the father of this fiery publicist, and the revitalizer of the Hebrew tongue, was still alive when we settled in Jerusalem. In his house in the Abyssinian Street his little lamp could be seen burning until late in the night. He had retired from public affairs by then, and the controversies engendered by his publications were forgotten, but his legend was growing in his lifetime. It was known that he was working as hard as his strength would allow at his great dictionary; his study lamp lighted up his enormous card index and the old books he consulted. Chancing to pass that way, my parents and I would look in for a chat with him. He was a little, thin old man with a reddish goatee beard, and he talked in a mannered Hebrew, studded with singular expressions and unusual turns of speech.

A sort of relief of the guard was going on among the heads of affairs. The outstanding figures of the pre-war period were still at the head of the public offices, but Labour leaders were coming into prominence beside them, newly landed young farmers and foremen. Fresh currents of opinion were making themselves felt, and there was a general mood of effervescence. In the Emek the partisans of the big *kibbutz* and those of the little *kvutsa* engaged in passionate discussions, and in the tents and corrugated iron huts of the roadmakers the young *halutsim* spent the night arguing about the collectivist society, the struggle for Jewish labour and the society of tomorrow. Jewish masons trundled their wheelbarrows along the sands of Tel-Aviv, labourers newly disembarked formed the 'Maavar' group, working in the orange groves, sinking wells, seeking to drive a road towards the future. From Beth-Alpha, at the edge of the Valley of Jezreel, we heard strange, exciting tales of pioneers seeking new ways of life.

But in Jerusalem we were still living in another world. The Emek was far away, and the noise of the roadmakers' hammers did not reach us. We still had some years to go before an encampment would be set up at the top of King George Street for the bearded youths in ragged shirts, marking out roads for the new quarters of the city. Meanwhile the Jewish community there lived so to speak in a retort, centred upon itself. Even in Jerusalem, with its mixture of races and religions, foreigners seemed to us to exist only on the fringe of our reality. In the Russian Square the Orthodox popes strolled about majestically in their long black cassocks; ebony-skinned Ethiopian priests attended their church near the Street of the Prophets, sheltering their heads under white parasols, and the muezzin called to prayer from the top of the mosque of Zikhron-Moshé. In Jaffa Street the shops were kept by people of every complexion. There were a Greek photographer who dressed his window with coloured photographs of young couples in wedding dress, an Armenian selling ice cream, a Christian Arab displaying dress goods, and the shops in the American colony sold photographs of the Holy Land and souvenirs for tourists. The most luxurious of the hotels was the Fast, whose proprietor was a German. The city was surrounded by Arab villages, and camel and donkey caravans brought vegetables to the Mahane-Yehuda market, while fellaheen piled up red-fleshed, green-skinned water-melons at the foot of the wall near the Jaffa Gate. Visitors to government offices were received by persons in red fezzes. As for the British, they lived in the green German or Greek colony; isolated from the inhabitants of the city they pursued their special way of life, and nobody dared approach them. Officials, soldiers, policemen, to us they were all just Englishmen, strangers within our gates.

It took me only a few weeks to become permeated with this feeling of belonging to ourselves, and ourselves alone. We did not look upon ourselves as a small minority in the country; the fact that Jewish Jerusalem was enclosed in the alleys of its few quarters, and that our future was dependent on the immigrants brought us by the ships dropping anchor in Jaffa, never occurred to me. We boys went to school of a morning along narrow tracks through stony wastes, living in a world of our own. The train of events that had brought us here was our personal destiny, and nothing could deflect its course. Some day the country would be the Jewish State. Inevitably. We saw Jerusalem, a motley jumble of quarters, lanes and streets, clothed in the splendour of its future, and took no heed of its present plight.

When the Treaty of San Remo was signed, officially endorsing the principle of a Jewish National Home in Palestine, there was great rejoicing in the streets of the city, and a few years later the ratification of the Mandate was the occasion of public celebrations. But we really had no need of sanction by international law: the country had belonged to us from all eternity.

The Wind of Spring

I

THE years fled. Up early of a morning, winter and summer, we bolted the breakfast Grandmother prepared for us, seized our knapsacks crammed with books, and made our way to our school, across the stony fields stretching endlessly behind our house, up steep paths to the Bokharan quarter, meeting schoolfellows, boys and girls, chattering, discussing the latest news, or running over the Bible chapter given us to learn, until the school bell sounded.

On the sabbath, after the siesta, I often went to visit friends. If they were Sephardim of an old stock, I should find the family seated on low divans along walls painted pale blue, enjoying candied oranges, pink and white sugared almonds and platefuls of pumpkin seeds. The walls would be hung with rugs from Bezalel, embroidered with the figure of an Arab woman carrying a pitcher on her head, or the tower of David, or a portrait of Herzl, or of Herbert Samuel, cork helmet in hand. The tables would be covered with lace cloths and the hostess would ply her guests with sweets.

On a Saturday in the Ashkenazi quarter there would be a smell of *tsholent* and jellied calves' feet or highly seasoned fish. The whole family, young and old, would assemble for the *kiddush* ('blessing of the wine'), and the father, returning with measured tread from the synagogue, would exchange a few words with his guests, to discover the views of the young generation. Small children hung around the bigger ones, and the narrow court rang with feast-day shouts and laughter. The chanting of prayers issued from the synagogues, and Ashkenazi, Sephardic and Yemenite strains mingled in the peace of the morning in a sabbath symphony.

The schoolboys of that day were not yet interested in politics, or in the clandestine, semi-military organization of the *Hagana*. There was only one cinema in the town, the Zion, the corrugated iron roof of which had collapsed under the weight of the snow in the hard winter of 1920. It had since been rebuilt, but still looked like an enormous barn, broken down and patched up again with difficulty. For a few piastres one could watch serial adventure films, with accompanying music that an old pianist adapted to the demands of the plot. Sometimes a hand-written poster announced that on such a day, at such a time, a whole serial film would be shown in a single evening. Nobody missed the opportunity, and the story of *Les Misérables*, or *The Adventures of Eddy Polo*, would unroll endlessly over the screen, with the pianist tirelessly thumping the old piano till three in the morning.

The main excitements of our life were the theatrical performances given in the same building—where, incidentally, all important events took place, from the sittings of our Representative Assembly, party congresses and films, to concerts by amateurs. There was no permanent theatre in Palestine so far, though at Tel-Aviv a company was formed now and then, which might pay a visit to Jerusalem. They gave plays translated from Russian or Yiddish, and every new company opened its season with *Uriel d'Acosta*, and closed with a play by Leonid Andreiev, which the youth attended, wild with enthusiasm, sometimes paying—after a tussle with Mother—sometimes not, gate-crashing under the nose of the helpless ushers.

On winter evenings, if we had nothing better to do, we went to the People's House at Zikhron-Moshé, where in the light of a hissing incandescent lamp we listened to lectures by well-known speakers, or public discussions on questions of the hour, echoes of some stormy polemic disturbing Palestinian public opinion.

Every guest of importance was asked to speak, and party leaders carried on their eternal quarrels, slashing their opponents before an audience of young people, and of old men who sank at once into a beatific doze. For lack of other entertainment, we listened to innumerable commentaries on the Bible, history lectures by Joseph Klausner, and descriptions of archaeological wonders by Nahum Slousch or Eliezer Sukenik, the young teacher with a passion for relics of the past, who collected old stones and flints. It was he who, a quarter of a century later, discovered the Dead Sea scrolls, which were to revolutionize historical knowledge and the history of religions.

The Wind of Spring

This peaceful existence was suddenly interrupted by a fresh wind that changed the quiet atmosphere of our own school.

The new headmasters who had been appointed to succeed Shlomo Schiller came from Germany, equipped with long experience of teaching in the Hebrew schools of Lithuania. The twenties were years of ferment and educational experiments in Central Europe, and Moshé Calvari had thrown himself into the movement with all the ardour of his nature. He allowed his pupils complete autonomy, and avoided formal discipline and the use of the strong hand, not only on account of his educational ideas but from his natural propensity to tolerant mildness. The discipline of the school soon collapsed. His pupils led him a hard life, although they were attracted and even fascinated by his innovations. Stories of his absent-mindedness were exchanged in the corridors, and the clowns of the class imitated his heavy German accent behind his back and parodied his ways of speech.

The new headmaster having decided to introduce us to the beauties of democracy, meetings were held to elect committees for the different forms, and even a super-committee for the whole school. He encouraged us to find our own means of expression, and insisted on our exhibiting our talents as singers, musicians and orators. He spared no effort in acquainting us with western culture; bringing us reproductions of famous paintings in European museums, talking to us on the history of art and trying to widen and deepen our interest in literature. A Hebrew version of the *Iliad* appeared at that time, and Calvari, who was a great classicist, attempted to demonstrate the beauty of Greek poetry through the translation. The novelty of it appealed to us, but the buffoons made us all laugh by marching round the yard, declaiming Homer's 'Sing of the anger, O goddess, of the son of Peleus, Achilles', in hexametric rhythm and in biblical Hebrew pronounced with a Berlin accent.

All this seemed rather absurd and remote to boys born and bred in Jerusalem. Where was this Muse, daughter of the gods, where were Olympus and the heroes of Greek mythology? To us, Calvari was a being from another world. When he dictated a lesson, we listened with only half an ear to his explanations; we giggled, we exchanged notes, and he gazed at the culprits with his melancholy eyes, without reprimanding them.

111

He was profoundly convinced that man was born good, and did not despair of finding a way to the heart of these thick-skinned lads.

The fancy took us one day to publish a magazine of our own, and I was appointed editor, being accounted one of the seniors, and an expert in literature because I knew Russian and was a great reader. The magazine mobilized a legion of contributors, and a 'talent hunt' was set going in the upper forms. We bought some gelatine which I took home and boiled in one of Grandmother's pet saucepans, to her great indignation. The resulting paste was poured into a square tin that became the hand-press of the magazine. This was all part of the editor's duties, besides distribution and sale (two Egyptian piastres a copy, to cover costs). But this was nothing compared to the task of selecting articles worthy of publication and throwing the rest in the waste-paper basket, at the risk of quarrelling 'forever' with the offended authors. The editorial staff recopied articles and poems until the small hours, besides 'studies' and 'slices of life'. I must confess that no literary celebrity made a first appearance in our Review, but the editors responsible were proud to detect their friends secretly reading it during some particularly boring lesson in maths or chemistry.

We often went for excursions, and the Head, faithful to the tradition of Youth Movements in Germany, and used to long walks after the *Wandervogel* pattern, often took the lead. We went to Mount Herodium or the Cave of Adullam, across Bethlehem and the bare hills of the Desert of Judea, or down a steep descent to Ein-Guedi, spending the night in the open round a camp fire on the chalky rocks of the desert. One day we chanced to stop at Hebron on the eve of the sabbath. Hostile eyes took stock of us, and we were surrounded by a company of young Arabs who began throwing stones at us, till with great difficulty we reached the shelter of the yard of one of the Jewish houses. But security reigned at the time, and this alert did not deter us from walking back by moonlight, stopping by the way at King Solomon's Pools, and threading the sleeping streets of Bethlehem to arrive home at daybreak.

We came to know and love the Desert of Judea. We could find our way about its tracks better than among mathematical problems and the philosophy of the Middle Ages. Whenever we saw Calvari standing in the empty yard of the school, knapsack on back and green hat on head, we knew he was preparing to carry us off to the hills. He attached a greater educational value to these walks than to the intensive study of the Bible, with which we were already saturated by our other teachers, for he gave the highest importance to the formation of character and the development of a spirit of observation. In the shade of a spreading fig-tree or at the foot of an old oak, he would tell us stories of real life and the internal conflicts of young Jews in Germany, or evoke a forgotten episode in the history of Israel. He was bent on introducing us to the world of literature, awaking our aesthetic sense to the appreciation of art as well as nature, and took infinite trouble in answering his pupils' questions, which were not always prompted by a thirst for knowledge.

The period was of short duration. The days of Calvari's reign were counted. Discipline was relaxed, and more time was given to outside activities than to learning. We were terribly behindhand in the curriculum, and getting worried at the thought of our school-leaving exams. We had heard rumours of stormy discussions between the Head and the teaching staff, and when term began again, in September 1923, the red beard of the enthusiastic innovator had vanished. The new headmaster was a moderate man, kind and rather conservative. School life returned to its usual course and the pupils to their routine; but we often thought with a twinge of regret of that brief period of turbulence, when a little fresh breeze from the great world had reached our small circle.

II

In winter, when the days were short, and fog covered the hills, we were prisoned in our quarters in Jerusalem. But after the rainy season the wind of spring transformed the country. Our Passover excursions, and the summer holidays, introduced us to another Palestine, sometimes dusty and somnolent like the roads rutted by the wheels of the diligences, sometimes young and aquiver, throbbing to the blows of pickaxes, preparing to face the future. From Metulla in the north to Gedera in the south the traces of the past were being wiped out and the countenance of the future was appearing, blurred at the moment, but alive.

We spent our first summer holidays on Mount Carmel. Every time I visit Haifa I look in vain for the bare hill of my youth among the wide streets and tall buildings, the café terraces, shops and cinemas of the Mount Carmel of today. We had taken then two rooms in an old stone house that was built by a German Templar and belonging to one of the old families of Haifa. It was surrounded by tall pine-trees, and the terrace on either side looked over deep wadis thickly carpeted with vegetation. It was isolated, secluded from the noise of the town: only the whispering of leaves and the howling of jackals disturbed the silence of the night. A stony track ran down to the sea, and another led to a narrow ravine where a little gang of labourers had pitched camp. Half a dozen young men were trying to found there a new settlement, but they were eventually beaten by the arid soil, and scattered to the four winds.

Our landlord owned a shop in Hamra Square in the Lower City, near the harbour, where all the trade of the town was concentrated. On weekdays he rose early, saddled his white donkey and rode down to the town by the steep path on the hillside. Sometimes we went with him, jumping from rock to rock, stopping now and then to get our breath and glance at the view. The port was not yet built and there were no quays; ships dropped anchor in the open sea. The river Kishon drove its winding course through the marshes in the Plain of Acre, full of little pools sparkling in the sun, and covered with vegetation looking, at a distance, like a vast cornfield. The dunes stretched white and immovable to the keeps of the fortress of Acre, and beyond them to the steep white rocks of Ras-el-Nakura on the frontier of Lebanon.

One evening we went by moonlight, a little party of boys and girls, down the heights of Carmel to the Lower City, planning to go to Acre. After lengthy bargaining with the Arab drivers, we piled into some back-firing old Fords. There were no hard roads, and the cars travelled over the wet sand along the Bay of Haifa, their wheels sending up spurts of sea water at intervals. After going round the inside of the fortress we stopped in the market-place of the Arab town, and seeing the twinkling light of a little cinema, we sent some friends who spoke Arabic to negotiate with the cashier, who, impressed by the number and quality of his customers, agreed after much bargaining to the price of one piastre per head, and so we spent the rest of the evening watching the jerky shadows of an old adventure film.

That summer, in the solitude of our house on Carmel, was a luminous time, joyful and carefree. There was a girl of my own age, with lovely brown eyes; friends came to see her from Haifa and the villages of Galilee. A troop of scouts from the secondary school were camping in the wood near by, and I was soon allowed to join them and share their games and dances and excursions. We roamed about the deserted tracks on the mountain, scrambling up and down, and lighting camp fires in the scrub. Sometimes we got up early on a fine day and ran down to the Mediterranean. There was no road yet running like a black ribbon along the coast, and the foot of the Carmel Range slid into the powdery sand, white and pure as on the Day of Creation. The quiet waves lapped us in a cool freshness, and we stayed there till it was time to return, climbing the rocky slopes, faces aflame and sweat running down our thin shirts. The forest covering Carmel was then the only one in Palestine, and the boys of Jerusalem were fascinated by the trees, used as they were to the Judean hills, grey and bare, their slopes parched by the sun.

The new streets, and the frames of houses being built in the new suburb of Hadar-Hacarmel, heralded a new era in Haifa. Further north, Galilee still slumbered round its black basalt houses, in Baron Rothschild's settlements, far from the impetuous rhythm of Tel-Aviv and the littoral. I often went there, either on a family visit to Beth-Gan or on school excursions. Nothing had changed in the Yavniel Valley since our arrival in Palestine. I walked along the Lake of Tiberias, up a path over the hill and down a dusty track to the village. There were not many boys of my age at Beth-Gan, and I spent most of my time with my uncle, riding with him on an old horse across the fields, listening greedily to the wealth of stories he had to tell. We rode along narrow paths between the almond plantations to the top of the hill from which we could see the Lake of Tiberias, beyond the deserted houses of Poriah. The people of Beth-Gan told me proudly one day that they had some new neighbours: a few newcomers from America had settled at Sarona, on the plateau opposite the valley. We often crossed the rocky mountain ridge to contemplate this American village, a marvel of white houses, shining with cleanness, furnished with every amenity available at that date, including a gramophone screeching out the high-lights of transatlantic music.

In the villages of Upper Galilee nothing had changed since before the war. The guards still went their rounds at night behind the basalt wall, protecting the livestock from the raiding bandits from the Hauran hills. Arab labourers still tilled the fields. The wooden huts of Kfar Giladi still stood desolate, and near by, in the farmyard of Tel-Hai, you could still see the marks of the bullets, reminders of the tragic events of the spring of 1920, when a band of Arab aggressors killed eight of the defenders of the little settlement, among them Joseph Trumpeldor, whose heroic deeds had since been the inspiration of the youth of the country. Metulla stood up like a ruined hill fortress on the crest that formed our northern frontier, and a mud path ran along the foot of the hills beside the Hula marshes, where lean-flanked buffaloes wallowed, and clumps of papyrus waved among the reed-mat tents of the Black Beduins. Nobody had dared to venture into the tangled vegetation of these marshes, and no new village had sprung up on the soil of this enclave, incorporated in Palestine after protracted political bargaining.

Our school excursions into Upper Galilee led us by day along desert tracks, and at night into school-yards where we slept in the open. We came to know the young peasants of Galilee, a type apart, bred in these solitudes, even pronouncing their Hebrew in a strange way so that every *v* became a *b*. They were the product of an artificial experiment, made in this case by a famous pedagogue and philologian, who introduced a different pronunciation into the schools of Upper Galilee to create a dialect, which, according to him, was indispensable to any living language. The experiment only lasted the length of a generation. The road system ramified, distances shrank, Galilee emerged from its isolation, and the Galileans went back to talking like everybody else.

The Wind of Spring

But a wind of change was soon to invade the calm of the Galilean villages. *Halutsim* songs were heard in the labourers' camps where modern roads were being laid out in the north of the country. Girls in shorts and wide-brimmed hats sat on heaps of stones, breaking them up with their hammers to make road-metal, and boys were busy emptying barrowfuls of earth along the line of the road to come. In the white domed tents and tin shanties newly arrived pioneers discussed their plans, and formed separate working gangs, some of which were to settle and people the whole of the Emek, while others sought work as masons in the towns or farm labourers in the region of the old settlements. These labourers' camps were the crucible of a new world of thought, visions, polemics and discussions whose reverberations spread beyond the frontiers of the country to reach the young people undergoing training in farm schools in Poland and Roumania, and in those still carried on clandestinely in Soviet Russia. But the greatest importance was attached to the new settlements in the Valley of Jezreel, the focus of Palestine's new ideas, aspirations and hopes.

It was usual for the pupils in their last term but one to end their Passover holiday by an excursion, before returning to prepare for their school-leaving exams. The fortnight spent in long walks through Samaria, the Emek and Galilee, was passionately looked forward to and excitedly discussed afterwards.

This was how we came upon the great valley, after an endless march along the mud track traversing the Wadi Ara. When we broke out of the mountains by the path leading up to Megiddo, the whole of the Emek lay spread out before us in all its primitive splendour—a vast untilled space with no sign of human life. Then we came upon the new *kibbutsim*, with their huts and tents facing the slopes of Mount Gilboa. They looked more like military camps than agricultural villages. Their pioneering inhabitants were still busy draining the marshes, clearing their land of stones and digging the soil for their vegetable gardens. A plough drawn by a pair of mules was driving the first furrow in a field, shrubs had been planted along the approaches to the village, cows lowed under a roof of branches; but the whole did not yet suggest a village settled on its own soil. A long hut of blackwashed boards served as a refectory. Piles of tomatoes in deep dishes and thick slices of black bread were the only food provided, and people sat eating there as if to get over a boring task, without pleasure, with a sort of contempt for a function unworthy of idealistic pioneers, to which one resigned oneself solely to appease one's craving stomach. There were shower-baths roofed with mats, and when we went in to wash off the dust of the road, the *halutsim* exchanged jokes about the Jerusalem lads. They appeared contemptuous of us young townsfolk who spent our time doing God knows what, while a new world was being created in our valley.

Their clothes were torn, their hair unkempt and their chins unshaven; the girls protected their heads with old scarves or floppy hats. The wind swept into the huts and under the tents, swinging storm lanterns shed a dim light in the refectory; but we were aware of a spirit of ardent faith and confidence that impressed us, we who were so proud of belonging to the youth of Jerusalem. In our heart of hearts we knew it was here that the miracle was being accomplished, and many of us looked at these great, strapping fellows with envy and respect.

The villages of the Emek were going through a crisis. Ever since the gates of Russia had been bolted and barred, the human stream of reinforcements had dried up, the subsidies allotted by the Zionist Executive were meagre, and the *kibbutsim* had been largely left to their fate. As poverty increased, quarrels became sharper. Many of the younger members were unable to stand the test, and the ships leaving the port of Jaffa carried away departing *halutsim*. The third *Aliya* was petering out and disaster was felt to be imminent.

But the year I left school things suddenly took a turn for the better. Ships crowded the port of Jaffa once more, and the quays were piled not only with the scanty baggage of the *halutsim* but with solid trunks, and crates containing complete sets of furniture—tables, sideboards, easy chairs, and sometimes even a black piano belonging to some well-to-do middle-class family. Immigration from Poland had started again, and the

Palestine Offices in Warsaw and Vilna were once more being stormed by would-be emigrants.

This was Tel-Aviv's greatest period of growth. Going down from Jerusalem we found the new town looking like a builder's yard. New houses sprang up daily in the dunes, and we often made a detour to admire some new factory set up in one of the suburbs. We had inherited from our elders the classical dream of the return to the land, the new Jewish man living in the land of his forefathers, every peasant resting beneath his own vine or his fig-tree, but even in our wildest dreams we had never imagined that Palestine might undergo a great industrial development. So we were doubly proud when we saw the first chimneys of little new factories rising skywards in the dunes of Tel-Aviv.

Meanwhile, orangeries were being planted north of Petah-Tikva, and new settlements founded. In the streets of Tel-Aviv and in the cafés along the promenade, Polish was taking the place of Russian as the language of intellectuals and snobs.

The Labour camp was undergoing a transformation too; new immigrants were knocking at the doors of the national institutions, demanding land for the settlement of their villages. An inflow of agricultural labourers found work in plenty in the new orangeries on the littoral. On the sands of Tel-Aviv, along the edge of the sea, tents were hurriedly set up for the gangs of navvies employed in levelling the dunes, trundling barrow-loads of sand, piling up bricks and leading caravans of camels heavily burdened with *zifzif*, a gritty form of sand used in building the new town.

New faces made their appearance at home. Besides the young pioneers there came good bourgeois from Poland with starched collars that turned limp in the Jerusalem sun, and ladies in well-tailored white dresses. The Polish language, with its polite flourishes, poured out in an easy flow. Tourists had been unknown in Palestine before; people came there to settle, or not at all. But now friends of my parents, old acquaintances from Warsaw and Vilna, came on a fortnight's tour of the country —and stopped several months. There were journalists sent by their weekly papers to write reports on Palestine, and well-to-do Jews come to prospect the land for the chance of an investment. I often acted as their guide, to show them the beauties of the Old

City, make them admire the Wailing Wall, and climb Mount Scopus, panting and sweating, for the sake of the magnificent view over the Jordan and the Dead Sea.

This was the beginning of a period that came to be known as the fourth *Aliya*. We felt that the crisis was coming to an end, and were convinced that we were about to turn into the royal road to prosperity and progress. How could we foresee that it was merely the beginning of a cycle of ups and downs that would mark for years the history of the emerging Jewish fatherland?

IV

I was coming to the end of my schooling. After the Passover holidays lessons were suspended to allow us to prepare for the school-leaving exams. We formed a little group among ourselves—boys and girls—for study in common, re-reading lesson books and the notes we had taken in class. The test itself was probably not very severe, but the strain of preparation gave us a feeling of great importance. We got up at four o'clock for the sake of the cool morning air, and met in the little Schneller coppice to work until midday; then, after a short siesta, we carried on through the afternoon till late in the evening. After a few weeks we had become experts on the Bible, had delved deep into Hebrew philosophy, could solve mathematical problems with ease, and were prepared to hold forth on any subject in Hebrew or English.

But the nearer the exams approached, the more formidable they appeared. Our familiar teachers had suddenly become a Grand Sanhedrin, prepared to decide our fate. Some of the girls were in tears on the eve of the maths exam, and our hearts beat wildly as we each drew the slip of paper with the question to be answered, or the subject for an essay. Our parents found excuses to visit the Bokharan quarter, to see how we were getting on, and hand us a bar of chocolate or a bunch of juicy grapes. But the most excited of us all was Shlomo, the Yemenite doorkeeper, who had grown fond of us over the years, and shared our pains and pleasures.

The last day was one of intense strain. Our whole destiny might have been at stake behind the closed doors of the professors' sanctum. But when our English teacher, who had never spoken to me in any language but the one he taught, smiled as he said in stilted Hebrew (actually addressing me ceremoniously in the third person!) 'The gentleman may take his leave', I knew that my schooldays were over.

After the distribution of diplomas, the family sat in council to settle my future.

The general lines had been laid down before: I was to continue my studies abroad. There was no university in Palestine; the foundation-stone that had been solemnly laid on Mount Scopus in the idyllic days of the Balfour Declaration was still there, all alone. But nobody thought at that time that a young man who had finished his schooling in Jerusalem could start work in a *kibbutz*, as thousands did later on. The Zionist Youth Movements in Poland, Lithuania and Roumania were in full swing, but the pioneer idea had not yet found its way into the Jerusalem schools. My generation clung to the old routine and went to university.

Our home atmosphere had much to do with this, as well as the conservative climate of Jerusalem at that period, in which the new ways of thought and life developing in the rest of the country had not yet been assimilated. It had even more to do with our teachers, who might have endued us with the pioneering spirit if they had been interested in anything but the restoration of the Hebrew tongue. They looked upon their task of teaching and moulding souls as a sacred mission, and performed it with fervour. Most of them had been born abroad, and their migration to Palestine had been preceded by a profound internal crisis. They had wanted to spare their pupils the moral torments they had suffered, and breed up a generation of normal, natural Jews, speaking Hebrew as their mother tongue, and in this they had succeeded.

The political parties were absorbed in their domestic quarrels, and had no time to pay attention to us. The thousands of immigrants pouring into the country meant more to them than the boys scattered among the schools, who were more or less bound to fall into their hands sooner or later, so they probably thought, and need not be recruited now.

Nobody then considered it wrong for young Jews living abroad to leave home for Palestine, to build houses and drain the Emek marshes, while young men who had grown up here went abroad to complete their education, and the little community, still so weak, was impoverished by the dispersal of its sons throughout the world.

Many of them returned, but others settled where they had studied, especially in America, where all those who had relations there had gone. The sons of well-to-do families chose England, whence they might return with a chance of good appointments in the Mandatory Government. Ordinary mortals went to European countries, where living was cheaper; attracted by the promises of the Italian government, offering great facilities to foreign students, I decided, with my family's approval, to go to Italy.

I went to the Italian hospital in quest of someone to teach me the rudiments of the language, and was given some lessons by a young, shy priest. My father ran across a friend just come from Rome, who gave him some letters of recommendation to the Zionist leaders in Italy, and at the end of the summer I went to the station at Lydda, accompanied by the whole family. Grandmother had baked me some cakes, and Mother had spent a whole evening sewing bank-notes into the hem of my shirt, so that I should not be left penniless if I was robbed on the journey.

So, late at night, I found myself on board the ferry over the Suez Canal, three years after crossing the Egyptian frontier to go to Palestine. A short time, even in the life of an adolescent; but I had become so used to the country, and so much a part of it, that when I boarded my ship at Alexandria, I had no recollection of myself as a young immigrant from Europe. I had thrust deep roots into the rocky soil of Jerusalem, and was bound to it by every fibre of my being.

PART THREE

Italian Interlude

Florence, Year III

I

TO OUR eyes Italy was no different from any of the other countries mentioned in our geography books. The world was still a
wide one, distances still counted, and a journey abroad was an
adventure. We had opted for Italy because of its boasted
beauties, and because of its reputation as a cheap country to live
in, with reduced travelling and educational expenses. We did
not know its language, we had no idea what its people were like,
and as for the political upheavals it had lately gone through, we
thought them no more important than the changes of government in foreign countries to which our newspapers devoted a
few lines in small print on the back page.

After some hesitation our little party had chosen Florence, in
spite of friends who had persistently recommended the University
of Rome. Perhaps, subconsciously, we had wanted to settle in a
smaller, quieter city, fearing the turmoil of the great one that
might distract us from our studies.

On arriving in Florence we went roaming round the streets,
admiring its art treasures, discovering a new world at every step,
like villagers let loose in a metropolis. The new régime that was
taking over by force hardly caught our attention, and we should
have been very surprised if we had been told that its doctrine
would spell the ruin of a whole generation. The word 'Fascism'
meant nothing to us. We had heard of the Roman lictors'
fasces, and the 'March on Rome' called up vague memories.
Black shirts, castor oil, Roman salute—all that sounded like some
childish game. Revolution? Forgive me if I smile, I who have
been through the bloody battles of Russia, murders, street fighting, a whole world falling into ruin!

World events, as seen from Jerusalem, centred round a
young, weak community, anxiously awaiting the arrival of a
shipload of immigrants, fearing the Arabs, suspicious of British
intrigues, appealing to the sympathy of the noble souls of
London. This was the scale of our interests, which our news-

papers reflected fairly exactly. Now and then we had come across an article on Italy, relating an episode of the struggle between Fascists and socialists. From time to time the Labour press published an article warning us against the danger with which the new nationalism *à la* Mussolini threatened the world. These warnings made us prick up our ears, but they met with a certain scepticism.

I had sailed in the *Helwan*, of the Lloyd-Triestino Line, and one evening I had gone up alone on deck to breathe the air of the open sea. Leaning on the rail, I was watching the twinkling lights on the Greek islands, when a lean young man wearing spectacles stopped beside me, eyeing me with curiosity. 'Student?' he enquired.

'Future student,' I replied, with a touch of pride.

'Where d'you come from?'

'From Jerusalem.'

He asked my name, and it turned out that he knew my father. He introduced himself as Dov Hos, and I remembered having seen him sometimes at the Jewish National Council. Young as he was, he was already considered a political leader of importance, and I kept silence, convinced that he would think it beneath him to talk with a boy of my age. But he went on questioning me. What Faculty had I chosen? What did my old school friends think? How much did we know of what was going on in the country? Had any of us joined the *kibbutsim*? I answered as best I could, criticizing the teaching methods and the little ideological education given us. Then he told me about the pupils of the Herzlia secondary school, where he had been educated, how they had organized themselves and taken part in creating the Labour Movement. He asked what university I was going to attend, and I said, 'Florence, in Italy.'

He was silent for a moment, then he put his hand on my shoulder, looking into my eyes as though trying to drive his words into my inmost soul, and said: 'What is happening in that country will probably seem very childish to you. Make no mistake. Open your eyes and take notice. This Italy will bring great misfortunes upon us, and who knows but you and I may suffer from the consequences. Fascism is a doctrine of hate, and nothing succeeds so well in this world as hate. We Jews must be specially on our guard against this régime. So be careful, while you are living there, to pay attention to all you see. We are perhaps on the threshold of a new era, which may be a hard, very hard one for us all.'

This warning seemed at first greatly exaggerated. Florence was a beautiful city, gay and hospitable. The old streets, the Renaissance palaces with their delicate stone traceries, the narrow alleys and little squares, the varying faces of a city saturated with history, soon had me in thrall. The townspeople were kind to foreigners, and newly arrived students, talking a halting Italian, were treated like old acquaintances. The Florentines acted as their guides, and professed admiration for the rapidity with which they were learning the language.

At the beginning of the university year we were greeted by a crowd of young men, second- and third-year students, wearing caps with long peaks, red for medicine, blue for arts, and so forth, filling the streets and chanting their university song:

Evviva Firenze, città delle belle donne!

Friends in the know told us that the same song was sung, suitably adapted, in Bologna, Pisa and all the university cities of Italy, but the Florentines defended their version with ferocity, swearing by the gods that the hymn had been composed in the Tuscan capital, and the others were mere vulgar plagiarisms, the best proof being that the girls of Florence were the most beautiful in Italy.

Like all freshmen, we had to submit to the traditional ceremony of baptism, which cost us half our monthly allowance. The old hands kept watch at the doors of the University for the newcomers hurrying along the corridors, looking a little lost. They were immediately encircled and dragged away captive to the most expensive cafés of the town, where the veterans seated themselves comfortably in the easy chairs, ordered drinks, devoured cakes, and then made off, leaving their victims to foot the bill. To save the student from suffering a second time, he was presented with a diploma on stamped paper, in macaronic verse, laying down the ten commandments he was bound to observe, the only repeatable one of which forbade him to attend lectures and pass exams. But all this, and other details of the *Matricola*, was carried out with good humour and frankness, and no suggestion of sadism, contempt or xenophobia.

A few months later, however, the streets were thronged with a crowd that was not in quest of pleasure or amusement. In the middle of the year 1924 the socialist leader Giacomo Matteotti was assassinated, and the Opposition was convinced that this was an act of the party in power. Cesare Rossi, a well-known Fascist, was one of those imprisoned, and he was said to have revealed everything in captivity, especially the Duce's share in plotting the crime. The event is hardly remembered now, after all the tragedies we have witnessed since then, but the Europe of that day was not used to seeing a legal government liquidating its opponents in cold blood. The press was still free, and public opinion was soon roused. The fate of the Fascist régime was at stake. Mussolini had been in the habit of sending his cohorts into the streets, but now that he was in power he affected to respect order and the law. Liberals and socialists held up their heads again, and the March on Rome appeared forgotten. The name of Matteotti became a war-cry, and the Duce, determined at all costs to regain his prestige, launched his followers into the streets by the thousand to bring the Opposition and its leaders to submission. Fascists were assembled in squads in all the towns of Italy, and in Florence the Blackshirts spread through the streets and squares, attacking newspaper offices, setting fire to buildings and beating up their political opponents. An atmosphere of terror soon reigned in the city.

I was then in lodgings opposite the headquarters of the Fascist Party, and was able to watch not only the rioting in the street but the regrouping and organizing of the Blackshirts, mainly composed of very young men, and thugs recruited from the underworld.

A few days later the Fascists decided to bring the University to heel. Gangs of roughs suddenly made their appearance in the buildings and found their way to the lectures given by professors known to be opposed to the régime, interrupting them with insolent interpellations, attacking the socialist students, overturning the benches and tearing up notebooks and papers. When the socialist students attempted resistance, Blackshirt

128

reinforcements were called in, and the police maintained a kindly neutrality. The University, famous for the struggle it had waged in defence of its independence ever since the Middle Ages, and the fighters for the liberty of Italy it had produced in the nine-teenth century, was soon muzzled. Few of the professors could stand up to the spate of persecutions; some were forcibly ex-pelled from their professorships, but most of them were obliged to bow to the inevitable and join the ranks of the Fascist Party.

I was then attending lectures by a young professor of psy-chology, Enzo Bonaventura, considered one of the leading lights of Italy. He was a proud Jew, one of the heads of the Florence community and a leader of the local Zionist organization. He maintained close contact with the Palestinian students enrolled in the Faculty of Philosophy and Letters, and often invited them to his study. His lectures were brilliant and very popular, and he was greatly liked in university circles.

Entering the lecture hall one day, I realized at once that the atmosphere was electric. The amphitheatre was full, and lining the walls were a lot of young men I had never seen before. The professor had hardly begun his lecture when he was interrupted by cat-calls from every corner of the hall, followed by howls and farmyard noises. I did not know the meaning of all the invectives being hurled at him, but I suddenly recognized with a shock a word that was being shouted on all sides: *Ebreo!* Jew! Bonaventura remained seated, awaiting the end of the demon-stration; but when he realized that the hooligans had no inten-tion of leaving off, he collected his notes and left the hall. The non-Fascist students stood up and applauded him. And this, I believe, was the last demonstration the opponents of the régime dared to make inside the walls of Florence University. Before the end of the year silence reigned in all the institutions of higher learning in Italy. The militant Fascists had assumed complete command, and their opponents dared no longer raise their heads.

Some years later Bonaventura left his native city for Palestine, and was appointed Professor of Psychology at the Hebrew Uni-versity in Jerusalem. He had many friends in the city, and meet-ing him at one of their houses I reminded him of the savage demonstration that had put an end to his academic career in Florence. At the University on Mount Scopus he taught in his clear, precise Hebrew, enhanced by a soft Italian accent. His end was a tragic one. He was assassinated on his way to Mount Scopus in a convoy of university professors in April of 1948, and was denied the happiness of witnessing the creation of the State of Israel.

I have a vivid recollection of a historian whose lectures in the Faculty of Letters were universally admired—Gaetano Salvemini, a prominent historian of Italy, whose fame had spread beyond the frontiers of his country. He was known to be a resolute opponent of Fascism, and he did not conceal his opinion of the régime.

The Jewish students once invited him to give a lecture in their university *Mensa*. His address was followed by a lot of questions, and a Hungarian student said to him, 'Can you tell us, Professor, on the strength of your profound knowledge of Europe's past history, whether any inference can be drawn from it as to the future? What future developments do you think we should expect?'

The old professor looked at his interlocutor with a smile, stroked his beard, and replied, stressing each word, 'My young friend, every man of science knows it is possible to indulge in previsions and predictions in any sphere governed by the laws of logic. On the other hand, nothing can be foreseen of what is about to happen in a lunatic asylum, because the actions of the insane are not susceptible of any rational explanation, and the laws of logic are unknown to them. Unfortunately we are living at a time when the affairs of the State are in the hands of idiots and madmen. And I am not excepting my own country.'

A few days later, a gang of young Fascists attacked the professor during his lecture. He succeeded by a miracle in escaping from the University, and eventually in leaving Italy. He spent his last years in England, where he went on with his historical researches, and had the sad privilege of witnessing the accomplishment of his prophecy when the Second World War broke out and his native Italy came near to ruin in the conflict.

II

We lived at first in a closed circle, restricted to our own company, like chicks hardly out of the egg. But the circle soon widened to include the Jewish students from Poland, Hungary and Roumania pouring in their hundreds into the Italian universities to breathe the air of the West, safe from the anti-Semite persecutions raging in those of their own countries.

We had little contact with Italian students; there seemed to be a dividing wall between us, first because of our ignorance of the language, and later, when we had become more familiar with it, because of the difference in our make-up. They probably considered us shy, timid, young for our age. Our mixed education had accustomed us to relations of frank comradeship with girls, and we had no taste for the dissipation that formed the backcloth of the life of young Italians. They had all grown up in austere, practising Catholic families, under the rigid surveillance of their parents, and now that they had left home they felt suddenly free of their fetters, with nothing to hinder their imagination or their instincts. They must have thought us incorrigible simpletons, quiet, well brought-up, absorbed in our studies, preoccupied with the problems of our distant country, of which none of them had ever heard.

Our way of living was different, too. Coming from a poor country, and aware of the great sacrifices our families had made for the sake of our education, we did not allow ourselves to waste a penny of the money our parents allowed us. But those of our Italian counterparts who managed to extort a few extra lire from their people boasted of it. The more money they wasted, the more their friends admired them, even if they were later reduced to taking their possessions to the pawnshop, the *Monte di Pietá*, an institution venerated in the students' circles, and crowned with garlands of verse.

The character, origins and nationality of the Palestinians were a puzzle to all of them, and even to the university authorities. Palestinian citizenship did not yet exist, and we held only provisional *laissez-passer*, a sort of second-class passports, in which our nationality was not stated. We had all been born in some remote town of Europe: Warsaw, Bucharest, Kiev or Vilna. The university officials tried to find their bearings, and for want of any definite solution contented themselves with a compromise. I still have my student's card giving the place of my birth as 'Vilna, Palestine'.

The Florentines were friendly people, ready to enter into conversation. When we lunched in a *latteria*, drinking a cup of very white *caffè latte*, or went for walks in the Cascine, the beautiful park in the neighbourhood of the city, they were surprised to find us describing ourselves simply as *Ebrei*, Jews, without adding a nationality. They knew there were Italian Jews, and that some had come from Russia, Poland, and countries beyond the seas. They knew, too, that Jews practised a different religion from their own, but this one looked to them like a bizarre version of their own Catholic faith. We tried in vain to convince them that our religion did not recognize the divine character of Christ, and did not oblige us to obey his Roman Vicar. They listened politely, but obviously refused to admit that perfectly normal people could profess so strange a faith, even if they were Jews— human beings like themselves in every other way. These Tuscans were so entirely without prejudice against the Jews that I was surprised, later on, to hear that the Fascists had succeeded in inspiring even them with Hitler's racialist doctrine.

Even the language we spoke did not surprise them. It was a language like all the others spoken by foreigners belonging to that queer world where people did not understand Italian. We were not often asked about our language as we were one day, during the interval in a play we had gone to see together. We were sitting in the gallery, chatting together in Hebrew, and some Italians near us were discussing something in low voices. Finally one of them addressed us, saying 'Excuse me, gentlemen, can you tell us what language you are talking among yourselves?'

'Hebrew,' I replied proudly, expecting to be assailed with questions on the language of the Bible, revived after centuries of oblivion.

But the questioner turned to his neighbours with a note of triumph in his voice. 'You hear that? Didn't I tell you it sounded like Latin?'

Florence, Year III

So we discovered suddenly, from this brief exchange with men of the people, the extent to which our Palestine, the focus of our existence, was ignored abroad. Nobody was interested in the struggle we were carrying on there. Even in Italy, a country bordering like ours on the Mediterranean, our difficulties were unknown, Zionism aroused no sympathy, and nobody had heard of the *kibbutsim* of the Emek, or the new life sprouting in Tel-Aviv. There was never any mention of Palestine in the Italian press; our fellow students knew the Arab world only from Rudolf Valentino's films, and as for the immigrants streaming towards Haifa, nobody was aware of them, except perhaps the dockers of Trieste, who met them once a week on the Lloyd-Triestino liners, on their way to the East.

On the Banks of the Arno

I

MY SCHOOL friend and I rented a room from a kindly old Italian woman on the Lung'Arno, bought a few books with which to teach ourselves Italian, and set to work. Our landlady had the greatest respect for students, whom she addressed as *signor dottore* even before they had crossed the threshold of the university. As soon as I could do so in Italian, I asked her what title we should have a right to at the end of our studies, when we were really D.Litts. She looked at me in astonishment and said, 'Why then, signorino, you will be signor professore!' Meanwhile she waited on us faithfully, mending our shirts, sweeping out our room, and when she decided to give it a more thorough cleaning, put her drawing-room at our disposal, with its old-fashioned heavy furniture, a table with a plush cloth, and walls adorned with the regulation gallery of family portraits—uncles and grandfathers with drooping moustaches and bushy beards, their chests covered with decorations, memorials of forgotten wars.

The house was curiously silent: there seemed to be no children about, nor any of the street singers whose fame had spread beyond the frontiers of Italy, and when we were fed up with slogging at Italian grammar and translating the insipid phrases of our manual, we longed for something to happen. But the only event ever to disturb our calm was the arrival of the postman, who announced himself by ringing the door-bell and shouting 'Posta!'

At once every window of the five-storied house was opened, and from each there descended a little basket suspended by a string. The postman rummaged in his bag, distributed the letters in their respective baskets, and consoled those who had received none, saying 'Don't worry! People haven't stopped writing!'

We Palestinians laughed at the postman's ways and the strange habits of the Italians, but when Wednesday came, the day of the Palestine mail, none of us went out. We waited, ears strained, and the moment we sighted the postman with his bag, we implored our landlady to lower her basket. As she drew it up again we seized the letters bearing stamps showing Rachel's tomb or the mosque of Omar, and nobody bothered any more with Italian conjugations or grammatical exercises. We were deep in the letters in which Mother told us how anxious she felt about the approach of winter, and the thin overcoat that would not protect us from the cold of Europe, adjuring us not to overwork and be sure and wear our flannel vest, and a muffler round our neck. It was a moment of communion with our home, a return to the world of childhood. The boy of eighteen, shaving the down on his cheek with a razor given him by his father at parting, forgot for a moment that he was in a foreign land, independent, a *signor dottore*, free to study or idle as he chose, and in receipt of a substantial cheque every month. Every Wednesday, homesickness pervaded our rooms.

Autumn soon brought grey days, a fine rain fell incessantly on the cobbles of the old alleys, the wind whistled under the bridges over the Arno, and we kept to our rooms most of the time, still busy with the mysteries of the Italian tongue. The old houses in which we lodged were innocent of central heating, and an icy wind blew through the chinks in the window-frames, penetrating to the marrow of our bones. Our landlady brought us a sort of iron cauldron filled with red-hot coals, over which we warmed our hands. The *scaldino* came into general use in our students' quarters for the duration of the winter.

As usual in Italy, lectures at the university were late in beginning. The Faculties were officially open, but not all the professors were there. One had not yet returned from his holiday, another was detained by matters of State. At the Faculty of Letters attendance at lectures was optional, and students could choose the disciplines and lecturers they preferred. Foreign students were not obliged to attend until they knew enough Italian not to be reduced to watching the professor rattle off his lecture with writhing lips, banging the desk with his fists, while they understood not a word of it. At first the rapid Italian speech struck me as a uniform, headlong stream of vowels without content, and it was only by degrees that separate words emerged from the fog and became organized into sentences. The meaning of the lectures began to take shape as the months went by. Reading books, which had been tiring and tedious, became suddenly a pleasure; I no longer had to look everything up in the dictionary. I was even able at times to do without it altogether, and the more I progressed the more I enjoyed the victory. The only foreign language I had known up to then was Russian, which I had learnt as a child; my English, studied at school, was clumsy and limited, but sufficed to make our Italian colleagues rate me as an expert. The only dictionary I possessed on arrival was an Italian-Russian one, and my room-mate, a native of Jerusalem knowing no foreign language at all, constantly disturbed me at work by asking the meaning of a word, so I ended by teaching him the Russian alphabet. The Cyrillic script hampered him, but I soon learnt to guess the word in spite of his Jerusalem pronunciation, and the translation became easy.

The first books I read in Italian were easy to understand because they were translations of some I had read in the original or in a Hebrew version. Soon I was able to run through the local press and the *Corriere della Sera*, which was still an independent paper. I was soon reading books with pleasure in the university library, beginning with Manzoni's historical novel *I Promessi Sposi*, which reminded me of the romanticism of Walter Scott that had attracted me so much as a child. So, I followed breathlessly the adventures of the young lovers, whose union was prevented by endless obstacles, until a turn of fate united them on the last page of the book.

I enjoyed reading *Le mie Prigioni* by Silvio Pellico, thrown into prison by the Austrian Occupation before Italy broke free. Then I took a leap backwards through the centuries to the adventures of Benvenuto Cellini, whose *Perseus* adorned the Piazza Signoria, and whose statuettes and jewellery were to be seen in all the museums. From there I came back to d'Annunzio, then at the peak of his fame, and made an attempt at reading his books. I knew too little Italian to appreciate his style, and his pride and masculine self-conceit did not appeal to me.

Reading contemporary writers brought me in touch with the futurist school, whose star was beginning to decline after the considerable prestige it had enjoyed in Europe in the days of Marinetti. The term 'futurist' was itself of Italian origin, and the revolutionary pranks of the doctrine were attuned to the spirit of revolt and negation of the period before and after the war. But the Fascist régime, which had sought support at first from these sources of revolt, ended by turning its back on them, and Italian literature soon foundered in a desert of monotonous and pretentious boredom, the common fate of all literature in times of restricted freedom.

Among the writers of that time I remember Giovanni Papini, whose *Down and Out* (*Un uomo finito*) made a great stir in Italy and throughout Europe. I should be surprised to hear of anybody reading it today, but post-war hearts and minds had been easily won over to his sceptical, disenchanted conception of the world, his nihilism, his revolt against convention, enhanced by a caustic, disdainful style. In that troubled period, in a disillusioned Europe, this gratuitous negation found favour, and a mediocre author like Papini, one of the epigones of futurism, could assume the mantle of a prophet. Towards the end of his life he seems to have figured as one of the glories of Fascism, but his writings and his antics had lost their attraction; greater people than he had appeared on the stage, and he was gradually forgotten, even in his native country.

By the end of my stay in Florence I was capable of enjoying the poetry of the great classics. I remember my emotional discovery of Dante and Petrarch as one of the profoundest experiences of my brief contact with Italian culture.

II

At first we used to feed in cheap restaurants as the fancy took us, or in the only *kosher* boarding-house in the town, run by a widow, Signora della Pergola, a descendant of a respectable Jewish family. But on the influx of so many Jewish students, the local community realized that it had a duty towards them, and organized a *mensa academica* with a strictly ritual cuisine in a little street at some distance from the centre. The room was a small one, with tables set close together, and the food was in the purest Italian tradition: macaroni with tomato juice, midday and evening, with little crumbs of meat from time to time. The place soon became the rallying-point of our group, and we held meetings and lively debates there. Florence was not used to such a concourse of foreign students, and our restaurant was soon known all over the town. As the notion of 'Jew' was not very clear to the Tuscans, they sent every foreigner with halting Italian to our table.

One evening, in the middle of a student gathering, the door opened and some ten sun-tanned, black-eyed young men were shown in by a handful of street urchins as 'Some of your people! You'll understand their lingo.' We seated the new-comers at one of the tables, but our attempts to understand them were unsuccessful. Nobody could distinguish a single word in the stream of talk. At last, with the help of explanations in a primitive Italian, we discovered that they were Albanian revolutionaries who had left their country after an upheaval of some sort and taken refuge in Italy. The doors of the *mensa* were opened to them, and they attended our gatherings, even to the lighting of candles on Friday evenings; they joined in our sing-ing, and contributed their own native songs, melancholy and monotonous, reminiscent of the oriental melodies we heard at home.

When they had mastered a little Italian they remained at table for hours at a time, with a plate of cold macaroni before them, telling us of their national aspirations, the revolution they were plotting, and their dreams of greatness for their country. But the hugger-mugger of Albanian home policy struck us as highly confused, even after their explanations, and we were not really sure whether they were of the left or the right, Liberals or Conservatives. The fact that they had been granted political asylum in Fascist Italy obviously laid them open to suspicion. We became quite fond of them, all the same; it was the first time we had come across other men devoted to an ideal of national struggle, fighting for freedom and dreaming of independence, under no matter what flag. We talked to them of Israel's glorious past, the kingdom of David, the prophecies of Herzl and the Jewish State, and they countered with Mehmet Ali, the conqueror of whom Albania was so proud, and Iskander Bek; all their tales breathing a longing for their barren, lofty mountains and their villages clinging to the rocks.

Our relations with the Jewish students of Europe, on the other hand, were complicated and contradictory. There was obviously a bond between us, but we criticized one another with acerbity. The Palestinian lot considered themselves the salt of the earth, looking down on these other Jews who did not speak their language, were hampered by their loyalty to their country of origin, and were trying to find some solution to their difficulties other than Zionism. This superiority complex affected not only native Palestinians but even those who a few years earlier were still members of Judaism in exile. I speak advisedly, for my letters at that time were full of harsh reproaches against these Jews of the Dispersion, their behaviour and their lack of dignity. 'What have we in common with them?' I asked, filled with fanatical pride in my 'Palestinism' of recent date. I denounced their defects, exposed their weaknesses, their propensity for endless palavering, their inability to rebel against the drabness of their existence, their tendency to bow the head to maltreatment, their resignation to every form of anti-Semitism. 'Look at them, unhappy in their native country, and yet incapable of devoting themselves to the fight for a real fatherland!'

'Compare them with the Palestinians—undaunted, their course clearly marked out. We had been educated in Hebrew schools, and Hebrew was our tongue. Our stay abroad was purely temporary; we should go home to share in the building up of our country, each as he best might. We were proud Jews, stiff-necked, and woe betide those that attacked us! Like them, we admired the beauty of Italy, but what was even this lovely city of Florence, compared with our Jerusalem, whose image was graven on our hearts for ever?'

The news reaching us from home seemed to justify our pride: thousands of immigrants disembarking on our shores, orange groves planted on the dunes of Sharon. Our Palestine was definitely looking towards the future, but what were the present cares of Italy, with all its glorious past? Fascism? Mussolini? The King and his family? How could these young Jews of the Dispersion refuse to recognize our great truth, our great reality, instead of clinging to the Europe to which nothing bound them, and which actually refused to accept them?

We erected a barrier, uncompromisingly, between ourselves and our Jewish comrades of West Europe. Youth is like that, hard.

absolute, dividing the world into black and white, the righteous on one side, the sinners on the other. As it happened, it soon became evident that neither the faults nor the virtues were all on one side. Most of the Palestinians did go home after completing their studies, but others yielded to the tempting pleasantness of life abroad, and scattered more or less in all directions. Our own little group was particularly incensed with one of our girl comrades, belonging to a family settled in Palestine for many generations, for marrying the son of one of the patrician Jewish families of Rome, and settling down there.

On the other hand there were ardent Zionists among the Polish and Roumanian Jews, who had acquired a sound knowledge of Hebrew, and were later to become famous in the scientific world, while others settled in Palestine and soon distinguished themselves among us.

Meanwhile our whole community led a lively life. The eve of the sabbath was devoted to debates, or readings and singing. We had established funds for loans and mutual aid, the beneficiaries being mostly students from East Europe, who were always short of money. Committees were elected and meetings convened, one of which resulted in yet another quarrel between Palestinians and 'foreigners'. The subject of debate was the recognition of Hebrew as the official language of the Jewish Student Association in Florence, and the inclusion of Zionism among its objects. The Zionist students from other countries joined forces with the Palestinians, and the motion was carried.

After this victory we decided to start on the ideological conquest of our East European colleagues. At meal-times, after devouring our ration of *pasta asciutta*, we scattered among the tables and started discussions with them. The Hungarian Jews were the hardest to convince. They knew very little about Judaism, and talked no language but Magyar. Conversation was carried on in near-Italian or a halting German that both parties understood with difficulty. However, we succeeded in forming a group among them prepared to learn Hebrew, and we became their zealous teachers. One of our difficulties was to induce them to trace their Hebrew letters from right to left, which they considered as a sort of philological aberration.

III

With the approach of Passover we all became immersed in preparations for the National Conference of Jewish Students to be held in Florence. We held several preliminary meetings, and political groups took shape. Delegations began arriving from Rome, Bologna, Turin and other university towns, and we now came in closer contact with our Italian colleagues, who, as we discovered, differed in no way from their non-Jewish friends, either in language, name, behaviour or way of thinking. This was a constant puzzle to the Russians and Poles among us, who had always considered themselves different from their fellow-countrymen. Very few of them observed any religious precepts, and the majority were practically ignorant of all the burning issues preoccupying the communities of Europe at that time.

It was at this Conference that I came to know Enzo Sereni, a young Roman Jew who was destined to become a leader of the pioneers of Israel.

At the end of the Conference Sereni was elected President of the Students' Federation. He was only two or three years older than the rest of us, but already famous in student circles. Small, thin, spectacled, he had smiling eyes that flashed in the heat of discussion. He waved his arms about and brandished his fists, all tension and energy. Even when standing still he seemed in perpetual motion. He belonged to an aristocratic family in Rome, where his uncle was president of the Jewish community, and his father private physician to the Queen. A few years earlier he had been converted to Zionism and had learnt to speak Hebrew, expressing himself with eloquence in a rich, varied style, to which his Italian accent lent a peculiar charm. The speech he delivered at the opening of the Conference was a brilliant one, proud and courageous, full of flights of oratory. I have a lively remembrance of him in our crowded *mensa*, his forceful personality standing out from among his rather colourless audience.

In later days, when I chanced to see him in his *kibbutz* of Guivath-Brenner, or at meetings in Jerusalem or Tel-Aviv, we reminded each other of the Florence congress, and our youthful excitement of those days seemed a little comical. A serious philosopher as well as a man of action, preoccupied with matters of faith and religion, he was considered by now one of the great hopes of the Socialist Party in Palestine. He worked indefatigably at his *kibbutz* among the dunes of the littoral, near Rehovoth, where, as in Florence, he seemed to be in perpetual motion, always in a hurry, talking rapidly, his ideas tumbling out as if to relieve him of their superabundance. Once he had reached a decision nothing deterred him, and he showed the same fearless resolution throughout the dangerous missions he accomplished in Hitler's Germany, and in the city of Baghdad in full rebellion.

The last time I saw him was in Cairo, during the war, when he was preparing for the mission from which he was not to return. Our leaders had done all they could to dissuade him from the attempt, but in vain. In charge of the intrepid Palestinian mission to be parachuted into Europe, he claimed the privilege of going with them, never demanding of others what he was not prepared to do himself.

We separated in the apartment of one of our friends in Cairo, after spending our last hours together in a passionate discussion that had gone on till dawn. His friends who were remaining behind did not conceal their anxiety; they knew the peril he incurred by returning to his native country wearing the Allied uniform. But Enzo Sereni went on talking as usual, rapidly and excitedly, proving by reasons of formal logic the existence of Divine Providence and its influence on the course of human history.

As we feared, he was never to return from his last perilous mission. Parachuted behind the German lines, he fell into the hands of the Nazis in Northern Italy, and was executed at Dachau.

From the Palazzo Vecchio to Mount Scopus

THE letters of recommendation I had been provided with on leaving home had remained at the bottom of my suitcase, but in time I came to know the leaders of the Jewish community in Florence, either at public meetings, or at the Convenio Ebraico, the Zionist Club of the town.

My people were by no means practising Jews, but a yearning for a Jewish atmosphere led me more than once, on the sabbath eve or on festival days, to visit the Grand Synagogue of Florence, a fine building in coloured marble, architecturally resembling a mosque, the style in favour in wealthy Jewish communities in the middle of the last century.

At my first visit I thought the temple cold and unfriendly compared with the little prayer-houses of Jerusalem. A handful of the faithful, in festal attire, sat solemnly in their chairs, while the verger, in swallow-tail coat and top hat, with a silver badge bearing his title in Hebrew and Italian hanging from a chain round his neck, bustled round the visitors. Saturday prayers were being sung to an organ accompaniment, and the precentor was intoning them in Sephardi plain-chant, but with a more melodious rendering, somewhat Italian fashion.

Contact with this little community opened my eyes to the profound transformation that was taking place in Italian Jewry. A wave of spiritual revival was spreading through intellectual Jewish circles, chiefly affecting the younger generation. In a strangely roundabout way these young Italian Jews had been brought in contact with the Zionist ideology, after passing through a phase of mysticism and awakening to the philosophical values of Judaism.

One of our friends, for example, brought up in an assimilated milieu, happened in the course of his studies to light on a book devoted to Jewish thought. His curiosity was aroused. He read and re-read it, and borrowed others from his home-town library, till he felt he had reached the roots of the Jewish religion.

He became gradually inspired with an ardent faith, reverted to this religion to his parents' great distress, and began observing all its ordinances, even to having himself circumcised at the age of thirty.

Another young man of the same milieu, son of a businessman who often went on trips round the country, heard his mother say to his father, 'You'd do better to put off your visit till a bit later. Tomorrow is the Day of Atonement. We're not religious, but it's a Holy Day we ought to respect.' His father was surprised at this sudden fit of piety, laughed it to scorn, and set out for the station. Next day they heard that the train he had travelled by had been derailed, and he was the only victim. This set the boy pondering. What was Judaism, he wondered, and what sin had his father committed? He began studying the law and observing its religious rites. Then he asked one of the Palestinian students to teach him Hebrew. He ended by settling in Palestine, and became one of the first Italian Jews to make his home in Jerusalem, long before Mussolini adopted his anti-Semite policy on the eve of the Second World War.

Examples of this kind constantly surprised us. Our own Zionism had originated in our doctrine of nationality. Our idea of Judaism was a part of the feeling that had been ours from childhood: that we were different from others because we belonged to another people. And here we had Jews devoid of any national feeling, who had yet been able to identify themselves with their people merely through the medium of their faith and their religious ideas.

The little Jewish community of Italy was firmly established in the country at that time. Its situation seemed assured, and anti-Semitism was unknown. Jews could become Ministers, one of them even rose to the post of Prime Minister. They included writers, and publishers, politicians and even Fascist leaders. All Jews were Italian citizens, free and equal. And yet this atmosphere had generated and confirmed a faith as ardent and total as that of Enzo Sereni, and brought Zionist convictions to flower among a handful of Jewish thinkers in Italy.

I went one day to see Alfonso Pacifici, looked upon at that time as one of the heads of Italian Zionism, since he was the editor of the weekly *Israel*. As soon as I knew enough Italian to read the paper I had been struck by its contents, its amount of information regarding events in Palestine and the Jewish communities of the world, and its long articles in small print on religious practice and Rabbinic law, with a wealth of supporting references and textual quotations.

A lawyer of repute, Pacifici belonged to the generation of Jews affected late in life by religion. Tall and handsome, with a long red beard, he was of exemplary piety. He apologized for receiving me that day lying on a sofa, instead of at his desk, because he was weak from fasting. He explained that as it was the Eve of the Passover, and he was the eldest son of his family, he was fasting in memory of the tenth plague of Egypt. I was deeply impressed. In the milieu in which I had grown up I had never known anybody to observe this recondite custom, even among our orthodox friends of Jerusalem.

Pacifici ended by settling in Jerusalem in the thirties. He identified himself completely with Palestine, but he was repelled by the secularity of most of the population. He could find no common language even with the religious parties, and shut himself up in the isolated world of the pious quarters of Jerusalem, where he spent his time studying the Law and observing its ordinances, cut off from the public life of Israel, leading an almost solitary existence, devoted entirely to the quest for religious perfection.

Sincere piety and faithful respect for religion did not prevent many Italian Jews from contracting mixed marriages. Once, on a Jewish holiday, a party of Palestinian Jews was invited to a meal at the house of a leader of the community. Our host's mother, a very distinguished old lady, was careful to see that all the rites were observed. I learnt later that she was a practising Catholic, and at the time of their marriage it had been agreed between her and her Jewish husband that their children should be brought up in their father's faith. She went to mass herself every Sunday, but was rigorously insistent on her children's observance of their own religious duties.

We went one day to the Institute of Jewish Higher Education in Florence, the principal seat of independent Jewish thought in Italy. In spite of its great reputation, it was little frequented, and that day we found only one student attending the lecture.

We had entered in a bunch, right in the middle of a lecture by Professor Umberto Cassuto, Rabbi of Florence, and Professor of Hebrew and Biblical Exegesis at the local university. Glancing at the newcomers, he at once recognized us as Palestinians, and apologized in excellent Hebrew for being obliged to continue his lecture in Italian, because 'the other students'—in this case the young man sitting alone in a corner—would not understand the sacred tongue. We had come in purely out of curiosity, sure of our superiority as Palestinians, even in the matter of Holy Scripture. But in a very few minutes we were conquered by the eloquence of this great Bible commentator and the beauty of his thought. He was analysing the origins and sources of the Psalms, and I think no one else can ever have revealed the poetical force and lyrical flights of great biblical poetry as he did. Later, when he was appointed to the University of Jerusalem, I sometimes attended his Bible lectures, but I never forgot that first one, given in his precise, melodious Italian.

At the end of the lecture we held a confabulation in a corner of the room, and decided to ask him to admit us to his lectures. It grieved us to see so eminent a teacher talking to empty benches, and we thought it our duty as Palestinians to support this seat of Jewish learning. But we all knew where the real attraction lay— in the sudden revelation, the profound communion with the Bible of our childhood. From that time onwards we made it a habit to attend Cassuto's lectures and those of Dr Isaiah Sonne on the philosophy of Judaism. The hours spent in this peaceful place were a harbour of comfort and meditation in our life of exile.

II

The bells of Giotto's campanile rang in the New Year of 1925, with the rain beating down on the streets of Florence, and the wind blowing under the bridges over the Arno. At night the arches of the Ponte Vecchio were lit up by the shop windows of the goldsmiths and silversmiths.

In the evening, after their discussions and meetings in the *mensa*, little bands of Palestinian students wandered about the deserted streets and gathered in the Piazza Signoria, near the

Town Hall, the Palazzo Vecchio that served as a model for the Italian Hospital in the Street of the Prophets in Jerusalem. The shepherd David stretched out his arm from the Piazzale Michelangelo over the slumbering city with its twinkling lights.

Visits to the museums, on Sundays, revealed the splendour of Italy's art treasures. In the spring we walked out to the neighbouring hills through the green fields, between vineyards and olive gardens. Sometimes we went without a meal for the sake of the fare to Siena, Pisa or Leghorn. We fell in by degrees with the peaceful, pleasant way of life in Italy, but we felt no closer ties with the country. We counted the days we still had to spend away from home.

Palestine was going through a period of great advance. The fourth *Aliya* was in full swing, and the whole country was preparing for the solemn opening of the Hebrew University on Mount Scopus. Workaday cares were pushed aside—unpaid salaries, the National Council without funds, strikes by teachers demanding their pay. My people's letters spoke of thousands of immigrants from Poland, some poor, some rich, with capital to invest. New houses were springing up in Tel-Aviv ('you won't recognize the town when you return'). The newcomers had planted citrus groves near Petah-Tikva and further north, in the Sharon plains, and the population of the country was increasing in number and strength. Soon there would be 200,000 Jews in Palestine, and we should have nothing more to fear— neither the Arabs and their plots, nor the British officials in the High Commissioner's palace, weaving their sinister plans. Even the redoubtable head of the British Colonial Office, Leopold Amery, would no longer be able to harm us.

My father wrote, always in a hurry, from Jerusalem, Tel-Aviv or Haifa, giving me accounts of the National Council's sessions and describing the villages of the Emek he had just visited for the sake of articles he was to write for the Warsaw papers. He complained, as usual, of quarrels, clumsy administration and insufficient funds, but he always ended his letters on an optimistic note. All these troubles would soon fade out; a new era was opening before us, we were already on the point of issuing from the impasse, and final victory was just round the corner.

My mother was more reticent, but she too wrote of friends arriving from Europe with the fresh waves of immigration, of new streets and local housing developments.

As spring approached, excitement reached its peak. Great scientists and eminent politicians from all over the world were coming to attend the opening of the Hebrew University. My parents' letters overflowed with pride. Balfour himself had promised to take part in the ceremony, and the High Commissioner would wear the black gown of the Hebrew University! A great amphitheatre was being built on Mount Scopus that would command a breath-taking view over the Dead Sea! Now the great men were holding forth: Weizmann had said this—Balfour had said that—even Einstein had put in a word. Now we should be irresistible. We should have a university towards which the eyes of all the nations of the earth would be turned. What did the Arabs and their hate-filled incitements matter now, or the British satraps in their offices at the Damascus Gate?

That week the mail was late. Every house in Jerusalem was overflowing with guests. At home, my father's friends and comrades in arms were unrolling their mattresses on the floors, and even after the ceremony on Mount Scopus fresh visitors continued to arrive. The old traditional songs were sung, and potatoes in their jackets were served hot with herrings from the grocer, as in the good old days of my parents' youth. Hasidic dancing went on all night in an explosion of joy in the houses of the city.

While all this was going on in Jerusalem, I was champing the bit—cursing the fate that kept me in Italy and prevented me from taking part in this historic event. Of course we celebrated the occasion ourselves, but what did that amount to, with the sea separating us from the rejoicings at home? A celebration took place in the *mensa*, and the Zionist *convenio* organized a grand demonstration with a crowd of participants and many enthusiastic speeches. The heads of the community asked the Palestinian students to choose their spokesman, and their choice fell on me. I spent the night at my desk, writing, scratching out, rewriting a speech appropriate to the event, to be delivered in Hebrew before this distinguished gathering. The next week's number of

Israel mentioned the speech of the young student from Jerusalem, 'delivered in a vibrant, forcible style', unaware that the distinguished speaker's voice had trembled with emotion during this his first address, lest the spokesman of the Palestinian students of the University of Florence should not prove worthy of the mission with which his friends had entrusted him.

We strode proudly round the assembly, as though the glory of Mount Scopus were reflected upon us.

The Polish, Hungarian and Roumanian students begged me to write to my father, in case they too could pursue their studies at the Hebrew University. Could they be given some financial support in Palestine with the help of the Zionist Organization? When would a Faculty of Medicine and a Faculty of Science be established? And where would the students be lodged who came to Jerusalem to study? A heavy mail left Florence for the towns of Hungary and Roumania, asking for parental advice, and to be told the rate of exchange between the Italian lira and the Egyptian pound, and an estimate of the cost of the passage to Palestine. Nobody doubted that after such a solemn ceremony on Mount Scopus the most eminent scientists of the whole world would throng to Jerusalem, and that a diploma of our University would be worth a hundred times more than those of the Italian ones. Those who knew Hebrew, learnt in the secondary schools of Poland or Lithuania or in the Rabbinic schools of their native country, felt that their hour of glory had arrived. They would be the first to study in Jerusalem without the language presenting a barrier.

I sent a letter to Jerusalem, saying that my friends and I had irrevocably decided to enter the Hebrew University early next year. I had made myself the spokesman for my friends, and begged my parents for a prompt reply.

But the first flush of enthusiasm did not last. No reply came for some time, and then bitterness and disillusionment crept into my parents' letters. It had become obvious that all the ceremonial and festivities had been no more than outward show, and it was hardly even certain that anything would come of all this business of a university.

Weizmann was said to have been aiming at nothing more than a political demonstration, and the wealthy patrons in

America, England and other countries who had advanced him money, had no intention of making the University a living organism, an Academy open to all. It was condemned to remain a modest, cramped Seminary, concerned with religious casuistry and affording an honourable livelihood to a few specialists whose researches would interest nobody. As for students—well, the governing body of the University had clearly stated that no pupils would be accepted, and there would be no exams or degrees, for the moment or even for some years, because the young institution must first of all consolidate its position. It had not yet sufficient funds to open Faculties other than an Institute of Jewish Science and a few chemical laboratories. Even this was only to please Chaim Weizmann, a chemist of world-wide repute, who sought the development of the only discipline dear to his heart.

Disappointment was everywhere intense, but nowhere so bitter as among Palestinian students abroad. I began by avoiding the friends who had fixed their hopes on the reply I had undertaken to obtain for them, but in the end I had to resign myself to telling them the truth. The Zionists were crushed, and their opponents greeted them ironically with satirical allusions to the 'bluff' manufactured in Jerusalem, and a Palestine that would never be able to solve their difficulties. The Palestinians were forced to come down off their pedestal and set their feet on the ground again.

In Palestine itself the situation deteriorated rapidly. Dark days followed the rejoicings, and disturbances broke out in Damascus when Lord Balfour passed through on his way back from Jerusalem. The Arab trouble-makers raised their heads, forcibly opposing the farming of the Afoula territory recently acquired in the Emek by the 'American Zionist Commonwealth', and the quarrel cost several dead and wounded—a thing that had not been known since the disturbances of 1921. The High Commissioner, Herbert Samuel, was about to leave his post, and there was anxiety in Jerusalem as to who would replace him. Of course we were far from the idyllic days of 1920, when the 'First Governor of Judea' was adorned with all the virtues. The Jewish press was not sparing in its criticism of his methods of government, denouncing his weakness and the extravagant concessions made to the Arabs. It did not hesitate to remind him of the original sin of the amnesty granted to the fomenters of trouble in Jerusalem, a weakness or a blunder that had elevated the Grand Mufti, a dangerous agitator, to the dignity of President of the Supreme Muslim Council. Still, we had a Jewish High Commissioner who believed in the Zionist ideal. It was rumoured that the Zionist Executive, especially Chaim Weizmann and Colonel Kish, were involved in his decision to resign. Without them, he would have liked to retain his office. But now, what would tomorrow be like? Perhaps they would send us a Jewish aristocrat from England, prudent and unimaginative, or far worse, one of their colonial satraps, a Commissioner from India or Africa, indifferent or hostile to the Balfour Declaration, who would abandon us to our isolation.

After the outburst of joy in the spring, correspondence reverted gradually to familiar subjects. My father was going to Tel-Aviv again to try and reach a compromise with the teachers, whose salaries remained unpaid and who were threatening to strike. He was again going to plead with the committees of Haifa, Hedera and Petah-Tikva for fifty pounds to ensure the functioning of the National Council, whose treasury was empty. So, in the greyness of disappointment, the wave of enthusiasm died down that had upborne the Jews of Palestine in that memorable April of 1925, when Balfour and Weizmann assumed their black gowns, while Bialik and Chief Rabbi Kook delivered their dedicatory speeches from the summit of Mount Scopus.

An Eventful Journey

I

WHATEVER the news from Jerusalem, I was determined to cut short my stay in Italy. It would soon be summer, and work at the university was slackening; some of the professors were already on vacation. According to the rules of the Faculty, I could not sit for my exams for another year, so why should I linger on here instead of spending a long holiday with my people in Palestine? While I was deliberating I heard that my parents had moved from Jerusalem to Tel-Aviv and my father had resigned his appointment as Secretary-General of the National Council. I knew they must be facing hard times, and was glad to think that even at my age—getting on for nineteen—I could give them a helping hand.

Out of the four pounds they sent me every month I had succeeded in saving enough for the fare to Jaffa, and just before I was due to start my parents surprised me by sending me a cheque for two pounds towards my travelling expenses. I decided to use this windfall for a detour through Rome and Naples, embarking at Brindisi instead of Trieste. This decision, so simple in appearance, was to change a banal journey into an adventure worthy of a bona fide *halutz*.

I sent a postcard to a friend in Rome, asking him to book a room for me with a private family. I could not afford to stay at a hotel, and I knew that housewives in Rome often let rooms to travelling students at a moderate rent. I packed my belongings in a suitcase, and the second-hand books I had picked up for a few lire in a wooden box, said goodbye to my friends and boarded the train for Rome.

Friends met me at the station and piloted me round the capital —so vast compared with Florence that I began to doubt whether my money would last for even a few days, and my doubts increased when I was shown into a large luxurious flat, furnished with taste. I murmured my fears to my friends, but they assured me the rent had been settled beforehand, and anyway the mistress of the house did not let her rooms for profit, but out of sympathy for Palestinian students. She was really a mother to them, looking after them, and even lending them money unobtrusively in case of need.

At that moment the door of the dining-room opened and a little thin woman appeared—rather old, as she appeared to me then, though I know now that she could not have been more than forty. She wore her hair in two plaits wound round her head, her eyes were kind and her lips were smiling. I introduced myself, adding a polite greeting in Italian, but she replied in Russian, 'How d'you do? My name is Xenia Pamphilova, and I shall be your hostess while you're in Rome. You won't have to depend on your friends, I shall show you the city myself. I love Rome, and it's always a fresh pleasure to show it to strangers. In return, you'll tell me about Palestine. I haven't been there yet, but I've heard a lot about it, and I feel as though I belonged to your country without having seen it.'

While we were talking, the door-bell rang and a girl of my own age came into the room. The likeness between the two women was striking: she too was small and thin, with delicate, regular features, but her hair was cut short in the prevailing fashion.

'This is my daughter Xenia,' said her mother. 'You won't see much of her, I'm afraid, she's always very busy.'

After a few evasive civilities the girl left us, and my hostess took me to my room. As I unpacked, I kept wondering about her. Xenia? I had never heard of a Jewess bearing that name, and even her surname was typically Russian. So why this attachment to Palestine and this motherly care of young Palestinians? With her slender figure, her dignified gait, her calm, smiling speech, she reminded me of Turgenev's heroines, aristocratic and subtle, always ready to sacrifice themselves for their cause.

A friendship grew up between us that was to last for many years. She never told me the story of her life, but from hints she let fall during our walks in Rome, and the touching diary she published later in a working-woman's miscellany in Palestine, I was able to piece together the story of this modern Ruth, who followed her husband beyond the grave, and for love of him attached herself to his people, whom he had never known in his lifetime.

Born of a Russian family in high society, she married, while still a student, a young Jew converted to Christianity. Whether this conversion was a voluntary act on his part or a decision by his parents is not known; but he joined the fighting wing of the Socialist-Revolutionary Party. After one of the terrorist attempts on the government of the Tsar, in which he took part, he was arrested and executed. Tradition has it that it was to him and six of his comrades that the Russian writer Leonid Andreiev devoted his harrowing tale *The Story of Seven Hanged Men*.

Xenia was left a widow very young, with a baby in arms. Her life was in danger, for it was known that she belonged to her husband's group and had taken part in acts of terrorism. Her party comrades helped her to flee the country, and she reached Rome, where she devoted herself to the education of her daughter.

Her misfortune led her to ponder her husband's fate and tragic death. Like Job, she tormented herself with questions: How had he deserved such a punishment, he so noble, brave and just? Her pure faith rebelled against the injustice of God. Delving into her husband's past and finding no blemish, she came to the conclusion that he had been punished for his apostasy. He had forsaken his people in distress and deserted to the other side. Up to then she had known very little about Judaism or the Jews, but as soon as she settled in Rome she sought contact with the Jewish community, and studied Jewish literature and history, more and more convinced that her husband had committed a grave sin—out of ignorance, perhaps, but Heaven's judgement had gone against him. So now it was her duty, although a Christian, to redeem his sin and reintegrate her daughter, his earthly heiress, in the bosom of his people.

A young medical student and talented journalist, Moshé Beilinson—later editor-in-chief of *Davar*, the organ of the Labour Federation in Palestine—introduced her to the Zionist movement, and she began to dream of the day, not too far hence, when she would settle in Palestine with her daughter and lead a completely Jewish life. Her closest friends in Rome were the Serenis, of the Jewish aristocracy. They had three sons, and her daughter Xenia was brought up with them. The eldest became an eminent scientist, and died young. The others, Enzo and Emilio, men of action and born leaders, had learnt Hebrew without difficulty, and the elder one decided to go to Palestine and settle in a *kibbutz*. To her delight, Xenia saw that love was springing up between her daughter and the youngest, Emilio.

The daughter was very young when she married Emilio. They had a baby within the year, but a few months later the husband was arrested by the police and interned in the prison reserved for criminals of State, the Castle of Sant'Angelo on the banks of the Tiber. It was thought at first that he had fallen a victim to some mistake or one of the denunciations only too familiar under the Fascist régime. But the truth came out in a conversation between mother and daughter. Emilio really was an active communist, and, although so young, he held a responsible post at the head of the Party's cell in Rome. Moreover, Xenia the younger shared in his beliefs. She had not dared confess this to her mother for fear of grieving her, but she no longer took any interest in Judaism, and as for Zionism, it left her completely cold. Why should one bother about a handful of people homesick for a distant country? It was only a childish effort compared with Communism, destined to set suffering humanity free. She had devoted herself to the revolutionary cause, and far from blaming her husband had encouraged him. If she had to wait seven years for his liberation she would do so patiently and resume the struggle on his return.

So Xenia was fated to relive her own experience in her daughter's person. Again the husband sacrificing himself in the cause of freedom, with his young wife by his side, and the story beginning in the same way, with the denial of one's origins, and voluntary separation from the destiny of one's people. Xenia's sacrifice to redeem her husband's guilt had proved useless.

Years went by, Emilio was set free and his friends helped him to leave Italy with his family. Xenia the elder decided to go to Palestine. Her devoted friend Moshé Beilinson was dead, but she had found others, who directed her to the Naan *kibbutz* in the plain of Judea. I often went to see her there, in her old age, in her solitary hut. She read and spoke Hebrew fluently, and busied herself with education and culture, always surrounded by friends and looking no different from other pre-war 'veterans' of our villages, in her long white linen dress, belted at the waist, with a scarf over her greying hair. But under this exterior of an ageing pioneer one discerned the features of the Russian aristocrat.

Time had only widened the distance between mother and daughter. They wrote to each other for a while, even during the war, when the young couple had taken refuge in the south of France. Then came a letter breaking off the correspondence. In spite of her great love for her mother, the daughter felt they should face the truth that their ways had diverged irretrievably, and sever all ties for ever.

Xenia narrated all this quite simply in the memoirs she published towards the end of her life, including the text of the tragic correspondence with her daughter. Knowing her as I did, I wondered how she could find the moral strength to reveal her secrets to the readers of the magazine. Perhaps her suffering had become too great a burden, and she could no longer keep it locked up in her heart.

Emilio Sereni reappeared on the scene after the war as one of the leaders of the rising that liberated Milan. He at once became one of the most conspicuous members of the Italian Communist Party and was elected to the Senate. His wife died of a malignant tumour, and old Xenia passed away soon after at Naan, surrounded by the love of her friends—the great new family that had replaced the daughter she had never ceased to mourn.

II

Rome, as I saw it under Xenia's guidance, was very different from the city the tourist gets a glimpse of from the top of a motor bus, or as he races from church to church and on to the catacombs. In the morning I used to wander off alone to the Vatican Museum or the galleries, widening the knowledge of Renaissance art I had acquired in Florence. I lighted upon old churches, roamed from one basilica to another, and wandered at random among the ruins of the Forum, discovering the various strata of the glory that was Rome. But in the afternoon my hostess took me for unforgettable walks. We explored the tortuous alleys of the old quarters, entering the *trattorie* where the men of the people came for a drop of wine and a plate of macaroni, and she translated the conversations I was unable to follow because the Roman dialect is so different from the Tuscan. One day we would come upon a dilapidated church, hidden away in a narrow side street, and on the next, the palace of some noble family, still miraculously intact among crumbling hovels, or a little square with a fountain centuries old, shaded by the spreading branches of an ancient tree.

I often came back to Rome in later years, and was always tempted to seek out the unexpected and unknown, forgotten corners where the pulse of life still beats to the rhythm of a small town. Such places are always to be found behind the busy façade of a great city—and as I went about it I felt as though I were looking for the traces of those bygone walks, that torrid week of a Roman summer with its motionless air, and the asphalt pavements melting in the heat.

It was nearly time for me to start, and though I would have liked to stay longer in Rome, I decided to give myself a short spell in Naples before embarking. I said goodbye to my friends and to Xenia, hoisted my suitcase and my box of books into a crowded railway carriage and was in Naples a few hours later.

I still had enough money to spend that night in a boarding-house near the station and take a trip next day to Pompeii and the Isle of Capri, besides one or two journeys by tram that my friends had listed in my notebook. On the second evening I was tempted to stroll by moonlight as far as the beach of Santa Lucia to listen to Neapolitan songs, mix with the singers, and sample their food, having first gone to the station and found that the last train for Brindisi left at midnight.

Santa Lucia was an enchantment. Lively lads, barefooted, open-shirted, vied with one another in song, girls sold bitter lemonade to operatic arias, fishermen sat mending their nets by moonlight, or playing the guitar and singing traditional songs.

The tunes were still echoing in my ears when I boarded the train about midnight. I was exhausted after a long day's walking, and had eaten nothing except a plate of *pasta*, standing at a counter. I had only a few lire left, but I should be aboard ship tomorrow and in no need of money till I reached Jaffa. I had hardly squeezed in between my fellow passengers on the wooden seat before I fell asleep.

A jolt awoke me. Daylight was glimmering through the window. I asked my neighbours if we were getting near Brindisi. The peasant next to me looked at me in astonishment. 'Brindisi?' he said. 'Are you going that far? We haven't reached Salerno yet.' By now I was wide awake and my heart was beating wildly. How could we be so near Naples still after all these hours of travel? My neighbours soon enlightened me. This was an all-stations train taking twelve hours to crawl from Naples to Brindisi. My boat was due to leave at ten in the morning, so I should arrive too late and have to wait a week for the next one. I had not even enough money left to wire to Jerusalem or to my friends in Florence, let alone for bed and board for a week in a strange town.

Seeing my distress, my neighbours tried to console me by assuring me that Italian liners hardly ever started on time, and there was every chance that I should find mine still in harbour; even if not, I should be sure to find another. But behind my back they shook their heads, full of compassion for the young *straniero* who had met with such rough luck. They were poor peasants, but I could see that if they had had the means they would have clubbed together to help me out of my difficulty. Meanwhile they opened their bags and invited me to share their bread and cheese and garlic sausage. In spite of my uncertain fate, I did honour to their meal. While I tucked into it, listening to their tales, fresh passengers got in as others got out, all of them ready to commiserate with the young lad who had missed his ship after coming all that way—from that *Gerusalemme* where they had crucified Our Lord Jesus Christ.

So the journey went on till the train puffed into Brindisi station.

A cab-driver was dozing on the seat of his cab near the platform, while his horse slowly chewed the oats in its nosebag. Without waiting for the train to come to a stop, I jumped out with my luggage.

'Quick, for the love of Heaven!' I cried. 'Take me to the harbour!'

The driver woke up, removed the nosebag and started off. Turning round to me he said, 'Which is your boat? The one for Egypt? I saw it come in this morning.'

I told my story all over again. He was an old man with a nice face, and I told him in detail how and why I had been delayed, and what would happen to me if the liner had left. Then, taking a plunge, I said, 'Look here, I've got forty lire in my pocket. If you get me to the boat in time they're yours. If not, I can't pay you anything, because what should I live on for a week till the next one comes in?'

The old man smiled. 'Done, young gentleman!' he said. 'That's agreed.'

When we reached the harbour the quay was deserted. A thin column of white smoke was rising from the horizon.

'There goes your boat, son,' said the driver, full of pity, replacing his whip. 'Now there's nothing for it but wait. Don't go to any of those hotels where they'll take all your money for a single night. I'll take you to a cheap place. For five lire a day you'll have a corner to lay your head. And who knows,' he added, by way of encouragement, 'you may even find another boat before the week is out.'

He took me to an old house in an alley away from the centre of the town, and rang the bell. A woman in a worn dressing-jacket opened the door, hair in disorder, eyes dim from an inter-rupted siesta. Sitting in the cab, I heard my driver explaining what had happened to the unfortunate *straniero*. His voice grew louder and I caught echoes of persistent bargaining over the price of the lodging. At last he came back, saying, 'Take your luggage and get out. You won't pay this woman a lira more than we settled on, you and I. She's agreed.'

When I prepared to pay him for his trouble, he refused. 'Business is business,' he said. 'That was the bargain, wasn't it?'

III

I have never been to Brindisi again, so I do not know what the town may look like after forty years. Four years earlier we had been through there on our way to Palestine, but all I remembered of it was the quayside, with piles of sacks and barrels of fruit for sale to passengers. It turned out to be a small place consisting of only a few streets of little two-storied houses, and on that first day I perambulated those streets in the vague hope of finding a friend. I had never heard of a Jewish community in Brindisi, and though I had caught sight of one or two churches, there was no sign of a synagogue. I waited till the afternoon to go to the Lloyd-Triestino office and explain my dilemma to the company's agent. He began by telling me that as I had missed my boat my ticket was no longer valid; then he softened a little, and after running his eye down a time-table, told me there was a cargo-boat due to call at Brindisi in three days' time, which would take ten days to get to Jaffa. He could give me a deck ticket, if I liked, without food or berth. I accepted the offer. I had no idea what I should live on for ten days, but I should at least be getting nearer home.

I begged the agent to send a telegram announcing my delay, but he refused. I thought of my people waiting for me at the harbour and picturing all the accidents that might have befallen me, and in my distress I sent a postcard to my friend in Florence, asking him to wire to my family. Then I returned to my lodging, wondering how I should get through the days before me, pockets and stomach empty.

The lodgings my kind driver had found for me were a mixture of hotel and *maison de passe* for seamen, such as I had read of in Maupassant's stories. Call-girls haunted the passages, dressing-jackets hanging open over their breasts, and the whole house was just a honeycomb of cubicles, the smallest of which had been allotted to me. The landlady immediately began a conversation with me; the young ladies joined us, and assailed me with questions as to my nationality, and what I had been doing up to now. An hour later I heard them informing their friends in the house opposite, from balcony to balcony, in loud voices and with a tinge of pride, that they had a foreign *signorino* under their roof, a real student, the kind that go to universities. After dark the coming and going was continuous until late in the night; the house rang with laughter, singing and mandoline playing, while I shut myself up in my room, trying to sleep and forget my hunger.

Next morning I went down to the grocer's shop to buy half a loaf and a bunch of grapes. At midday a goatherd came along the street with his herd of goats. I picked up a tumbler in my room, raced down the stairs and had it filled with milk 'warm from the goat' for half a lira. This was henceforth my daily diet; but do what I would, my scanty supply of cash trickled away—and there was still no boat on the horizon. I went to the Lloyd office every day, but the clerks there could tell me nothing definite. It was a tramp, with no fixed time-table. It might take longer than usual unloading at one of its ports of call, and that would upset the whole schedule. On the other hand, it might arrive before its time. It was all on the knees of the gods.

Several days had gone by, and I was still roaming round the streets, staring into shop-windows for the umpteenth time, when I suddenly heard a burst of laughter. Turning my head I saw two men who did not look as if they belonged to the place. They were wearing dark, well-tailored suits, hats, and gold watch-chains. They looked altogether Jewish.

Conquering my shyness, I addressed them in Yiddish. 'Are you Jews, perhaps?' I said.

'Of course we're Jews.'

'Do you happen to be going to Palestine?'

'To Palestine, of course! And you, young man, what are you doing here? Are you a *halutz*?'

They had come from Venice on the very boat I was on the look-out for, which was due to leave again that evening. There was a party of *halutsim* on board, travelling on deck. They themselves had cabins, and had only chosen the tramp for the sake of a longer cruise and a few days of rest.

I told them of my adventures, showed them my *laissez-passer*, part of which was in Hebrew—they had never seen a Palestinian document before—and my student's identity card, and begged them to help me out of my difficulty by lending me a hundred lire. One of them hesitated, but his friend laughed aloud and pulled out a hundred-lire note which he shoved into my hand. I took down his name and address so as to be able to repay him in Palestine; then I dashed into my hotel, paid my bill and went to the market to buy bread—enough to live on for ten days on board—picked up my luggage and hurried down to the landing quay, loaded like a pack-horse. I was beside myself with joy. I was going to be among my own people again; every day that went by would bring me nearer home, and the *halutsim* would be sure to share their provisions with me.

As I walked across the gangway I was hailed from the deck above, and a young man shouted, waving his arms, 'Hello, friend! Who are you?'

'A Palestine student,' I shouted back, panting under my load. 'Student? Then perhaps you've got fifty lire to lend us? We've had nothing to eat since Trieste!' I went aboard without answering. So, obviously I should not get any help from my fellow passengers. It was lucky I had laid in all that bread. At least I should not die of hunger.

On reaching the deck I joined the *halutsim*. They were not an organized group, like the many that were leaving Poland at the end of their agricultural training to go straight to their *kibbutz*. Some had lingered on at the farm schools after their friends had left, others had come straight from home with an immigration permit their parents had obtained for them, and a little money for the journey. Our boat was not included in the list of vessels ordinarily made use of by the office in Warsaw for the transport of *halutsim*. This was why there were so few passengers on board, except for those who had not been able to afford the ordinary fare. They had spent a few days in an Immigrants' Hostel in Trieste, waiting for the tramp; their scanty funds had petered out, and they had come aboard provided only with some old blankets, having spent their last lire on buying some bread. Some of them spoke Hebrew, others only knew a few words. Among themselves they chattered until well into the night in a drawling Warsaw Yiddish.

They fitted me at once into their 'commune'. I was given a corner on the deck, and allotted two partners to share my blanket. My bread was added to the general stock, and my wallet was lightened—according to the rules of the 'commune'—of the last remains of my Brindisi loan. As I was the only one among them to speak Italian, I was sent at the head of a delegation to see the cook, who agreed, in return for a small sum, to supply us every morning with a few kettlefuls of sweetened tea.

Under different conditions I should certainly have enjoyed this peaceful cruise among the Greek islands and the ports of Asia Minor. We dropped anchor every day in some harbour of the greatest beauty, and longed to visit the little white-walled places opening to our sight. But we could not afford a launch, and had to remain on board, leaning over the side, devoured by curiosity. Near the coast of Greece itself we ran into a storm. Our little tramp was pitching dangerously, and we started up in a fright to save our few blankets and belongings from the seas. For two whole days we remained in the shelter of the lifeboats, shivering with cold and drenched to the skin, warming our frozen bodies as best we might with the boiling tea the cook sent us by one of the crew. White-faced, dishevelled, seasick, we were still not allowed to go down to the passengers' cabins. The rules were categorical—deck passengers must be kept in their place.

IV

The sky cleared, and the hot Mediterranean sun took over. We were nearing the coasts of Cyprus and the Lebanon, and the summer heat of Jaffa soon set in. I was used to it, but the poor *halutsim*, hardly out of their cold Polish villages, suffered agonies under the pitiless sun.

Our provisions were dwindling rapidly. The hard bread, turned mouldy by the spray, was no longer eatable. Of an evening, when our insides cried hunger, we toyed with the idea of forcing the door of the galley, down in the hold, and stealing something to stay the craving. Then we noticed the sailors going up to the sacks on the deck, slitting them with a knife and filling their baskets with fruit. From now on our greatest need was at least partly solved. We filled our *cache* with the cherries, plums and medlars shipped at the little Greek ports, and reduced the pangs of hunger. There were more medlars than anything else, and for many years after such an overdose I could not bear the taste of them.

Tongues wagged at a great pace. From my new friends' chatter I gathered echoes of the discussions going on in Poland among political parties, agricultural training centres and youth organizations; of recriminations against the Palestine Office in Warsaw, injustice towards the *halutsim*, and the priority given to the middle classes going to Palestine to make money without actual investment, simply by hazardous speculation. I was asked about life in Palestine, and about the Arabs. What did they look like?

About the English and their policy, and the new life in Ein-Harod, and what did people say about the lads of the 'Maavar', near Petah-Tikva? They were curious about the ideological differences between the two brother-enemy socialist parties—'Ahduth-Haavoda' and 'Hapoel-Hatsaïr' and other topical subjects. In short they looked upon me as a Palestinian citizen of the old stock. I had carefully concealed from them that I had only entered the country a few years earlier, and allowed them to believe I was a native of Jerusalem, born and bred in Palestine.

We sailed the Mediterranean for ten days, calling at ports, weighing anchor, heading now north, now south, without even the crew knowing where we should be going next day, and then finally put into Alexandria, where we were joined by a lot of *halutsim* come from Trieste on their way to Jaffa. We old stagers were soon lost among this crowd of boys and girls who had just completed their training in Poland. They spread over the whole of the deck, as we had done when we were masters of the field.

These *halutsim* were disciplined and well organized. Each group knew exactly where it was going—to the farm settlements of Sharon or the labour units laying out roads in Galilee or the Emek, or as reinforcements for the existing new *kibbutsim*. The deck was full of their laughter and singing, and even the Italian sailors, who had ignored our little party, joined in the *hora* and danced Italian dances to attract the attention of the girls in their white dresses, Arab kefias on their heads, bought cheap from the Alexandrian hawkers. A shock-headed boy ran to the middle of the circle and, clapping his hands to the rhythm, began pouring out all our well-known songs, from the Yiddish ones of the first 'Lovers of Zion' to the refrain popular at that time in the farm schools in Europe:

> Ho—Haluts, little haluts,
> Little haluts of Poland. ...

The handful of Palestinians returning from Europe, who had joined us at Alexandria, contributed our own popular songs, while those from Brindisi, who were used to singing in chorus, started up a song to a tune my father used to hum when he was feeling happy, which always set everybody dancing, willy-nilly.

An Eventful Journey

Boys and girls were still singing and dancing wildly when the sun rose and the minarets of Jaffa took shape in the distance.

The joy of the *halutsim*, heartfelt and profound, broke out at the sight. They had been preparing for this moment for months, waiting feverishly at their training centres for their immigration permits or cooling their heels at the Palestine Office in Warsaw. They had come to a decisive turning-point in their lives, the start of a new existence they had dreamed of since their adolescence. They were going, open-eyed, into the unknown, aware that they would be forced to live in damp shanties, facing unemployment and poverty, but seeing, nevertheless, a radiant future taking shape before them. It was as though the thudding of their feet in the *hora* had stifled all doubts and dissipated all fear.

I was standing near the ship's side when I saw a girl, red-haired and very excited, slip out of the circle close by me. Suddenly she began to cry, and then, catching sight of me, smiled through her tears. She looked very young, almost a child—a tenderly affectionate home-child. She blew her nose, wiped her eyes and said, 'Never mind. Don't take any notice. I'm so dreadfully homesick, but I'll be better soon.' I wanted to comfort her, but could not think of anything to say, so I started telling her stories to amuse her, haunted all the while by the thought of her, so young and so lost, in a world without father or mother, where work is hard, and rain seeps into the shanty. But soon her comrades came to fetch her back, and I lost sight of her.

Brawny Arabs rowed us ashore in the harbour, where we were kept in quarantine for forty-eight hours, being scrubbed and steamed, and washed with black soap, and having our clothes decontaminated, just as I remembered this happening in Alexandria on my first journey to Palestine.

At last the harbour gates were opened, and my luggage was hoisted on to a swaying motor bus that took me to Tel-Aviv. Nobody was waiting for me, as the day of my arrival was not known.

I went stumbling through the sand, carrying my luggage, sweating profusely, with my shirt and trousers crumpled by their passage through the disinfection stove, trying to find my way among houses that had not been there ten months earlier, round scaffoldings, gravel heaps, piles of white bricks and lime kilns.

PART FOUR

The Sands of Tel-Aviv

The Falling House

I HAD been unhappy, from the first, about my family's removal to Tel-Aviv. Jerusalem, to me, was the haven of safety where we had cast anchor after so many years of tribulation. I had spent three peaceful years there, and had hoped to build up my life among the friends I had grown up with, and the surroundings that had become so familiar and so dear. The time in Florence had been a period of homesickness for my quiet corner of Jerusalem, the withered trees in Schneller's coppice, my home and my family. I had been borne up by assurances that our family affairs would soon be settled, we should build our own house in Jerusalem and put an end to our perpetual moves. The future had looked even rosier when I was told we had acquired a site at Beth-Hakerem, in the shade of some young trees that had sprouted among the rocks. The plans were ready, the banks were prepared to grant loans and mortgages, and soon the Kurdish stonemasons, with their long black beards, would be camping on the site and squaring stones for our future home.

Autumn had gone by, the calm, untroubled autumn of 1924; the rainy season had set in, but the building plans had vanished from the family letters. Soon afterwards I was informed, first by hints, then openly, that my parents had decided to leave Jerusalem and start all over again in Tel-Aviv. The decision was irreversible. My mother's health was declining. She was breathing with difficulty, spending most of her time in bed, and had been ordered by the doctor to move down to the plain. The air of the hills was too bracing for her, and the steep streets made walking too great a strain. In Tel-Aviv the sun was warmer and everything was on the level.

My father's salary at the Jewish National Council still existed only on paper, and there was no knowing when it would be paid. He had no idea what he would do in Tel-Aviv, but, confident by nature, he counted on his luck to find a livelihood in a Jewish city where he had so many friends. He sold the plot of land in Jerusalem for a song, and went to Tel-Aviv to rent an apartment.

The fourth *Aliya* was in full swing, and house property was increasing. Between the dunes and the deserted vineyards, along streets marked out by boards laid end to end either side of a track of flattened sand, the walls of houses were going up, built for the most part of white bricks from the Sillicat works, whose chimney reared up north of the town. Builders and land-lords advertised apartments at moderate rents, equipped with the latest amenities of European technique: carved doors in wood of every shade, tall, narrow windows, black-enamelled baths mounted on four legs, brass taps from which the water gushed with a roar, and even—unlike our Jerusalem apartments—lavatories with water flushing worked by a chain. It was a matter of *embarras du choix*.

Friends were mobilized, and my parents themselves spent days in the search. They ended by choosing a house built by a well-to-do Jew recently come from Poland or Russia, which was looked upon at the time as one of the architectural wonders of the new Tel-Aviv. It was a three-story building at the top of Nahmani Street, whose tall, narrow windows were set in frames projecting beyond them and widening at the top, which made the house look as though it was leaning forward, about to collapse. On the sabbath the people of Tel-Aviv came to stare at this daring creation, which soon became famous as 'the falling house'. Old inhabitants still call it that today, though it is already decayed, its entrance half blocked by a wall of dingy bricks, its plaster peeling off, its colour faded, its garden invaded by brambles. Its old tenants have moved long ago to more modern quarters, and it now shelters only a few shabby offices and some temporary occupants.

But at that time it seemed to promise a radiant future, with its large, sunny rooms. Mother went for walks among the young trees of the Rothschild Boulevard near by, and late in the afternoon, when the heat was less overpowering, she visited her friends, all living in the neighbourhood. My father still carried on several jobs at once, writing and doing odd office work. His articles were published in the *Haarets*, and his reports for the *Morgen-Journal* of New York were posted off more or less regularly. The country was beginning to prosper owing to the influx of immigrants and of well-to-do Jews coming to invest their funds. My brother and sister, now both attending the Herzlia secondary school, brought their friends home, and the house was full of their liveliness and laughter. To celebrate my brother's *barmitsva* the doors were flung open to all the old friends from Warsaw, Vilna and Jerusalem, besides writers and public figures of Tel-Aviv. Grandmother stayed tirelessly at her post beside the kitchen stove, while Mother, defying the doctor's orders, toiled night and day in preparation for the great event. The only fly in the ointment was my absence in far-away Italy.

II

For the first few days after my return I stayed indoors, venturing but seldom out in the heat. The family listened to my adventures in the wide world, and friends and acquaintances looking in in the evening were surprised to see me grown so much taller. 'Quite a man now.' Even Father listened with a tinge of respect to my praises of Italy, snatches of Italian, and references to literature. By way of exchange he gave me the latest news of the country—the party conflicts and political rivalries. When he came to the immigration his eyes shone and his imagination ran away with him. He saw Tel-Aviv becoming a fine, large town, its factories working at full strength, new quarters springing up like mushrooms, the population increasing to tens of thousands.

The town was unrecognizable. It no longer resembled the quiet garden city where I used to spend my holidays. When I went out I took my bearings by a few familiar points—Herzl and Nahlath-Binyamin streets, the 'gazoz' stall at the corner of the Rothschild Boulevard, the Herzlia School, dazzling white at the end of the street and appearing to set a limit to the expansion of the town. The sand was also unchanged, white to infinity, with narrow, sinuous tracks beginning where the asphalt of the streets came to an end. But elsewhere my astonished eyes met with discovery after discovery: new streets, unfamiliar buildings. How far would the town stretch, and what would it be like in a year's time?

When I recall the Tel-Aviv of those days I taste the salt, gritty sand and breathe the scent of the orange-trees in flower. From the door of our house we plodded through a sea of dunes stretching from Herzl Street to the end of Allenby Street and beyond it towards the land recently levelled on the coast. On hot evenings white shirts were damp, and the odour of humanity, mixed with the scent of the orangeries and the fumes of the lime kilns, formed a thin, odorous haze round everything in the clean, white town, so different from Jaffa, its great neighbour full of dark alleys and huge, decrepit houses.

Old Tel-Avivians, and those of my contemporaries who had known the place from its foundation, talked regretfully of the little township that was no more. Where were the days when the houses stood close together along Herzl Street and in the neighbouring alleys; when everybody knew everybody and nobody locked their door? On Saturdays the young people used to wander down to the beach, or as far as the spreading sycamores beyond the land recently acquired by a new allotment society. Such were the tales told to every newcomer, and everyone who had arrived after the war was regarded as such, with a hint of pity, as if to say, 'Poor devil, he never knew the good old days!' The rigours of war, the forced evacuation of the Turkish era, famine and distress, were all forgotten. Of those far-off days there remained only a secret feeling of superiority mingled with nostalgia.

Since the resumption of building on the morrow of the disturbances in Jaffa, everything had changed. Tel-Aviv had grown out in all directions and could no longer be crossed on foot. One was forced to take the motor buses that jolted over the asphalt from Herzl and Nahlath-Binyamin Streets, as far as the Casino on the seashore, between the sand-heaps barring their way, rounding concrete foundations not yet dried out.

The cottages of the founders of the town stood in a line near the Herzlia school, surrounded by little gardens, among them that of Achad Haam, the great philosopher and thinker, lately come to Tel-Aviv, and already suffering from a serious, incurable disease. When he grew worse the street bearing his name was closed at both ends by chains, to prevent the passage of carts and motor-cars. But at the end of Nahlath-Binyamin Street there were houses of several stories, and even, on a terrace, a Hungarian restaurant, whose highly spiced cuisine was famous throughout the town.

Sand drifted between the houses and could apparently never be got rid of. It was useless to lay down strips of concrete, which the workmen watered with their hoses; there was always sand left at the sides, which with the help of the wind would seep between the slats of the green shutters, and fill up the date round a Star of David that the owner had proudly engraved on the front of the house as if to erect a memorial to himself in his lifetime. Building went on at such a pace that concrete had hardly been laid in one street before a heap of bricks showed the site of yet another one, and anybody looking for an address had to wade among the dunes of the new, nameless quarters which the inhabitants called after the owner of the first house built there, or of the neighbouring plot.

The biggest Jewish tradesmen still had their shops in Bostros Street in Jaffa, but they no longer felt safe there after the tragic events of 1921. So one day the palm-trees that had been planted behind the railway barrier in Herzl Street were cut down, orange groves were uprooted and a new shopping centre was laid out, modern and elegant, where in time the big Jaffa stores would be transferred, and perhaps the first branch of Barclays Bank, that estimable financial institution of the Mandatory Government, would be opened. The mania for building seemed insatiable. Roads were being laid out, and houses erected, on the vine-covered hills. Soon there would be nothing left of the belt of green verdure surrounding the sands of Tel-Aviv.

The city fathers took anxious note of this, and decided that parks and shrubberies must be laid out without delay in the expanding town. The sand was first levelled from the end of the Rothschild Boulevard outwards, beyond the water tower, which till then had been considered the furthest point of the town's future development. This building, which blocked the end of the boulevard, had long housed the offices of the Town Hall, and on the ground floor, of the municipal police, the first Jewish police in the world. Its members were under the authority of the municipality, which paid them their salary, and they enjoyed certain concessions in consequence, such as the right to wear the

blue caps of the British police instead of the *kolpack* of the
Turkish period, part of the uniform of the native police, Jews
and Arabs alike, in all the police stations of the country. After
this, seedling trees and shrubs began to sprout on the boulevard
laid out at right angles to Allenby Street; and in the heart of the
town, in Nahlath-Binyamin Street, a little fenced plot was laid
out as a public garden. The pines planted in it were no taller
than a bed of onions. Young Tel-Avivians met there of an evening, to look lovingly at these tiny plantations and improvise
burlesque descriptions of the wonderful days to come, when their
children would walk arm in arm beneath the shade of this future
park.

One spot only seemed to have been forgotten by time. In the
middle of a wide sandy road, a few minutes from the centre of
the town, stood a group of old sycamores, the last remnants
of an ancient forest. Some of these trees have survived to this
day, solitary and as if overwhelmed by the tall buildings of King
George Street and Habima and Museum Squares, like poor
peasants lost in the turmoil of the city. But at that time they
were scattered in groups in the sandy waste, each casting a wide
circle of shade. On hot summer evenings young people gathered
there, sitting astride the enormous roots or climbing on the
drooping branches. It was the favourite retreat of the solitaries
unwilling to join the crowd by the seashore, of loving couples
seeking quiet, and of parties of adolescents intent on their endless discussions on the meaning of life. The noise of the town was
far away, the scent of the orange-trees close and intoxicating, the
howls of the jackals and the desperate laughter of the hyenas
louder than the roar of the traffic on the asphalted streets of the
encroaching, effervescent city.

III

'Look at this! We're becoming a regular metropolis!' exclaimed
the citizens of the new town, in a tone of pride mingled with a
little regret. A big hotel, the Palatine, had been erected at the
corner of Nahlath-Binyamin Street and Achad Haam Street, and
old members of the second *Aliya* had fond memories of the first
hotel in Jaffa—the Chaim-Boruch Inn, where you slept on the

floor and where the pioneers of Galilee and the labourers in the orange groves of Judea had shivered with malaria. Stories were told of the bed-bugs in the first 'hotel' in Tel-Aviv, of the rent that was never paid, and of Chaim Boruch himself, who, giving it up as a bad job, used to hand his insolvent customers a few piastres to get to their village in Galilee. Artists and young writers ate ices now in a café called Snow of the Lebanon, at the lower end of Allenby Street, entering their debts in the proprietor's register—half an Egyptian piastre for a glass of tea and seven mils for an ice—and engaged in violent discussions, in which the standard of revolt against conventional literature was brandished by the poet Abraham Schlonsky, tossing his black mane over the open collar of his Russian rubashka.

A casino had sprung up beside the sea, on the bare rocks against which the waves broke. It was an ugly building, made of convoluted iron girders and green-painted boards. The architect who designed it imagined no doubt that the future town would be greedy of night life, but his casino had none of the attractions of those overseas, neither luxury, roulette, dancing nor music. A lethargic pianist played there occasionally for the sightseers, tired of wandering aimlessly along the shore. A few peaceable, pot-bellied citizens forgathered there of a Saturday morning to resume a conversation of the evening before and exchange the latest gossip, or play a game of chess, watched attentively by *kibbitzers* who had no hesitation in offering their advice upon occasion.

It was in the summer of 1925, a few months after my return, that the crisis of the fourth *Aliya* supervened. The sudden prosperity produced by the influx faded out as suddenly from one day to another. The ships dropping anchor in the port had no immigrants on board, but when they left again they carried away a cargo of men who had not succeeded in striking root in the country. Families that had settled in Tel-Aviv at the time of the Grabsky rule in Poland had lost their meagre fortune and were going back stripped of everything. Building was virtually at a standstill: not only was nothing new being undertaken, but many half-finished schemes were abandoned for the next ten years or more. However, daily life in Tel-Aviv went on by mere force of inertia.

There were still tents left on the seashore, where the *halutsim* had camped when they were engaged in levelling the dunes, laying out roads and building houses. Gangs of workmen roamed the streets in quest of employment before disappearing in search of fresh openings in the citrus belt or in the *kibbutsim* of the valleys of Jezreel or Sharon. Young men and girls in broad-brimmed hats, khaki shorts and heavy army shoes lived alone or in groups, or two or three to a tent, on the dunes at the edge of the town.

At the first streak of dawn long camel caravans went by, heavily laden with *zifzif*, the fine gravel dug from the banks of the river Yarkon, and American and Polish tourists, overcome with emotion at the sight of the Jewish camel drivers, levelled their cameras at them. Everything was new and stirring to their astonished eyes. An old lady-teacher from Russia flung her arms round the first Jewish policeman she saw regulating the traffic at a cross-roads in Tel-Aviv. Veteran Zionists visiting the land of their fathers for the first time talked enthusiastically to the workmen—who listened somewhat sceptically—standing on scaffoldings under a leaden sky. But in the workers' canteens the soup grew thinner as the unemployed's accounts grew longer, while the all-powerful Secretary of the Workers' Council organized strikes against employers who had reduced wages or kept back the few piastres they owed their workers.

It was rumoured that a wealthy Jew of Iraq, a certain Mograbi, was going to build a real theatre at the bottom of Allenby Street, but this proved to be only an empty scheme like so many others. Theatrical troupes gave their performances in the hall of the Herzlia School or on premises hired at random, and young people spent their free evenings at the Eden cinema, which showed a selection of silent films from overseas. But the mood of the time was such that the greatest success was reaped by the meetings held in the *Beth Ha'am*—the House of the People in the new Ben-Yehuda Street, running out through the sand on the west of the town.

This House of the People underwent many metamorphoses before its total disappearance. But to the young Tel-Avivians of those days it was both a club and a university. It consisted of a large area of sand surrounded by a low palisade, with a little kiosk at the entrance for the sale of tickets. Gate-crashers had no difficulty in digging their way in under the fence or jumping over it. On the raised ground inside stood rows of benches, discoloured and eroded by the winter rains, with a platform for the speaker, monitor, spiritual guide and manager of the institution, Dr Blauvstein-Sela.

I never spoke to him, but I was one of the crowd of young people who spent hours on the wooden seats listening to him. Tall and thin, he contorted his body as he talked till it looked as though his backbone must crack. His Hebrew was rapid, with the strong Russian accent of his generation, plus something unusual about his pronunciation that was personal to himself. From the first moment he had provoked grins and smothered giggles, even at times a shout of laughter or an ironical remark from a member of the audience, but he went on imperturbably with his lecture. After a particularly boring evening we often swore we would never set foot in the place again, but it was not long before we were back there, and in the end, going to the House of the People became an inveterate habit.

Dr Blauvstein was said to have completed his education in Italy, and decided, on coming to Palestine, to devote himself to the spread of culture among the masses. He certainly made good use of his platform. Several times a week he introduced lecturers, writers, militant Zionists and other speakers, but what he adored most of all was taking the floor himself. If a lecturer left him in the lurch, he would take his place without hesitation, organizing verbal 'news columns', staging public trials, and dispensing his knowledge without stint. He talked with the same ease and competence on poetry, the history of art, European history, Jewish history, the progress of science and the great geographical discoveries.

All the political controversies of those years found expression on the platform of the House of the People. It was there that electoral meetings were held for the Representative Assembly, and party disputations, quarrels between workers and employers, and meetings of the unemployed. At that time relations between the Jewish community and the British authorities had eased, and protests against the Mandatory Government, frequent towards the end of Herbert Samuel's rule, seldom occurred. The new

High Commissioner, Lord Plumer, was an old general, an upright, energetic soldier. From the very first he gave the Arab leaders to understand that he, and he alone, was responsible for the safety of the country, and he would not tolerate any disturbances. He kept his word. His administration was a period of calm for the country, and people had greater confidence in him than in any other British High Commissioner since. The Jewish leaders, on the other hand, were absorbed in their internal difficulties: unemployment, decreasing immigration, lack of funds, and strained relations between employers in the cities and planters in the villages and the unemployed workers who saw themselves threatened with famine.

One evening, after his usual scientific lecture, Dr Blauvstein told us that next week he would exhibit to the honourable assembly the latest marvel of modern technical skill—a wireless set—with the help of which it was possible to hear speech and music broadcast from a great distance. Posters on the hoardings announced that on such a day, at such an hour, Engineer D. would give a lecture on the radio, show the audience this marvellous apparatus, and allow them to hear music transmitted either from Europe or Egypt.

On the appointed evening the arena of the House of the People was full to bursting, and groups of children hung on the fence. A shy young man mounted the platform and began explaining the construction of the apparatus in a hardly audible voice. The audience understood not a word of his disquisition, but sat patiently awaiting the miracle that was to take place before their very eyes. Their attention was riveted on a large box from which protruded wires, levers, handles and knobs. When the lecturer had ended his laborious introduction, he went up to this machine, and began pushing things here, pulling wires there, and fiddling with levers. Whistlings and collywobbles suddenly broke the silence of the arena, and as the cacophony continued, the audience began booing and applauding ironically, while the engineer, his forehead bathed in sweat, went on struggling with his instrument. Finally, giving it up as a bad job, he turned to the audience, apologizing for the fiasco and explaining that he had not been able to trap the music on the waves because atmospheric conditions were bad over the Mediterranean.

The evening was windless and warm, and the sea calm, so the explanation was hardly credible. The audience refused to leave, and hung about in the hope that the magician would end by bringing off his trick. But the miracle refused to occur, and the lecturer dismounted his apparatus and took it home.

This was my first encounter with the great invention of the twentieth century. Ten years were to go by before the Mandatory Government decided to set up a broadcasting station in Jerusalem, and the Hebrew tongue made itself heard on the waves.

IV

The liners still brought thousands of Jews to the shores of Palestine. Warsaw was near, the Jewish newspapers from Poland were sold in the streets of Tel-Aviv hardly a week after publication. But our native Russia drifted further and further away. The memory of our relations in Moscow and Kiev became gradually blurred, and we seldom got a letter from the USSR. A curtain of oblivion was falling over the members of our family who had remained there, and when we discovered one that had survived the shipwreck of the war and the revolution, we felt this to be a miracle. Miracles of this kind happened that summer.

To begin with, there was a sign of life from Mother's only brother, who had been mobilized in the Russian army in 1914. It was for the sake of freeing him that Mother had gone to the other side of Russia, where she had contracted the lung disease that was to overshadow the rest of her short life. Ten years had gone by since then, the Germans had marched across Russia, the revolution had turned everything upside-down, and we had lost all trace of him. He must almost certainly have perished somewhere at the front. Grandmother mourned him in secret, wringing her hands, murmuring words of affection; but in her inmost heart she never ceased to hope that one day he would be restored to her, safe and sound. For the good God, in his infinite pity, could surely not refuse this boon to a poor woman who had borne and bred six daughters and this only son. We used to listen patiently as she recalled her memories of the handsome boy, beloved of his comrades in their little town, so clever at business in the great city of Lodz, where he had lived in safety till the Tsar's government had called him up. She used to take a packet of photographs from under her pillow and pull out the one of a young man in Russian military uniform, wearing a sheepskin cap and high boots. Bending her head, she feasted her tear-filled eyes on the beloved face, with her ritual wig tossed back and revealing her scanty white hair.

We had so often deplored his loss that he had acquired almost legendary dimensions by the time when, one fine summer day, I opened the door to the postman who had ploughed through the sand round our house with his heavy postbag. He held out a long envelope bearing an American stamp and an address in a familiar handwriting. I had known my uncle's hand since childhood, and had even tried to imitate it when I was learning Russian. He leant his letters backwards, lengthening and widening them in a fashion peculiar to himself. There could be no doubt: this was the same writing, though in Latin script and the English language. I rushed into the room with a shout of joy, and the envelope was opened with emotion. Uncle Berl had reached America after years of tribulation in Russia and Poland.

As a private soldier in the Tsar's armies, but able to read and write, he had been appointed official scribe of a company posted to Siberia. At the beginning of the revolution he had tried, like most of his comrades, to desert from his unit and rejoin his family in Russia, but his battalion had mutinied against the Bolshevik régime and gone over, with arms and baggage, to General Koltchak's White Army. He had knocked about from battle to battle and ended by falling into the hands of the Red Army. When the Bolsheviks realized that he was not an inveterate enemy of the revolution but an involuntary captive of the White Army they made him an infantryman and sent him into the Ukraine to fight the Poles. His company was soon routed, and he was captured by Pilsudski's army. He succeeded in proving that he had been born in Poland, and that Polish was his mother-tongue. He was immediately consecrated a Polish soldier, but was soon after suspected, God knows why, of being a Bolshevist sympathizer, and interned in a camp near the German frontier. On a moonless night he escaped, crossed into Germany, lived in hiding in one village after another, and wandered from town to town till he reached Hamburg, where he remained for several years, working in the port, trying his hand at various trades, and still ignorant of his family's fate. He was discovered one day, by the merest chance, by a sister who had emigrated to the United States before the war, and she procured him a visa and his fare to America.

I had to wait many years before meeting him on one of my American tours. He came to see me at my hotel in New York; a white-haired old gentleman, his tall frame a little stooping, but still elegantly dressed as in the days of his youth. He had made a long railway journey to see me, from the little town in Vermont in which he had been living since he came to America, and was not to leave till his death. He had built up a small business there, and led a dull existence into which he had retreated as if seeking to forget the vicissitudes of his young years. He died as he had lived, a bachelor, the slave of his habits and his dull, monotonous work. When the State of Israel was founded I invited him to come to stay with us, if only for a short visit, but he declined the invitation. He could not bear to leave his home. A strange end to the adventurous life of a hero *malgré lui*, who had been dragged into the flood of Jewish suffering by war and revolution.

We were still in a state of excitement over the letter from America when another light dawned on the world we had left behind in Russia.

One evening the door-bell rang. I opened the door to a short young man of rather dark complexion, with a small pointed beard, who asked to see my father. Father got up and held out his hand to the stranger, smiling as was his wont, but obviously puzzled by the unfamiliar face. The visitor bowed with true Polish politeness and introduced himself. 'My name is Joseph Barzilai,' he said. 'I've come from Esther.'

It was a dramatic moment. Esther, a sister of my mother's, had grown up in our house and had followed us in our peregrinations in Russia as far as Kiev. She was the young aunt who had remained in Moscow with us when my mother went to the Crimea and my father to Kiev, and had been such a great help to us owing to her relations with the authorities. She was a fervent communist, and her faith in the Revolution had hardly been shaken by the trials and sufferings of the civil war, so she had remained in Soviet Russia when we left for Palestine. Since then we had occasionally had news of her from Moscow, where she had a government post. Then her letters came only at long intervals, and the younger members of the family had only a faint recollection of her.

Tea was served, with biscuits out of Grandmother's tin, and the young man was assailed with questions. When had he seen Esther? How had he met her? And how had a young Palestinian risked a journey to Moscow and returned to Tel-Aviv? Had the Soviet authorities allowed him to leave the country?

He was obviously a Palestinian. He spoke fluent Hebrew and used a rich, precise vocabulary. With his goatee and his reserved manner he looked older than his age, which was really not much greater than mine. His replies to our questions were careful and guarded, even a bit vague, but none of us took much notice of this, because he ended by telling us that he not only knew Esther but had married her in Moscow, and she would soon be joining him. In a few weeks she would be in Tel-Aviv, with a bona fide passport issued by the soviet authorities, visa'd by the British consulate in Moscow.

By that evening the young man had become a member of the family, all the more warmly welcomed because he turned out to be familiar with the ancient texts and well versed in Hebrew. He had even succeeded in learning Russian during the few months he had spent in Moscow, although he was a native of Galicia, with Polish as his mother-tongue. Next day my father went the round of our friends, singing the praises of the newly-found relation. But his enthusiasm soon cooled. 'Barzilai?' they said. 'Don't you know who he is? He's the recognized leader of the communist splinter-group—those opponents of Zionism that are doing their best to destroy what we are accomplishing here!' And sure enough, my father soon discovered that Joseph had been invited to Moscow to be indoctrinated with Bolshevism, and had come back to lead the party in Palestine. Torn between his liking for the young man and the distrust of his subversive activities, he did not know what to think. At that time we were no more than a handful in Palestine, and even a few mischief-makers could put our position in danger. Besides, we had not forgotten the doubtful role played by the Palestine communists at the time of the Arab disturbances of May 1921.

The family's enthusiasm changed to discomfort. The young man went on visiting us, but violent disputes broke out more than once on the subject of the aims and activities of the small sect he belonged to. He was a clever controversialist, full of arguments and supporting proofs, and more than once my father was beaten in their verbal jousting. Sometimes he addressed himself to me, but at that time I was very indifferent to political questions, and the young man deafened me to no purpose with quotations from Marx and Lenin, statistics of the economics of Europe and the Middle East and sombre prophecies of the West's future, to which we had hitched our wagon. He drew up a violent indictment against everything that was being done in Palestine, trying to undermine my naïve faith in our leaders. With no arguments left, I seldom replied, but inwardly I was certain that this fine logical edifice was founded on a tragic error, and that my interlocutor, so full of his subject, and so puffed up with knowledge and learning, was unaware of it, and was sliding down a slope that was carrying him towards the abyss.

Thirty years later I met him in Warsaw, on his way to Israel, and we reminded each other of those early discussions. He was burdened then with the memory of twenty terrible years in the soviet concentration camps, and haunted by the fate of his Jewish brethren in the Soviet Union. In the snows of Siberia he had returned to the faith of his childhood, and set himself to observe the rules of religion with the utmost rigour. He wore a skull-cap, and never missed a prayer. He and his wife Esther, as if they had come back from some other world, assailed me with questions about the friends they had known in Palestine, some of them dead, most of them long forgotten. The Palestine of their youth had remained the only concrete reality to them, as if time had stopped during the years of their exile.

Joseph thought of himself as he had been then, fighting for world revolution in that little remote country of the East. He reminded me of a workers' meeting in Jaffa in the twenties, where he had delivered a speech as a communist delegate, proving that the revolution was on the way, nothing could stop it, it was already knocking at the gates. Suddenly, at the far end of the room, a young worker with broad shoulders and a rough voice thundered out, 'I say, comrade, where did you get that? Did you see that revolution of yours checking your passport at Kantara?'

Communist or not, an aunt is an aunt, and the house was turned upside-down to welcome her. Everybody went to the Immigration Office in Jaffa, and I was sent to the port to meet her. It was one of those broiling summer days when the over-powering heat of a Jerusalem *hamsin* joins forces with the humidity of Jaffa. I spent hours in the customs buildings, among boatmen in baggy trousers and multicoloured belts and Haurani porters clad in rags. The clamour of the Arabs, braying of donkeys, shouts of the boatmen, drowned the siren of the ap-proaching liner. My throat was dry—I had eaten nothing since the morning—and I was tormented with thirst. Suddenly I heard the sound of two little brass platters being clapped to-gether and the cry of the vendor of the Arab drink 'Barad! Barad!' I dashed up to him and swallowed glass after glass of the delicious brew, made of crushed ice and lemonade, and having quenched my thirst, went down to meet the longshore boat that the head boatman was steering between the harbour rocks.

A few days later I was laid up with a high fever, racked with pain, talking deliriously, throwing off my sheets and returning in fancy to the noises of the port, the shouts of the boatmen and my torturing thirst. I saw my mother's face bent over me, and beside her my young aunt wringing her hands as Grandmother did in times of distress, ceaselessly murmuring, 'Darling! What's the matter with you?' The doctor diagnosed severe dysentery, and next day I was transferred to the hospital.

This was a white building of silicate bricks, with thin, fragile partitions, standing on a dune in Nahlath-Binyamin Street. There was no fence between it and the street, so that passers-by could see into the wards where, on beds ranged close together, lay patients injured at work and victims of malaria and dysentery, the two diseases raging in the country at the time. Most of the patients were newly arrived *halutsim*, young ones exhaling the atmosphere of their little native town, others more mature, speaking Yiddish, their mouths adorned with gold teeth, sure sign of a wealthy past. The nurses were very young and inexperienced, in starched caps that gave a graceful touch to their faces.

My illness lasted a long time. The fever kept rising until the crisis set in, when I found myself drenched with sweat, thin as a skeleton and very weak, but filled with a great internal peace, as if returning from far away.

One night I was wakened by strangled sobs. I raised my head from the pillow. All the patients were asleep, and the dim glow of the night lamp left the ward almost in darkness, but I could see a white cap bending over my bed, with fair curls escaping from it.

'What's the matter? Why are you crying?' I whispered to the young nurse on night duty, whom I had seen sometimes attending to the patients in my ward.

'He's dead. Just this minute. He's just died. He'd been in this hospital for three weeks, and tonight, when you were all asleep, they took him away.'

'Did you know him well, then?'

'No,' she said, 'but it's the first time in my life that I've seen anybody die. I can't bear it!'

We talked for a long time that night, in low voices. She ended by calming down and going back to her work, to prepare the thermometers and the glasses of morning tea for the patients, who were beginning to wake up.

She was very young, a new immigrant just arrived from Russia. After that sad confession at dawn she often came to see me.

Sometimes she lingered after she had finished work, to exchange a few words with me near the hospital. After my convalescence the friendship became an institution, and we spent summer evenings together, walking with friends, or sitting in her room in a new street in the north of the town. My family chaffed me, pretending to think I was suffering from an incurable disease, and when she came to see us the children called her 'your dysentery'. This new disease did not last long, however. Our meetings became less frequent, and finally ceased. But my aunt, the ardent communist, was sensitive about family propriety in spite of her revolutionary principles, and still kept questioning me—with assumed innocence—about the girl's family and social background, fearing no doubt that I might be contemplating a misalliance.

A Young Town and its Citizens

WAS IT on a sudden impulse, or because I heard my parents talking of their money difficulties and increasing debts? Be it as it may, that summer I decided to prolong my stay in Tel-Aviv instead of returning to Florence.

We wanted for nothing at home, the apartment was comfortable, food plentiful, and we lived in the same style as our friends. Mother spoilt me as if to make up for our long separation, and Father had long talks with me on an equal footing, proud of the son who had become a real student. He never had the advantage of a systematic education himself, and had regretted it all his life. One of the dreams he indulged in at times was to free himself from family cares, if only for a year, to study languages or take courses at a Swiss university. Middle-aged though he was, with nearly grown-up children, he did not feel that his day was over. His elder brother, ten years older than himself, a learned rabbi and specialist of Jewish Law, had set himself to study at Lausanne during the war, and had even taken his Doctor's degree there. Now a professor at an American university, he was publishing scientific works that were bringing him universal fame. My father, meanwhile, was condemned to the hasty writing of newspaper articles that would be forgotten as soon as read, or to wasting his time on tiresome jobs merely to earn a living.

He often talked to me of all this of an evening, to encourage me to go on studying. But I took his regrets to heart, full of remorse and feeling that I could not go on living at my parents' expense without doing anything to help them.

After leaving Jerusalem my father had been forced to ply many trades. Even in Jerusalem his salary at the National Council had never been paid regularly, but here in Tel-Aviv there were few official institutions and every post was occupied. He had been obliged to accept part-time work, temporary jobs, and writing articles to order. He wrote regularly for the *Haarets*, but the editor himself, his friend Glickson, seldom saw the colour of a cent. The American Zionist Commonwealth society had appointed him a regular correspondent, and commissioned reports on the new towns it was building at Herzlia and Afula. Now and then he drew up a prospectus for an insurance company, and the cheques from the Warsaw *Moment* and the New York *Morgen-Journal* enabled him to reach the end of the month. But we spent a great deal, keeping open house and living well; the children were growing up, and Mother's illness still confined her to the house.

One day, plucking up my courage, I told my father of my resolve to interrupt my studies and remain in Tel-Aviv to help him earn his living. There was an armed rising. 'What! Sacrifice your chances, your future, for a few miserable pounds that really don't matter! We've always been poor and always shall be, and the four pounds a month we sent to Italy won't make all that difference.' Father and Mother pleaded, implored, persisted, trying to dissuade me.

I stuck to my guns. I knew that in their heart of hearts they did not want to part from me again. I insisted that I was no longer a child, that I had the right to share in the family troubles, and that it was shameful to live at their expense. I was not only thinking of them but of myself and my future. If I stayed on at the university, what experience should I acquire? It was time to prove to myself that I could work as well as plough through books. Was not life itself the best of schools? Should I not learn more there than in all the universities of Europe? And after all, why be in a hurry? There was no urgency, and the loss of a year was nothing compared with the feeling of independence that would give me more self-confidence.

My parents' resistance weakened visibly. My sister was jumping for joy at the idea of keeping her big brother now that her little one was not much use to her, with a bicycle and a football awaiting him in the street. Grandmother was wiping her eyes with her apron from sheer happiness. When the question was settled, my father told me a secret. A few days earlier, Meir Dizengoff, the Mayor of Tel-Aviv, had offered him a permanent, well-paid appointment, as editor of the *Bulletin of the Municipal Council*, which published, among other things, the minutes of the Municipal Council's meetings. But he had too much on his plate to undertake this fresh burden, the only one that would ensure him a regular salary. Since I had decided to stay at home, I could help him with the work and be given half the salary. The money would be paid into the bank in my name, and by the end of a year I should have saved the price of my fare and even enough to live on for a few months abroad. Instead of returning to Italy, where there was not much work to be had, I could go to Paris, where Jewish life was in full swing, and where, thanks to his relations with Zionist milieux, I could easily find a job that would allow me to complete my studies.

I fell in with this at once. Paris? Paris be it! I still had a year before me, and meanwhile I should be relieving my father of some of the burden that was weighing so heavy upon him. One day, therefore, we went to the new Town Hall in Bialik Street, and my father introduced me to the Mayor, Meir Dizengoff, as his deputy, who would occasionally draw up the minutes of the Municipal Council meetings in his stead. The Mayor, who had known me as a child, hesitated for a moment to entrust me with so much responsibility, then looked at my father and said, 'All right, we'll give him a trial.'

A week later I was seated at the Council table, armed with a battery of sharpened pencils and a black-bound exercise book, noting down rapidly and precisely the complicated debates between the members of the Council 'of the first Jewish town in the world', as it was called at that time. I filled page after page, trying to report the proceedings in a clear style and a legible hand. At the end of the month I took the manuscript to the type-setter of the *Hapoel-Hatsaïr*, who printed it in clear type in the *Bulletin*, alongside of municipal notices, decisions to increase the water tax by half a piastre, the paving of side-walks, and regulations concerning sea-bathing on the beach opposite the Casino in Allenby Street.

II

It was to Lord Plumer, the High Commissioner, that Tel-Aviv owed the autonomous municipal status that put an end to its dependence on Jaffa. The autonomy was a very relative one, however, and the young town was still dependent on its elder sister in many matters. In the official documents of the Mandatory Government it was still described as a 'township', a less flattering title than 'municipality'. But none of this had any real importance. It was Jerusalem that actually administered all the municipal corporations of the country. Important decisions had to be ratified by the British authorities in Jaffa, the budget was controlled by the High Commissioner in Jerusalem, and important undertakings like the building of a road were referred to the Colonial Office in London for a final decision.

The debates of the Municipal Council were none the less lively. The Council behaved in every way like the parliament of a sovereign Power. I attended the meeting every week to make an accurate record of the debates, and as the numerous members talked volubly, without notes, I often came home after midnight, my fingers stiff from so much writing and my ears deafened by the councillors' shouting invectives and accusations at one another, interrupting the speakers and drowning the sound of the Mayor's hammer. In winter the sessions were held in the Council Chamber, in summer in the open air, on the terrace of the second story. People on their way along the street sometimes stopped to listen intently to the vehement outpourings of their municipal councillors.

It was during that year that relations between the right-wing councillors and the workers' representatives became acrimonious in the extreme.

When the first houses had been constructed in Tel-Aviv, it was clear that the business of the town should be administered by the owners of these houses, who had invested their capital in them. The few tenants of single rooms or apartments were mostly unmarried, or birds of passage who had no interest in the management of public affairs. The change came about after the disturbances of 1921, when thousands of Jewish families had then moved out of the suburbs of Jaffa; the population of Tel-Aviv increased, and a new class of citizens came into being— long-term tenants, living in rooms or rented apartments. Then one day these unpropertied citizens demanded to be represented on the Municipal Council. Their claims met with open hostility on the part of the landlords, who had the monopoly of the vote.

The sittings of the Council were spent henceforth in interminable discussions on the drawing up of electoral lists and on a minimum tax to be paid for the right to vote. The landlords ended by complaining to the High Court of Justice in Jerusalem, alleging an old Ottoman law giving the right to vote only to citizens owning landed property.

Jewish public opinion was stirred to great indignation. Was not this a first attempt on the autonomy of the young town? How had any Jews dared to submit their differences to a foreign court of justice? Disputes became so violent that the Council had to be dissolved and fresh elections ordered.

Meir Dizengoff had been Mayor of the town since its foundation before the war, and nobody imagined that he could be replaced. He was an affable man, tall and in the prime of life. In spite of his merely relative eloquence and his poor Hebrew with its strong Russian accent, Tel-Aviv was not imaginable without him. Every morning, mounted on his white horse, he went the round of the streets, inspecting the houses under construction and the roads being laid out, stopping for a brief chat with the sweepers and workmen levelling the dunes in the new quarters. In the Purim Carnival and the schoolchildren's processions he was always at the head of the troop, on horseback, in riding-boots and cork helmet, and the townsfolk, proud of their Mayor, applauded him as he went by.

His house, on the Rothschild Boulevard, was a rendezvous for writers, artists and old militant Zionists. Even high British officials went there, welcomed by his wife Zina, famous for her beauty in her youth, but with her figure already distorted by disease. These Englishmen were actually the only foreigners to be met with in Tel-Aviv. In Jerusalem, a cosmopolitan city, British officials and Arab notables still mixed with Jewish families, but in Tel-Aviv one met Jews, and Jews alone. The British Governor and his staff lived in Jaffa, in houses surrounded by gardens in the suburbs on the south of the town, while Arabs were only seen in Tel-Aviv on public holidays, attending a 'fantasia' by the Jews or admiring the window displays in the smart shops, in Herzl and Nahlath-Binyamin streets. The population of the town amounted only to a few thousand, but it was already a Jewish kingdom over which Meir Dizengoff reigned.

I had hardly started on my duties when an event occurred that convulsed the whole town. Meir Dizengoff had resigned. The Tel-Avivians were dumbfounded, and even the Workers' Party, which had brought this revolution about, seemed stunned by it. I can still remember that evening, the oratorical duel, the violent criticisms of the Mayor and his administrative methods. This excited tone of discussion was normal in politics at that time, but we saw Dizengoff rise suddenly from his chair, his face flushed with emotion, strike the table with his hammer and leave the Chamber hurriedly, shouting to the Assembly, 'I've had enough of this, I'm resigning!'

There was a momentary silence: the company seemed horror-stricken. Then some members of the Council rushed after him. But he remained inflexible. The first Mayor of the first Jewish town had resigned, and I can think of no other event having upset our little world to the like extent, unless it was Ben-Gurion's resignation from the Government of Israel thirty years later.

At the next session of the Council the Labour Party came into power, and the Right went into opposition. David Bloch-Blumenfeld was elected Mayor. He was an old militant trade-unionist, founder and manager of the Labour Fund. I had often heard him speak at Council meetings, and wondered how he could take Dizengoff's place, for he had neither the noble presence nor the authority of his predecessor. Tall, thin, spectacled, slightly stooping, he had a pleasant, rather shy manner. I never saw him get angry, and he always appeared to hesitate before coming to a decision. He was a man of action, nevertheless, with a clear mind, and the old residents of the town appreciated and respected him; he merely lacked vividness and go.

If the new Mayor lacked the qualities of a leader, his two young assistants possessed them in plenty. Eliezer Kaplan who, twenty years later, was to become Minister of Finance of the State of Israel, was in charge of the technical department. A moderate, prudent, well-balanced man, he did everything he could to introduce modern methods of administration into the out-of-date structure of the municipality. We had reached Palestine together, and during our months of waiting in Vienna he and his wife had made friends with my parents and often came to see us. Nahum Tverski, the official in charge of the town's finances, had preceded us in the country, and I had only come to know him well through attending the Municipal Council meetings. The Mayor was all for conciliation and compromise, but Tverski inaugurated a bold, energetic policy, and soon became the real ruler of the town.

He had a lively imagination and great aspirations, but Tel-Aviv was poor, and taxes were imposed on a population that was having great difficulty in making ends meet. Even the wealthy of those days would hardly belong to the middle classes today, while the masses consisted of new immigrants, barely paid by insolvent builders who had lost everything at the time of the crisis in Poland. It was on this shaky foundation that Tverski tried to build the future of a town that he was not afraid of involving in heavy obligations, so sure was he of its destiny. He was profoundly convinced that its difficulties were merely transient growing-pains.

The greatest service he rendered it was his purchase of the land to the north of the town, the only direction in which it could develop. On the south it was barred by Jaffa, in the east by the Germans settled in the rich, flourishing colony of Saroma, a suburb that became the provisional seat of government after the constitution of the State. But on the north the dunes stretched to the green shores of the river Yarkon, separating the Jewish town from the Arab villages of the coast.

The Right made a violent attack on the administration, accusing it of risking undertakings without heed to the municipality's empty purse. Debts increased, and the Governor of Jaffa threatened to dissolve the Municipal Council if order was not re-established.

Tverski held his ground; but after the elections he left his post and retired from public service. The purchase of the land was a *fait accompli*, however. Soon, black ribbons of asphalt began winding through the northern sands, little white houses sprang up along the new streets, and Tel-Aviv made a fresh leap forward towards its future.

Unlike Jerusalem, where government officials and those of the Zionist Organization formed a natural élite, Tel-Aviv had no governing class. Really well-off families were rare, consisting mostly of a few orange planters and pre-war notables, landowners who had contrived to sell their property during the brief period of prosperity, and merchants who had succeeded in saving a little capital from the Russian débâcle.

With no moneyed aristocracy, 'good society' was mostly composed of intellectuals: community leaders, secondary-school teachers, trade-union leaders whose influence had increased owing to the influx of immigrants, and men of letters; for Tel-Aviv had evolved into an important Hebrew literary centre.

Writers led a hard life there. Many were on the fringe of penury, and could only make ends meet by taking on small jobs in education or administration. But their books were read and admired, their names were known to the reading public, and their reputation made up for the royalties whose payment bordered on the miraculous.

This was my father's natural milieu. After his years in Russia he had made friends with the masters of Hebrew literature, and on settling in Tel-Aviv he immersed himself in the affairs of the Authors' Society, and played a lively part in the launching of a literary weekly to be called *Moznain* ('Balance'). A group of young writers connected with the *Ketuvim* ('Writings')—Shlonsky, Steinman and their friends—had just rebelled against the traditions of Hebrew letters to the point of contesting the authority of Bialik, the great poet, considered supreme. I had little to do with these young recruits to literature, and only came to know them many years later. Our family was more in touch with Bialik and his acolytes from Odessa, who often visited us, spending the evening talking, planning the publication of books, recalling memories and discussing the events of the day. I was often present, sitting silent in a corner, looked upon as a mere adolescent, part of the young generation they were so proud of, but hardly to be taken seriously.

A few days after my return from Florence I was walking in

Allenby Street with my father, when we met Bialik, walking-stick in hand, hat pushed to the back of his head as usual. My father had taken my arm and was leaning slightly on me. Bialik took a look at me and said, 'That your son? This tall young man?'

'My son,' replied my father with obvious paternal pride. 'A student, just back from Italy.'

Bialik held out his hand to me, and addressing my father with a smile, half serious, half amused, said, 'That's fine, Shmuel. Happy the man that has someone to lean upon.'

My father, who knew how it grieved Bialik to have no children, said hurriedly, 'What do you mean, Bialik? You have the whole people of Israel as your support!'

Bialik wiped the lining of his hat and waved his hand. 'The people of Israel?' he said. 'A broken reed!'

School had impregnated us with the biblical spirit; the literature we knew derived from the Scriptures—and from Bialik. The two were thus connected in our minds, surrounded by the same aureole of veneration. In our little circle, in which we all knew one another, down to our mannerisms, habits and weaknesses, no aloofness was possible. Bialik himself was the subject of innumerable jokes and anecdotes. When he mounted the platform of the People's House, or in the sabbath study sessions he had initiated in Tel-Aviv, his young audience smiled sometimes at his rather dusty Hebrew and the length of the tirades his thoughts involved him in, as he leapt from one subject to another as the fancy took him. But with all that he was one of those rare masters whose authority no one dared contest. Meeting him in the street or watching him on the platform—ordinary in appearance, pot-bellied and bald—we still could not forget we were in the presence of the poet who had written *The Fire Scroll* and *The Desert's Last Dead*, the creator of the great poetry we had grown up with from childhood.

Meeting him at home, or in company at his own house, I was always secretly exasperated with him for wasting his time in unprofitable conversation. He seemed to give himself entirely to his interlocutors, preaching, commenting, squandering treasures of thought. He had published nothing for many years, and the mystery of his silence preoccupied lovers of great literature and provoked comments in the press. Listening to him talking—he was an inexhaustible talker—I mourned the works that would never be written. Did he not realize that all this talk would be lost in oblivion, whereas his poetry was eternal?

Many years later, after my father's death, chance gave me the key to the mystery, and I realized that instead of diverting him from literary creation, human contact paved the way to his work. Once I had gone to see him to ask his advice on some matter or other. As usual his front door was wide open. I found him seated in his easy chair, talking to someone who had come like myself to consult him and was sitting bolt upright on his chair, waiting impatiently to state his errand. But Bialik pursued his monologue. Seeing me, he motioned for me to sit down, gave me a smile, and went on with his lecture. He was talking about a king's son, describing his looks, his clothes, his love for the princess. Dropping the prince, he began describing the queen's daughter, sitting in her tower, her lonely life, her sadness. Then, suddenly interrupting his narrative, he said as though puzzled, 'And what shall I do with the snake?' After a moment of silence he went on, 'You see, even in a fairy story you must be logical. The elements must be linked up coherently, not merely as a result of miracles.' He then went on weaving his tale, making the snake creep and the eagle fly; his words flowed, the threads were woven into a multicoloured tapestry, while the young visitor sat on the edge of his chair and I on the edge of mine, till the Master concluded, as if emerging from a dream, 'A lovely legend, I must take it in hand again some day.' Having thus looped the loop, he returned to profane conversation, first with his earlier visitor and then with me, pertinent and lucid, asking question after question, as though nothing interested him so passionately as our miserable selves and our infinitesimal problems.

Years later, when his *Legend of the Three and the Four* appeared, based on a tale from the Talmud, I understood that I had witnessed the process of creation of one of his finest poetical works. And when, after his death, variants of the legend were published, I realized that all these monologues had been the hesitant tunes the composer tries out with one finger, to drag from the depths of his creative spirit the burning force of his symphony.

I have a vivid recollection of a Friday evening spent with a circle of poets and writers at the house of a man of letters who was teaching Hebrew literature at Mikvé-Israel, and lived in the precinct of this famous School of Agriculture, five miles from Tel-Aviv. The trip there was an expedition. We hired one of the old two-horse cabs still to be seen in Jaffa at that time. After zigzagging along sandy tracks through orange groves, we rejoined the Jerusalem road and entered through the old stone gateway, near which, thirty years earlier, the historic meeting between Theodor Herzl and William II of Germany had taken place. We dined in the refectory, together with the pupils, who were notorious all over the country for their mischievous pranks and the Hebrew slang they had invented.

Our host then took us to his apartment and settled us on the big terrace. Everybody began reminiscing, recalling forgotten episodes in the literary life of Europe, ending up with their favourite subject, the Palestinian theme in modern literature. These seasoned writers had never been able to detach themselves from their well-springs, their little towns in Russia, Poland or Bessarabia. Most of them had not even attempted to describe the new life of Palestine. They returned again and again to their small world and the events of their childhood and youth, under the spell of which they still lived. When a young author ventured to publish a tale of Palestine, the older ones' criticism was unanimously ferocious and devastating.

Z. I. Anokhi, who had had his hour of popularity in his youth, had left off writing after his arrival here. Taciturn and modest, he had taken a little job in one of the trade-union institutions, and published nothing except an occasional short report. That evening people were talking ironically of a story that had just appeared in one of the newspapers, describing life in a *kibbutz* in the Emek. It was a sentimental, high-flown bit of writing, the heroes of which sang as they drained their marshes, and talked in a grandiloquent style, the whole smelling strongly of propaganda. Anokhi, who had remained silent in his corner, coughed, cleared his throat and said, 'Why should that surprise you, gentlemen? Why not admit, once for all, that not one of us is capable of describing the scenery or the life of this country? It's as if a painter had been given tubes of dark paint and ordered to produce a picture of dazzling houses in the sunlight. Impossible, what? Well, we've all come from the small Jewish towns of East Europe, the back streets of Warsaw or the *Schulhof* of Vilna. It's among those Jews that we lived and grew up, however much we may have rebelled against their way of life. So where on our palette can we find the colours we need to paint these sands, these white houses, the *hamsin*, the scent of blossoming orange-trees? Or the generation born here, in these fields, among these rocks, breathing the burning air of a Palestinian summer? Are you going to clothe it in the caftan of the Polish *hassidim*?'

He smiled at a young poet in our company, adding: 'Of course, you poets ... love, the moon, sighs. ... You can move from one country to another with your lute and your portable scenery, and go ahead. But relating, describing in prose. ... It will be years before a real novelist is born in this country!'

IV

I enjoyed my work at the Municipal Council; making up the Council's Bulletin recalled the printing-press atmosphere, the noise of the machines and the smell of printing ink, that had attracted me as a child. But soon the job became a routine one, and I found I had a good deal of spare time.

I had always dreamed of going in for journalism, and when the *Haarets* announced that it was about to publish a weekly for children, I asked Glickson, the editor, if I might join the staff. Calling on Mr Ben-Eliezer, the prospective editor, I went to his room at the *Haarets* office, and was received with a critical glance over the top of his spectacles. He asked me if I had any literary experience, and my answer was evasive. He also asked if I had had any teaching training. Discomfited, I told him I had nothing but my matriculation diploma. However, either because the manager of the paper had said a word in my favour, or because my father's name had made some impression, I was asked to supply a weekly report adapted to young readers, at a salary of half a pound a week. As I was leaving, Ben-Eliezer repeated, 'Don't forget, the style must be very simple, but the language must be good, very good.'

I was to write five or six paragraphs, after reading the papers attentively, walking about the town, and making a note of every fresh event. I envied my father, who had only to seat himself at his desk to write his article straight off, without a correction or an erasure, whereas I found myself racking my brain for the right word, striking out and correcting every line—a regular torture. Like a poet taking his first poem to the press, I handed my chronicle to the editor-in-chief, who eyed me with the severity of a short-sighted man. Holding the sheets close to his eyes, he ran over them slowly and finally turned to me, saying, 'Good, quite good. Well written. You can go on.'

After this I devoted myself enthusiastically to the shaping of my chronicle, and delivered the script week by week to the office. My contribution appeared in large type. It was not signed, but I fancied the readers of the 'Haarets for Children' liked my work.

My literary ambition satisfied, I did not bother at first about the money side, though I should have been glad to earn a few pounds by my pen, independently of my father. But the weeks went by and I had not been paid. At last I summoned up my courage and spoke to the editor-in-chief. He assured me that I should be paid in time, and repeated this assurance from week to week—until the day when he told me reluctantly that I need not provide any more copy, because publication was being held up for want of funds. I asked for what was owing to me, and was told to be patient; accounts were not settled yet, and the publishers were deeply in debt. So my first author's fees have remained unpaid to this day.

I was rather at a loose end, therefore, when I met my friend Gdalia Jukhovitzki, returning from his first year at the Sorbonne. He gave me a rapturous account of Paris and its marvels, his fellow students and the university lectures, and his infectious enthusiasm strengthened my decision to continue my studies in the French capital. We were the same age, and had been promoted in the same year, I in Jerusalem and he in Tel-Aviv. Although very young, he had acquired transient fame in Tel-Aviv by his ardent defence of Hebrew. The town had been invaded by a mass of immigrants threatening its special character as the citadel of spoken Hebrew. The newcomers crowded the streets, talking Yiddish as they had done in their little native towns, and Hebrew, a frail plant barely rooted, was in danger of being crushed by the language of the Jewish masses, whose partisans were preparing to carry the war against Hebrew into its sanctuary, in Tel-Aviv.

A language crisis was approaching, when events took a sudden turn for the worse. Posters appeared, inviting people to attend lectures and meetings in Yiddish, an unheard-of thing in Tel-Aviv. The communist party took the lead in the fight for the *Mamé-Loshen*, the mother-tongue, as they called Yiddish, declaring that eliminating it from public life was an attack on the rights of the proletariat. They were reinforced by the Poalé-Zion of the left, vehement defenders of Yiddish as the national language even in Palestine. It was rumoured that a Yiddish theatre was about to open in the town, an audacity that verged on provocation. As the controversy increased in violence, a few young zealots, mostly pupils of the Herzlia secondary school, organized a counter-attack on the 'language of the Diaspora', prepared to resort to force in preventing the use of a foreign language in public demonstrations.

The Poalé-Zion organized a meeting of new immigrants for the Friday evening, at which speeches were to be delivered in Yiddish. When the evening arrived, a number of young men gathered round the hall, distributing leaflets bearing the slogan 'Jew, talk Hebrew!' They started a free fight in which windows were broken, and the audience had to be dispersed. The municipal police were called out and arrested a few young men, chief among them Gdalia Jukhovitzki, the leader of the gang, who was fined a token sum as a disturber of the peace.

The matter did not rest there. Next day a few hundred young men assembled at the end of Allenby Street, opposite the Casino, to make a noisy demonstration against the implantation of foreign languages. Gdalia climbed on the roof of a stationary car and made a speech. Although he had only recently entered the country, he spoke Hebrew fluently, because it was the language he had been brought up in. He had, moreover, some experience in public speaking, having often taken the floor in young Zionist circles in his native town. He knew how to stir his audience by his picturesque language and a certain popular humour which he made use of to perfection.

The audience greeted his speech with enthusiastic applause. A hat was passed round, and enough money was collected to pay Gdalia's fine. The young hero was carried home in triumph, accompanied by a crowd of admirers.

Soon after this the youth of the town organized a 'Brigade for the defence of the language', encouraged by the teachers at the secondary school. They went about the streets in groups, dogging couples they heard talking a foreign language, and remonstrating with them, leaving their leaflet 'Jew, talk Hebrew!' on café tables, and sticking fly-bills on windows and doors. They even attacked the notables of the town: Bialik himself got one of these fly-bills for having talked Russian in the street with one of his friends.

All this had happened some years ago, and the young militants no longer had to put up such a hard fight. But their presence could still be felt all over the town. The streets were still, though to a lesser degree, a Tower of Babel, and according to a popular refrain every language was spoken there, 'even a bit of Hebrew'.

Gdalia persuaded me to join the 'Brigade', which he had left when he went to Europe. I went one evening to their head-quarters in a little house near the Herzlia School, where I found young men and girls bending over maps of the town, or huddled in a corner, telling one another amusing tales of their daily round, while a sound of voices and laughter came up from the courtyard. Seeing no one I knew, I looked about for a member of the committee, and a stocky fellow, seated on a table, asked me what I wanted. I gave him my name and said I wanted to join the Brigade.

'All right,' he said. 'We'll see what we can give you to do. My name's Aaron, and I'm the Head of the Brigade.'

With the important air of someone used to command, he sized me up with a critical eye, asked me a few questions, and sent one of the girls to summon the members of the committee, who were outside in the yard. The door of the adjoining committee room closed, and I was left under the scrutiny of the old guard. I was absorbed in the various notices when the Head of the Brigade came out again, patted me on the back (we were the same age, but I was a new recruit) and said, 'Well, we've gone thoroughly into your request, and decided to appoint you to the committee as Secretary General. You can start work at once. The next committee meeting will be on Thursday. Here is the Agenda.'

I fulfilled my functions until the end of my stay in Tel-Aviv. All the work of organization and correspondence was turned over to me, but I never regretted the sacrifice of those evenings, and made lasting friends of my new comrades. They were a very good lot, devoted to their cause. Most of them had been educated, like myself, at one or other of the schools; but there were also some young workers among them, recently arrived, who had learnt, and learnt to love, Hebrew at their schools abroad. Few of them made any mark in public life later on. The movement had been a marginal one; its task accomplished, it disappeared from a society whose structure was thenceforth always determined by the political parties.

Even when I joined the Brigade the initial phase of enthusiasm was over. There were fewer street demonstrations, fewer still of the acts of violence that had been severely censured by public opinion. But its members were convinced that they were serving a good cause. The danger of the Hebrew tongue being ousted from everyday use was real then, and though the tracts they handed to passers-by were looked upon by many as misplaced childish pranks, they were able none the less to show concrete results. No more public demonstrations could be made in a foreign language, and the idea of a Yiddish theatre was dropped. But the newcomers still spoke their own language, and a lot of Russian and Polish was heard in the streets, to be supplanted by German after 1933.

The Brigade soon realized that people could not be forced to speak Hebrew by street propaganda alone, and set itself to conquer the public by teaching. Volunteers began giving lessons at Brigade headquarters and in school class-rooms. Their pupils included new immigrants, workers, the lower middle class, and townsfolk who had not succeeded in learning the language of the country. Lessons were given every evening, the improvised teachers taking the work in turn on a fixed time-table, with the town divided into centres of operation. Some of the pupils disappeared after a lesson or two, either because they had left Tel-Aviv and returned to Europe, or they had no time, or they were queuing for jobs at the Labour Exchange, but a faithful few persevered, acquiring a vocabulary and learning the grammar, to the satisfaction of their teachers. When the current of immigration set in again many years later, Hebrew was in such a strong position that competition from other languages was no longer to be feared.

The Stricken Tree

I

THAT year in Tel-Aviv was the most peaceful, relaxed period of my youth. I had deliberately given myself a breathing-space, a halt beside my life's road. My work was only temporary and did not bind me to anything; I had a whole year of study in Italy behind me, and my plans for the future were unsettled. I was back in the climate of my home, sharing its daily joys and cares. Mother's illness, which had overshadowed our lives from childhood, seemed to be abating; her strength was returning and her pallor disappearing. The present was more or less free from care and the future was far away.

But I could not help being aware of the malaise that was creeping upon the Jewish community, and I cursed my luck that had kept me in Italy during the prosperity years, and now that I was back at home all the miraculous achievements seemed about to topple like a house of cards.

The country had gone through hard times before. Even in the brief period of prosperity of the third *Aliya* many people had earned their bread with difficulty, institutions and undertakings had paid their employees very irregularly, and tradespeople had failed under a load of debt. Penury was endemic in Palestine; with the old families of Jerusalem it was almost a way of life, and it was not this that was depressing us so much as the threat of ruin after our brief hour of high hopes. A powerful arm had been raised, as if by a miracle, to erect the edifice of our dreams; a little further effort and the work would have been completed, but ill luck had intervened and the arm had remained in the air, motionless and powerless. The young people we had attracted from all over the world, prepared to work, afraid of nothing, were condemned to idleness. A few months earlier the victory had seemed ours, the goal within reach. Now all this was over.

Once again we saw workers queuing at the Labour Exchange for a day's job, unemployment pay doled out to hungry *halutsim*, girls of the latest *Aliya* waiting at street corners for the chance of a job—washing floors, or laundry work for the towns-folk. Soon whole families were crowding the landing quays in Jaffa, under a hail of gibes and insults from the Arab boatmen, as they waited for the ship to carry them away from the country where they had lost all their material possessions, and return them to the Poland from which they had fled.

At home again on the banks of the Vistula, they began sowing hatred and resentment. In Warsaw and Cracow they cursed the barrenness of Palestine; and the local Zionists, absorbed in their little internal quarrels, did nothing to stop them. The Jewish press in Poland, unfailing in its praise of life in Palestine only a few months before, took care not to mention the subject, 'which no longer interested the reader'—as one of the editors of *Moment* wrote to my father, asking him to cease sending in copy.

And as misfortunes never come singly, the disaster of the Polish *Aliya* was soon followed by the bankruptcy of the American Zion Commonwealth, whose correspondent my father was, commissioned to write articles to which he devoted all his talent and enthusiasm.

Going nowadays to Herzlia, which can be reached today in a few minutes by the wide coastal road leading to the handsome residential quarter of villas and seaside hotels, I find it difficult to visualize it as it was when I first saw it: an expanse of dunes with a few huts scattered over it, little plots of sand separated from one another by ropes fastened to stakes. Tanned workmen, stripped to the waist and shining with sweat in the sun, were levelling the dunes.

In those days one went there by the old road full of ruts as far as Petah-Tikva, and thence along tracks through Arab villages and moving sandhills. We interviewed the pioneers in the town, who were dreaming of their future orange plantations—little artisans or simple Jews attracted by the mirage of a city with a wonderful future. Then we seated ourselves on a cliff by the sea-shore, near the ruins of Arsuf, the Crusaders' castle, where the Company's agent, an old Palestinian who had settled in America, spread out some maps before us, and described the luxurious buildings to be erected on the sandhills—hotels, theatres and public buildings—and the bustling life of the future town, which would be bigger and finer than Tel-Aviv, because it was to be laid out on a new urban pattern.

My father's eyes glistened. He made rapid notes in his notebook, alternately looking about him and scribbling. At home that evening he said to me, in his usual emotional way, 'As you can see, son, this has been a day to remember. We have witnessed a Day of Creation. We arrived a bit late in Palestine. Tel-Aviv was there by then, and so were the *kibbutsim* in the Emek. But do you realize what we've seen today? I may not live long enough, but you, at any rate, will be able one day to tell your children that you saw with your own eyes how Herzlia came to birth—the second Jewish town in the world!'

He seated himself there and then at his table and wrote his article, jotting down his impressions while they were fresh. The words gushed from his Zionist heart, overflowing with passion. I can remember the beginning of the article, written in Yiddish, to be sent to Warsaw or New York. 'Here I'm travelling from one town to another. Fifteen years ago my town, Tel-Aviv, had hardly emerged from the sand, and it has a rival already: Herzlia.' And so on, in the same strain, with the same fire, with no suspicion that in a few months' time the company promoted by American Zionists with such vociferous propaganda would go bankrupt, and the flow of money would cease. The plots would remain unsold, the agents would vanish discreetly, and the dream of the future great town would fade out. Work was kept going at first by the force of inertia, but the motor soon slowed down and came to a stop. There was nothing left of Herzlia but isolated houses, skeletons of buildings, tarred huts lost in the dunes, until the day when the wheels started turning again, and Herzlia re-entered the cycle of the country's development, without, however, becoming the 'second Jewish town in the world', as its creators had hoped.

Still worse was the fate of Afula, also a product of the Zion Commonwealth. Old Israelis still exchange tales of those days, of plots sold 'near the Opera', and the good little immigrant bourgeois, just disembarked, going to Afoula in quest of the luxurious residential quarters they had been promised.

This town, which was to have become the urban centre of the Valley of Jezreel, was unlucky from the first. The land had hardly been bought in due form, when the few Arab peasants living in the village at that time refused to evacuate it. Riots and bloody disturbances ensued. Colonel Kish, the head of the political department of the Zionist Organization in Jerusalem, instituted legal proceedings, appealed to the authorities and tried to iron out the difficulties. It was the first post-war territorial conflict, and a presage of the agitation and veiled hostility inseparable henceforth from every purchase of land by the Jews in the thirties.

The Afula project had been launched to the beat of drums. The propaganda campaign covered the whole of America, but as few people there were anxious to buy land in Palestine, the Company's agents swarmed into Poland, Germany and Roumania, selling titles to property, promising houses, public services, shops and places of entertainment, and collecting advance payments. The engine was going strong. Builders' labourers were called in from all over the country, and gangs of *halutsim* engaged in roadmaking were dispatched to the new town. But even before the Polish immigration had begun to slow up, many Jews had lost their capital. Financial sources dried up, and the whole machinery came to a stop. Afula was now no more than a living grave, a witness to a brief prosperity, a township with unfinished streets, half-built houses, a modern ruin at the heart of the Emek.

I was coming back from Galilee one day in the little Emek train that forged its way slowly among the green fields and shanties of the young villages at the foot of Mount Gilboa. The ancient locomotive emitted a final death-rattle, and stopped at Afula station to take in water and couple and uncouple wagons at this important junction on the Damascus line. Leaning out of the window, I beheld a sight that haunted me for many years: young lads with unkempt hair, in patched shirts, khaki shorts and torn sandals, lying or sitting on the bare platform, or on mats and blankets, with fevered eyes and haggard, ill-shaven faces. When the train stopped, with grinding brakes, these workless labourers approached the compartments with outstretched hands, begging for bread or cigarettes.

I had known famine in Russia during the war and the Revolution. That was a collective misfortune, a plague from heaven which none escaped. Could I have imagined that this could happen here, in Palestine, among these *halutsim* who had left home only yesterday full of hope, driven by their youthful enthusiasm to create a new society in this country? Here they were in the heart of the Emek, the Valley of Jezreel of which the Jewish youth of the Diaspora had dreamed, perishing in this miserable station, condemned to starvation. I could not bear the sight. I was tortured by the thought of the safe, pleasant life that was mine, even now in these terrible days, in the shelter of my home, ignorant of privations and humiliations.

That year I re-read the works of Brenner, the harrowing, pessimistic writer who had left his mark on the thought of our pre-war generation, and I suddenly understood the whole immensity of his cry of pain. Up to then I had disliked his confused, impassioned narratives; his clamorous anguish, his icy despair repelled me. My Land of Israel was sunlight, love and perfection. Brenner, to my mind, was distorting and uglifying the face of my country to a reflection of his own weak, distorted soul. The sight of Afula station had suddenly opened my eyes.

II

Like a tree felled by the woodman's axe, Tel-Aviv groaned under the economic disaster. With wounded trunk, severed branches, withered leaves, the town lay there, suffering and helpless, while at a distance young shoots were springing up, preparing in their turn to thrust their roots deep into the soil.

The further one went from Tel Aviv, whose growth had been arrested, the more one met with scattered signs of life and presages of renewal. By its very nature, the big Jewish town had formed a nerve-centre more sensitive and vulnerable than any other.

Jerusalem, hardly touched by the main immigration, had been affected neither by its benefits nor its set-backs. The streets of my youth had gained a few new houses here and there. The trees planted at Beth-Hakerem had grown taller, the rocks were covered with verdure, and rows of young cypresses shaded the narrow streets. Near Beth-Hakerem, on the road leading to the town, Yemenite and Kurdish stonemasons, seated on the ground, were squaring blocks of stone for a new suburb to be built with money from the Montefiore Foundation, as the latest of the chain of suburbs bearing the name of the old British philanthropist Sir Moses Montefiore, the first builder of new Jerusalem. The economic crisis was barely noticeable in Jerusalem, and would not have altered the situation anyhow. Officials and teachers had grown used to going without their salaries, and strikes were organized only for form's sake.

The town was still without electricity. The Mandatory Government was engaged in endless lawsuits at the International Court of The Hague against a certain Mavromatis, a Greek who had earlier acquired a concession from the Turks, giving him the exclusive right to provide Jerusalem with electric light. Now as yesterday, parties of young people met together of an evening under the incandescent lamp at Zikhron-Moshé, while boys and girls ran out in the moonlight into the great stony stretches separating the different quarters of the town.

Every time I went to Jerusalem I came back to Tel-Aviv in a more acquiescent frame of mind, realizing the abyss dividing the two worlds: that of my youth, stagnant in its immobility, and that of Tel-Aviv, impetuous and changeful, whose fall was all the giddier for the boldness of its initial rise.

Even during those months of depression some seeds germinated and grew. Here and there new fires were lighted in the plain of Sharon. In spite of disappointments and penury, the agricultural and social experiment was still going on in the Emek, and the young villages were emerging from their isolation. In the initial phase many *halutsim* had allowed themselves to be discouraged; but most of them had stayed on, to join the young settlements in the Emek. And in their training centres in Poland erstwhile candidates for the *Aliya* were slowly recovering from the shock of the crisis, and the ships dropping anchor at Jaffa brought little parties of them, to be admitted parsimoniously by the Mandatory authorities.

Invited one day by Shmuel Jukhovitski—father of my friend Gdalia and a friend of my father's from the Warsaw days—we paid him a visit in the new village of Magdiel, which had just been built by some Polish Jews in the north of Sharon. Our host met us at the door of his shanty and took us round his property. With visible pride he showed us the fruit and eucalyptus trees planted in his yard, the levelled sands all round, and the extensive orangeries of the village. His neighbours joined us. They had come like him from Poland, little tradespeople from towns and villages on the banks of the Vistula. Instead of investing their capital in building schemes in Tel-Aviv, in the hope of making a speculative profit from them, they had bought their allotments co-operatively in the sands of Sharon without any hope of gain, and had been rewarded, since they had not lost their fortunes in the crash of land speculation. Our friend Shmuel took us along the paths in his orangery, where in three or four years' time the trees would begin to bear fruit. He told us an asphalt-surfaced road would connect Magdiel to Petah-Tikva, and thence to Tel-Aviv, so that the people of Magdiel would no longer have to go by bad, winding roads to buy their groceries or take their cases of oranges to the packing shed.

We sipped boiling tea, listening to their plans and dreams for the future. These new-type settlers assured us that when their plantations began to bear fruit they would not do like the Petah-Tikva planters and take on Arab labour. Here in Sharon Jewish labourers would do everything, trenching, watering, pruning and gathering. And this not merely because of their Zionist principles (had they come to Palestine to let Arabs and Beduins do their work?) but in their own interest, because the presence of Jewish workers would strengthen the new villages, and some day they would settle in their turn and help to fill these desolate sands with a chain of Jewish villages.

We got into the habit of visiting these remote places on the coastal plain, feeling heartened by the new spirit these modest middle class people from Poland had breathed into the country by their faith, as worthy followers of the pioneers of the Emek.

Everybody knew the Emek, but few of us had friends there, although from time to time some young writer from Ein-Harod or Beth-Alpha would bring my father a manuscript—narrative, poems or article—in quest of advice or a recommendation to a publisher. Now, however, we made contact with the young co-operative settlement at Nahalal, in the Valley of Jezreel, our link being Nadia, whom we had met by chance at the house of some mutual friends. Ever afterwards she looked in on us on her way through Tel-Aviv, and our friendship with her and her husband,

Tsvi Yehuda, endured till their last days in their house at Nahalal, hidden among the blossoming orange-trees.

Nadia, to us, was a being from another world. She was a native of Chicago, which was unusual to begin with. There were few immigrants from America at that time, and we had met no other example of a young woman deserting a comfortable transatlantic bourgeois home to settle with her husband in a *moshav* of the Emek.

She was then in the prime of life, tall, attractive, well-educated. She had led an ordinary middle-class life, her first husband being a prosperous businessman, and they had a son and daughter of about my age. Then Tsvi Yehuda had turned up one day in Chicago, on some Palestinian mission. He was a pioneer of the co-operative idea and one of the founders of Nahalal, the incarnation in the extreme of all the characteristics of the men of the second *Aliya*: the fanaticism of the idealist, the practical sense of the peasant, the spirit of renunciation and contempt for material wealth of the pioneer, and at the same time the sharp, shrewd intelligence of a man inured to party struggles. He was perhaps less of a peasant than he sought to appear, for he was always anxious to stress his rustic simplicity, concealing his deep and genuine Jewish culture. In his youth he had always taken care not to betray his knowledge of Judaism, devoting himself entirely to his village and its crops. Gifted with a pungent humour, he concealed his acquirements under the manner of a rough farmer who was not to be 'had'.

Nadia, who was a distant cousin of his, met him in Chicago and fell in love with him on the spot. She had felt the emptiness of her existence at their first meeting, and longed to find some way of escape from the bourgeois comfort surrounding her. She was sick of senseless ideological discussions, and wanted to accomplish her Zionist ideal for herself. She obtained a divorce, therefore, married Tsvi Yehuda, and had never left her Emek farm since she first set foot on the soil of Nahalal. She did all she could to shed her past, to forget her life in America and become a thoroughgoing farmer's wife. She had never done any manual work in her youth, but here she devoted herself night and day to her strenuous task, never losing her smile or her good humour.

Her children had followed her—the son was a talented painter, who later became my fellow student in Paris before returning to Chicago. The daughter remained and made her home in Haifa.

We often went to see Nadia and Tsvi Yehuda at Nahalal. The village was still in its early stage; the winter wind blew through the cracks in the huts, and in the rainy season the whole village was drowned in the sticky mud of the Emek. Nobody dared go out except in boots, for shoes sank into the black earth and disappeared in the mud. At night the village was plunged in darkness, surrounded by marshes where malaria mosquitoes swarmed, and always on the qui vive against attacks from the neighbouring Arab villages.

The way Nadia contrived to preserve her charm and her femininity always astonished me. She remained a woman of breeding through the roughest tasks of her rustic life. Early in the morning, when I awoke in one of the two rooms of the hut, I could see her busying herself in the kitchen and the yard, in her broad-brimmed hat, close-fitting riding breeches and black boots reaching to her knees. Always neat and tidy, she lived in her clean, whitewashed wooden hut, furnished with American comfort and their joint treasure of books. A gramophone with a fine collection of records was her solace through the long winter evenings.

When she went to the town she became another person. An American lady of high society, in tasteful clothes, with well-dressed hair and a fresh young face. Nobody would have taken her for a farmer's wife in a co-operative Emek village. As soon as she entered our house it was enlivened by her *joie de vivre* and her happy assurance. She could always cheer my parents by a word or a gesture in their hours of doubt and depression.

III

We became gradually used to living with the slump. The pessimists—and there were plenty of them—bewailed themselves, pointing to external dangers and signs of approaching catastrophe. What were we heading for? And what was to become of all our efforts? But those whose faith and confidence never deserted them—my father was always among them—were beginning to discern the first signs of recovery. The optimists soon proved right. The ships were still carrying away the last stragglers of the stampede, but the training centres abroad showed symptoms of revival, and the Trieste–Jaffa Line began bringing *halutsim* in their tens. Labour gangs were being organized here and there, and public works were again furnishing employment for the out-of-works. Agricultural labourers were being taken on in the Sharon orange plantations; *kibbutsim* and co-operative villages were growing up slowly but surely in the almost penniless Emek. Rents were going down in Tel-Aviv; the price of land, which had reached an astronomic level, decreased, and the Tel-Avivians could once more afford to buy an apartment. Now and again a contractor was able to complete a building whose bare framework had been an eyesore for months in the centre of the town, and little houses made their appearance on sites abandoned by their owners. The days of great hopes were over, and few of us still believed in a renewal of the flood of immigrants, but we had the feeling that the worst was behind us, and that at any time now we might expect better days.

It was now that a new force infiltrated into public life, in the foremost rank of the battle against depression and defeatism. The Labour Movement had never so far held the reins of authority; neither in the Zionist Congresses nor in the Representative Assembly had it been in the majority. The half-empty coffers of the Zionist Organization were in the hands of experts, or so-called ones, who considered they were fulfilling their functions in the best possible way by reducing expenses and lowering the estimates for education and agriculture. Arthur Ruppin, a man of lofty views, could not accept this narrow, niggardly conception, and ended by resigning from the Zionist Executive as a mark of protest against the liquidation of the Agricultural Settlements venture, of which he had been the chief promoter, and Sprinzak, a Labour leader, intelligent and courageous, fought a lonely battle against defeatism within the Executive. The Labour Movement itself was torn between two political parties, the Ahduth-Haavoda and the Hapoel-Hatsaïr, which had not yet amalgamated. But the *Histadrut*, the great Trade Union organization which they had created between them, was growing in importance and joining in the battle against defeatism. It put up an uncompromising resistance to the degrading system of unemployment doles, and demanded a resumption of public works. Both Labour parties were vowed to opposition towards any hampering of development, and to any attempt to limit immigration.

A new daily paper was launched in Tel-Aviv, founded and inspired by the *Histadrut* (Trade Union organization). It was called *Davar* ('The Word'), in allusion to one of Bialik's prophetic poems, condemning every kind of weakness and inaction. We had long discussions at home about this new venture. What was the use of a new paper when the *Haarets* was struggling with endless financial difficulties? Could the *Haarets* not defend the interests of the working classes just as well? Moshé Glickson, its editor, was both liberal and tolerant. He would gladly have opened his columns to articles by the leaders of the *Histadrut*. But the partisans of the new journal denounced its weakness and hesitations. Could one rely on a paper that avoided taking sides, trying at all costs to pacify, and shunning discussion, restricting itself to a wary, ill-defined posture? One of our friends, who had a gift for summing up a complex situation, defined the tone of the *Haarets*, and the tedious pedantry that characterized it, in this way, 'When you go into the *Haarets* printing office, all you see is tall figures in white overalls going from case to case looking for a dot to put on an "i".'

Our little community, barely amalgamated, not yet licked into shape, needed a new language, a guiding line. When the first numbers of the new paper appeared, they emitted a breath of freshness and strength. Open, merciless criticism of the government's policies, an urgent call to action and the continuance of the great work, and most of all, uncompromising faith in the future of the movement and the nation.

In its first phase, it gave the young people of the day the Labour party that had come into power, this daily fulfilled an educational mission. It gave the young people of the day the tonic assurance they were seeking. Beyond the impasse that was hemming them in, they could clearly discern a haven of safety they had the strength to attain, however distant it might be. The doctrine of the Labour Movement was no longer confined to a little sect of theorists. It was reaching the great masses.

The *Histadrut* turned its attention to the pioneers, organized the young labourers, and launched into the domain of culture.

One day I caught sight of a poster announcing the first performance by the *Ohel* ('tent') company, the theatre of the Palestine workers. This new theatre had been causing conversation for weeks. Everybody had been talking about this attempt by Moshé Halevy, the first of the Habima artists of Moscow to reach Palestine, to create a theatrical company composed of members of the *kibbutsim* and any workers engaged in building and on public works, with a turn for acting. A troupe of that kind could obviously not live by its dramatic activities—any more than any other of that day—and the actors would go on working, each at his own job, carting hods of bricks, or trundling their wheelbarrows, by day, and meeting in the evening for rehearsals.

The first performance took place in the Herzlia Secondary School. The scenery was not very sumptuous, but contrived to produce a fairy-tale atmosphere, and the young actors—all amateurs—seemed inspired by the tales of J. L. Peretz, the great Jewish author, they were interpreting. After the final curtain I roamed the streets of Tel-Aviv in a moonlight that seemed to have come from the play by the master of Jewish hassidic storytellers. I was still under the spell, as I had been, eight years before, after the première of the Habima in that little back street in Moscow, half ruined by the Revolution. The Habima had spoken to me then in my own language, the Hebrew in which I had been bred, a young boy in the wide wastes of Russia. Now I had seen the creation of a new theatre, in a Jewish town, a workmen's theatre unlike any other, in quest of new forms of expression. And all that was mine, a part of a new living body, the new society we were called upon to create, my people and I.

IV

The oppressive heat of the autumn *hamsin* heralded the approach of the rains. The French Consulate in Jaffa, where I had left my dossier with my request for admission to the Sorbonne, informed me that I must be in Paris by October at the latest, or I should forfeit a year of study. I set about getting a travel document, and the feeling of transience that had haunted me all through that year became more insistent. This time it was my mother who urged me to waste no time; she seemed less unhappy than when

I had set out for Italy. Of course I had ripened since then, while she had grown used to our separation. But now and then, when I looked at her unawares, I saw her eyes cloud with sadness, and I knew she feared this separation might be our last. She had recovered somewhat from her disease during this year in Tel-Aviv, but she had never had any illusion as to her condition. Even on her good days she knew her sickness to be incurable and that her days were numbered. France was far away—seven days by sea—and it was clear that I could no longer come home for the holidays. Should I be able to arrive in time if she grew suddenly worse? It was one of the thoughts one tries to repel, but which never cease to gnaw. She had suddenly grown older, her face was full of wrinkles, her hair had whitened, and she looked much more than her forty-five years.

I went to Jerusalem to get my letters of naturalization, having just become a Palestinian by virtue of a recently promulgated law. After filling in forms at the Government Immigration Department in the Street of the Prophets, I was taken to the office of a Jewish official, who asked me a few questions and made me swear an oath of fidelity—with my hand on the Bible—to the Government of Palestine, which I did with a willing heart. I was very proud of my *laissez-passer*, which specified in black and white that I was a Palestinian citizen, and had a right to the protection of the consular agents of His Majesty's Government. There were no Palestinian passports at that time, for the wheels of the London bureaucracy turned slowly, and my first one was given me years later, by an official of the British Consulate in Paris.

This document, which I had obtained with so much trouble, came near to delaying my departure. It disappeared utterly and entirely from the day when I had an entry visa stamped on it at the French Consulate in Jaffa. I looked for it everywhere, turning out every drawer, and searching all my clothes, every lining, every pocket. I had told nobody about it at home, hoping that one day, by some miracle, it would be found in a corner I had forgotten to rummage in.

Days and weeks went by—and no *laissez-passer*. I decided to confess to my parents, prepared to begin the weary business all over again for the production of a fresh identity paper. But that very day, when my father came home to lunch, he called me, and laid the document on the table without a word. I then confessed to my misadventure, and he told me how the paper had reached him. An Arab street porter, who had found it in an alley in Jaffa, had kept it in his pocket for some days, and then, not knowing what to do with it, handed it to the head porter of the harbour, who, unable to read or write, decided that the Jews would know more about it than he, and took the document to the manager of the Zionist Immigration Office, who knew my father well and realized that it probably concerned somebody in his family.

Italy no longer had any attraction for Palestinian students. Those who had begun their studies in Florence, Rome or Bologna went on with them there, but young students of Tel-Aviv and Jerusalem were all going to Paris, where the cost of living had decreased as a result of the devaluation, and one could live in comfort on a few pounds a month. I considered myself rich, having some fifty pounds left after paying my fare—enough to live quietly in Paris for six months. I felt sure, too, that when my funds were exhausted I should manage to earn my living, either by giving Hebrew lessons or doing translations, or some clerical work, without having to apply to my parents.

A dozen graduates of the Tel-Aviv Secondary School were leaving for Paris together. At the request of a family friend I willingly agreed to act as mentor to his son, younger than myself, but speaking French fluently. My own knowledge of the language at that time was limited to a few shreds of sentences, the last remains of lessons given me at school in Jerusalem, along with a few scraps of Latin, fruit of Dr Calvari's teaching, and the Italian I had learnt in Florence. I suspected that all these bits and pieces stuck together would not get me very far in Paris, and I relied on this young man to guide my first steps there.

On the day of departure we went to the port of Jaffa, laden with overcoats and luggage, with our parents discreetly wiping away a tear.

The head porter's little boat took us alongside the liner *Canada* of the Messageries Maritimes, and when she weighed anchor handkerchiefs went on waving from the quay long after we had passed the rocks outside the harbour.

PART FIVE

Epilogue in Paris

A Metropolis and the Wide World

IT WAS in Paris that I grew from youth to manhood, and I can think of no city in the world reflecting with greater intensity the spiritual torments of the post-war generation. Palestinian students landing up in some other university city of Europe or America might have been less affected, but if they had imagined they could carry on with their pre-war existence, still bound by a thousand ties to their home, the climate of Paris would soon have destroyed their illusions. The hot-house atmosphere in which we had lived was dissipated by the high wind from the open sea. Those years in Paris added a new dimension to our outlook; the fate of the whole world was to overshadow us henceforth. We should never be able to return to the idyllic isolation in which we had imagined we could order our future.

Paris was still convulsed in its inmost being by the massacres of the Great War: ruined towns, villages wiped out, a whole generation sacrificed at Verdun. Ever since the Armistice it had attracted those on either side of the Atlantic who were seeking new means of expression. Even we who saw ourselves as builders of a future State, a better world on the ruins of the past, were obliged to admit that we had been outstripped by events beside which our existence appeared calm and somnolent. A cataclysm was rumbling behind the façade of the busy city.

In later days the Americans referred to this period as 'the gay twenties'—and Paris was certainly noisy and excited, even 'gay' if you like. Night-clubs poured out the strident din of jazz bands, howling saxophones, banging drums, and the cacophony of negro orchestras. Men had taken to wearing wide trousers and short jackets inclining to mauve, with yellow shoes and broad-brimmed hats; and girls with Eton crops, and skirts hardly reaching to the knee, inhaling smoke through long cigarette-holders, paraded at night in an orgy of lights in cafés and night-clubs. People danced fox-trots and charlestons to exhaustion all night through. But, this noisy and stormy night life merely covered the deep and enduring malaise that lay behind it.

This was the time of a world-shattering intellectual upheaval. Painters, deserting the quiet colours and calm landscapes of their Masters, were distorting form in a desperate attempt to express the ineffable. Writers were rebelling against the sanctified rules of language and style, and poets had elected to be singers of the inexpressible. All was burgeoning profusion, schools of art arising and disappearing in defiance of the rules and the lawgivers.

Montparnasse was still under the spell of Amedeo Modigliani, whose friends recalled the bitter end of the young genius who went from table to table drawing portraits for the price of a glass of Pernod or a *croissant* to appease his hunger. Innovating painters—Picasso, Menkès, Chagall—spent the night over their drinks, discussing the new modes of expression that were to crystallize in the Paris School. They were already enjoying a certain fame; and there was no knowing but the hirsute painters one rubbed shoulders with in the cafés might themselves be destined to blaze a new trail in art. It was only a few years since the publication of *A la recherche du temps perdu* but the young generation was reading Proust. Gide's star was rising, while authors famous only yesterday were falling into oblivion. The poets were sounding fresh chords on the lyre that Apollinaire had let fall. Jean Giraudoux was laying down the law in the theatre, where production was being transformed by the bold innovations of Dullin, Copeau and Pitoeff.

This revolution had been born of doubt. 'We civilizations are henceforth aware that we are mortal,' said a great poet of the day. The pre-war world had believed everything to be known and settled. The post-war world believed in nothing. The rooms of the Louvre and the Luxembourg were crammed with sanctified works of art, witness to France's great past; the tragedies of Corneille and Racine were still being performed at the Comédie Française, and the great tradition of the French theatre still reigned supreme. We still wept over the dusty dramas of Dumas fils and the melodramas of the nineteenth century at the Odéon, but we all knew that this was no longer the language of the present.

Was the hecatomb that came to an end on November 11, 1918 to be renewed? Was the Great War really the last, as some enthusiastic journalists had declared when the fighting ceased? Nobody would have dared such a prediction now. Revolution was still raging in Russia, piling up ruins, though with a suggestion of a better tomorrow. Italy was aflame with a clamorous nationalist doctrine. Germany had not yet finished licking the wounds inflicted by war and defeat, and nobody knew what was being hatched under cover of her weak democratic régime. The disunited working class—some looking to Moscow, others faithful still to the tradition of French socialism—was becoming restless, and striving for power. Even in Conservative Britain the reins of government had passed into the hands of the Labourites, a surprising phenomenon, pregnant with consequences.

Parties were fighting each other, governments succeeding one another. The League of Nations was trying to impose its authority from Geneva, but true security, everyday peace, seemed very far off, and the man in the street was worried. He saw the franc falling, and nobody knew what tomorrow would bring: Bolshevism *à la russe*, or Fascism after the Italian pattern. Or would the two of them fight each other again on the battlefields of France? Would the Ville-Lumière stand up to the fresh assault?

It was not easy at first to fathom the minds and the fears of that time. We were merely a few provincial students living in the capital, secluded in our hotels, absorbed in our studies, on the look-out for the money order from home. We picked up a few crumbs of the great civilization spread out before us, all novelty and wonder, but we were far removed from it. Still, the months went by, winter was over and spring returning. Then came the second and third years of study. We took to a hurried reading of the paper in the tram or the Métro. We had begun to mingle with familiar figures on the café terraces of Montmartre and in the lecture-rooms of the university. We were buying new books at the local bookshop, listening to the play everybody was talking about—and thus, insensibly, becoming associated with the heart-beats of the period.

The newspapers reported the conferences of the Great Powers, discussions on war reparations and the occupation of the Rhine. Somewhere in Morocco Marshal Lyautey's troops were fighting the Berber rebels led by the fierce Abd-el-Krim. In Syria, close to the northern frontier of Palestine, the Druses had risen against the French, and General Sarrail's guns were bombarding Damascus. All these things seemed far away. More imminent was the feeling that something was afoot behind the apparently normal life we were leading in our Paris hotels and cafés.

II

When we first arrived in France, the *joie de vivre* of the twenties was already on the wane. Signs of the approaching depression could be detected, although the New York stock market was on the rise, and the slump of 1929 was not yet foreseeable. But the value of the franc laid up in the stocking was decreasing, and Poincaré had had to take strong measures to stabilize the currency. The new Premier, who had been President of the Republic during the war, was a cold, harsh, parsimonious man. The deputies listened resignedly to the long speeches with which he introduced the Budget in a monotonous voice; but when it came to voting, they gave him discretionary powers. The constant change of governments came to an end, together with the fluctuations of the Bourse; unrest was firmly repressed, and France sank into a state of boredom. White Russian emigrés, all of them princes or former Tsarist guards, were working as taxi-drivers, or mounting guard in front of night-clubs. The cafés were crowded with Englishmen and Americans with pockets full of pounds sterling or dollars. The Latin Quarter teemed with students of every country and every race. Big companies were doing business to the tune of millions, but the average Frenchman was chafing under restraint. He did not like foreigners.

The Faculty of Law was the hotbed of the royalist movement; the *Action Française* and the *Camelots du Roi* organized demonstrations in the corridors, booed the professors, booed the Jews, and waged pitched battles with the socialists—sons of schoolmasters and provincial bourgeois bred up in the radical spirit of the beginning of the century. Minor officials and hotel porters grumbled about the foreigners, come from no one knew where, and dubbed them indiscriminately as *métègues*, whether they were Bohemians, Americans, students who had exchanged their good currency for depreciated francs, Alsatian Jews living in the bourgeois quarters of the city, or White Russians.

We ourselves happened, more than once, to come up against this hostility, as we clung to the platform of a motor bus at the rush hour, forced our way into the Métro after the doors were closed, or raised our voices in a carefree conversation in Hebrew, in a public garden. But we attached little importance to these trifling incidents. France was still the harbour of refuge of all victims of persecution, and when irrefutable signs of anti-Semitism came to light in Paris in the early thirties, it was a revelation to all those who had known the city ten years earlier.

Poincaré's cabinet marked the end of the ascendancy of the Left. The radical party, led by Édouard Herriot, Mayor of Lyons, was not unscathed. The Leftist Coalition had come into power in 1924, after a wave of strikes, unrest in Labour circles and socialist demands. The Coalition was supported by the Socialists, although they had refused to join the government out of fidelity to their principle of non-alliance with the bourgeois parties. This turn of events had aroused great hopes, especially as the Cartel of Left parties had contrived to eliminate Millerand, the leader of the Right, from the presidency of the Republic. Herriot immediately became the recognized leader of France; but his rise was followed by a sudden fall when his government was faced with insurmountable financial difficulties. The value of the franc was falling, capital was fleeing abroad, and Herriot was forced to hand over to Poincaré, called upon by President Gaston Doumergue to form a new government.

The titular Defence Minister in most of the French governments of that time was Maginot. Germany was recovering little by little from the financial crisis which had wrecked the mark in an unprecedented inflation, and the man who was accomplishing this miracle was none other than Hjalmar Schacht, Hitler's future Finance Minister. Stresemann was Foreign Secretary of the Reich, and international relations were dominated by the spirit of Locarno.

The great hero of those years was Aristide Briand, Foreign

Minister in almost every government until the beginning of the thirties. His face with its big moustache adorned the front page of the newspapers; his optimistic speeches made headlines, and were reported by news agencies all over the world, and broadcast by the primitive, cumbersome wireless sets that were the delight of visitors to stores of electrical appliances. Entirely devoted to the cause of peace, he embodied the hopes of war-weary Europe. He was determined to put an end to the age-old rivalry between France and Germany, which had cost the world two bloody wars. With his opposite number Stresemann, the German Foreign Secretary, he set about accomplishing this miracle. They had behind them the Locarno Treaty, the resolutions adopted by innumerable international conferences, and the speeches of the delegates to the League of Nations in Geneva. Briand's will to peace won over Austen Chamberlain and his successor Ramsay Macdonald. By his faith and enthusiasm he conquered even the most sceptical of the journalists, in spite of the failure of the Reparations Conferences and the disappointment caused by the Dawes and the Young plans, which considerably reduced Germany's debt. The negotiations on disarmament dragged on endlessly, and still the public preserved its faith in the wizard of the spoken word, said by the newspapers never to write his speeches, improvising them on the spot in the glow of inspiration.

This faith communicated itself even to us, as we read *Le Quotidien*—the organ of radical circles—or Gustave Téry's *L'Œuvre*, a bold, intelligent paper that often bore as a motto the quip 'Fools don't read *L'Œuvre'*. The political column was written by a talented woman journalist, Geneviève Tabouis, who seemed to have a gift for seeing into the future. She had unlimited confidence in Briand, and communicated it to her readers.

One hot summer's day in 1928 we crowded against the gilded railings of the Foreign Office, opposite the steps of the Quai d'Orsay (which I was destined to mount many times, thirty years later), to witness the ceremony of the signing of the Briand-Kellogg Pact, which outlawed war once for all. We watched the luxurious limousines gliding, one by one, along the Quai towards the ushers, dressed in black, with white gloves, a heavy silver chain round their neck, who were opening the car doors for the great political figures of the world, delegates of sixty nations which had written, signed and proclaimed that the sword was to rest in the scabbard, and there was to be no more war. Never, never, never!

We felt excited and happy. Strangers though we were in the city, and excluded from its political life, we were convinced that we had witnessed an historical event destined to change the character of the world, promoting friendship between peoples and an enduring peace for us too.

Could war be possible, anyway, in this era in which the sky had been conquered and the laws of nature controlled? It was hardly a year since we had mingled in a delirious crowd, shouting, singing, dancing, laughing and crying at the same time, to welcome a fair-haired, blue-eyed young man, who had just crossed the Atlantic in an aeroplane and landed at Le Bourget, and who, leaning out of his cockpit, introduced himself shyly, saying, 'I'm Charles Lindberg'. A sublime, unforgettable moment, in which the crowd reached the limits of exaltation, suddenly aware of the grandeur of man's creative power. In the clamour of triumph celebrated at Le Bourget, we were not alone in thinking we heard the exultant voice of a new age.

III

Our first encounter with Paris had been a bit depressing, not to say lugubrious. Dark clouds covered the sky, and a diaphanous mist enveloped the roofs, when the smoky train entered the Gare de Lyon. A fine autumn rain was falling; green motor buses followed one another in an apparently endless succession; high-roofed taxis drove along, hooting aggressively. It was the end of the morning, but the street lamps were still burning in the foggy half-light, and it looked as though the sun would never break through in the murky sky. As far as one could see there stretched long lines of houses covered with an age-long accumulation of soot. Workmen in blue, wearing faded caps, were hurrying to their jobs. Trams went by with a metallic din, windows rattling, bells rending the air in sudden, nervous peals.

We stood there, hesitant and lost in the crowd of passengers issuing in a black flood from the station, out of the clouds of smoke and whirls of steam eddying through the great building. At Marseilles we had still enjoyed a little southern sunshine. Now, after a night journey in third-class wooden compartments, we stood there shivering in our thin overcoats, looking at the rusty autumn leaves, full of apprehension at the thought of the adventure awaiting us in this world-metropolis. This was not how we had pictured the Ville-Lumière, and we felt small and lost on its threshold.

We looked in vain for a cab. In Palestine, in Egypt, even in Italy, we had still travelled in horse-drawn carriages. Here the horse had disappeared; Paris was already at the motor age.

After a moment's hesitation, we approached a taxi waiting in the row beside the pavement, and piled inside it, four Palestinians, plus baggage. The driver growled something beneath his white moustache, settled our luggage between the seats and asked where we were going. Those of us who spoke French explained that we were students registered at the Sorbonne. This made no impression. He muttered something inaudible, as though to say there was nothing new about that, he had seen hundreds of lads like us at all the Paris stations. He straightened his cap, seized the wheel, and dashed off to the Latin Quarter at the speed of a whirlwind.

Crossing the river, he entered a labyrinth of by-streets, stopping at the doors of the hotels ranged along them, whose signboards promised every modern convenience, central heating, running water hot and cold. A leprous carpet covered the entrance steps, where a bored hall porter stood in attendance. By the end of half an hour our driver had succeeded in finding us a vacant room in one hotel, and a double room in another. He then pocketed his fare and made off.

We spent our years in France in the Latin Quarter. The Right Bank remained practically unknown country, into which we ventured only for a walk, to attend a theatre or to visit friends. On the Left we were at home, lost among the crowd of students, Frenchmen up from the provinces, Chinese and Japanese, Indo-Chinese with delicate features and slender waists, Americans and Englishmen, Negroes from Africa—the first we had ever seen, and were surprised to find studying along with us, talking French better than we did, laughing uproariously, showing their white teeth, and holding young French girls by the waist.

Our hotels were overcrowded, the rooms were let by the month, and students usually only made a short stay in them. Sometimes it was the proprietress who turned out her lodgers in the tourist season, or for a customer prepared to pay a higher rent. Sometimes the tenant himself decided to leave his badly lighted, mouldy-smelling room, whose window opened on a dark courtyard, opposite the dirty wall of a neighbouring house, and go hunting round the adjoining streets in the hope of finding a more attractive lodging in a hotel we had not yet discovered. Some went the round of the hotels in the Rue des Écoles and the Rue Monge, near the Sorbonne or behind the Panthéon. There was always an acrimonious concierge seated at an old desk in the reception office, making endless notes in a black book. She cast suspicious glances at the inmates taking their keys from the board in the passage, and at night, when we came in late, pulled sleepily at the frayed cord that opened the door in response to the bell, or the traditional cry of 'Cordon, s'il vous plaît!'

In the morning, before going to the Faculty, we went down to one of the many local cafés to drink a café au lait in which we dipped a crusty croissant. We drank hurriedly, leaning on the counter, wedged between taxi-drivers, crossing-sweepers, and postmen enjoying their early glass of white wine or an aperitif with purplish reflections. At midday we crowded round a table in some little restaurant where the meal cost only a few francs— bread ad lib and a carafe of wine included—immersed in conversation, enjoying the food cooked by the proprietor himself in the background, while his wife called out the orders, which he acknowledged by repeating them. We often changed restaurants. If a comrade discovered one that promised a better cuisine and more moderate prices, we all emigrated to the new place, greeted by the habitués with a toss of the head, as nomads come from God knows where, who would soon disappear again. The proprietress who waited on us always made a clear distinction between us casual guests and the serious customers she served with special attention—the police constable or the local postman, who had their reserved table with a bottle of their favourite wine. She greeted these with a broad smile, and turning towards the kitchen, called out '*Pâté de foie* for Monsieur l'Agent!' 'Veal cutlet to follow Monsieur l'Agent's *pâté de foie!*'

And Monsieur l'Agent seated himself at his table, tucked a corner of his napkin behind one of the gleaming buttons of his tunic, said good morning to his old friends, poured himself a glass of wine, and became gravely absorbed in the sacred rite of the midday meal.

Sometimes we went to one of the popular restaurants in the Latin Quarter, after carefully inspecting the menu at the entrance, so as not to come out again with an empty purse. The best known was the Chartier, at the corner of the Rue Racine and the Boulevard St Michel, which was always full, the waiters rushing to and fro, pitching plates on to the tables with incredible dexterity, and shouting orders to the kitchen.

This restaurant was destined to play a part in the Jewish history of our time. Passing by it early one afternoon, we found the street barred by the police. Boys were running about crying a special edition of the evening papers. An hour or two earlier Semion Petliura had fallen victim to a bullet at that very spot. He had been the Head of the Government of the Ukraine at the time of the Jewish massacres during the Civil War. Exiled in Paris after his defeat, he had been ambushed at the corner of the street by a little Jewish watchmaker, who fired his revolver at him on recognizing him. The former Ataman fell at his feet in a pool of blood. The trial of Shalom Schwarzbart, the evidence that recalled the sanguinary epic of the Ukraine pogroms, the moving speech for the defence by his counsel, Maître Henri Torrès, and the verdict acquitting the accused, kept Jewish opinion busy all over the world for many months.

IV

I had put my name down at the Faculty and received my student's pass. My halting French was no surprise to the secretary who was used to the stammerings of foreigners. I entered the Sorbonne for the first time with a feeling of respectful awe, pushing my way among the crowd of young men and women hurrying towards the lecture-rooms and stopping by the stone pillars to consult the time-table. Many were foreigners, others provincials, and the Parisians stood out from them by their assurance and the ease of their behaviour in this sanctuary of knowledge. I began studying the notices myself, and felt my brain reeling at the wealth of choice. On the advice of knowledgeable friends I bought the voluminous prospectus of lectures, practical work and exams of the Faculty; but the more I turned over the pages the more confused I became, faced with a programme whose subjects were all so attractive.

One thing was certain: the first thing to do was to learn French; so I spent several months pegging away at the grammar and learning to read fluently. My hotel room was ill-adapted to study, being badly lighted by a little electric bulb that had to be switched on all day. Besides which, the comings and goings of my friends distracted my attention. So I resorted to the public library. At first I was too shy to put my name down at the Bibliothèque Nationale, where I was to spend many days during my last years of study, and although the library at the Sorbonne was large and pleasant, students of every Faculty rushed into it as soon as it was opened. So I went to the old public library of Sainte Geneviève, opposite the Panthéon. This was a shabby old room with books covering its walls, and venerable librarians bending over desks that looked as though they had been borrowed from a court usher of the days of Louis-Philippe. They gazed in dejected boredom at the readers holding out their slips. These readers were mostly students of literature, the library being famous for the wealth of its literary collections. But as the doors were open to all comers, and there was no need to show a card or a season ticket, the readers were of every description: retired officials, sightseers, women dressed in black in the fashion of our grandmothers, and bearded individuals taking refuge from the cold, or merely killing time.

I soon began to recognize the most noticeable of these *habitués*. When I arrived, early in the morning, and took my usual seat at a long table in the middle of the room, I would find an old, round-shouldered man sitting on the other side, who, as soon as he began to feel a little warmer, would get up and fetch a bulky volume of eighteenth-century prints from one of the cupboards, return to his seat, blow on his red hands to warm them, open his portfolio, take out some squares of paper, select one, blow his nose noisily in it and replace it after folding it carefully, clear his throat, put a pair of steel-framed spectacles on his nose, and lose himself for hours at a time in beatific contemplation of an etching.

Opposite him sat a worn-out old lady, in a hat trimmed with two wooden cherries. On entering the room she had whispered excitedly into the ear of the uniformed attendant, scribbled a note, rubbed it out and rewritten it after a momentary hesitation. Her eyes had roamed all over the room, looking for a place to sit as though her fate depended on her choice. In the end she had come back to her usual chair, adjusted the lampshade, opened the book she had brought with her, and fallen straight into a blissful sleep, a happy smile on her face. So she remained until the midday closure, when the old keeper, a war veteran with a row of decorations on his worn uniform, walked round the tables announcing in a bass voice that echoed through the room, 'Gentlemen, closing time!'

It was in that room that I spent the long hours of my first winter in Paris. Once again, as in Italy, I had to struggle with a new language, forcing my way into a world of unfamiliar ideas and distinctions. Armed with dictionaries and grammars bought from second-hand booksellers on the Boulevard St Michel, I began by reading the tales of Alphonse Daudet, which I remembered, for the clarity and simplicity of the style, from the translations I had read as a child. I jotted down the meaning of new words, did grammatical exercises, and between two spells of reading ran to a lecture-room at the Sorbonne to seat myself at the top of the auditorium and listen attentively to the professor's delivery, trying to connect the sentences. I seized every opportunity of talking French to my neighbours at the hotel, listened to all that was being said around me in the restaurant, and spent my evenings reading the newspapers, translating and commenting. I was given the address of an elderly Jewish lady, a native of Lorraine, sympathetic and charming, who gave French lessons to foreigners. Her lessons were a great help to me, but I soon had to give them up for want of time or money, and return to my studies in the libraries of the Latin Quarter.

*

As I improved, I tried to increase my knowledge of French literature by reading the works I had heard of as a boy, from the novels of Victor Hugo to those of Georges Sand, then the comedies of Molière, and back again to de Musset and Chateaubriand, building up mentally, layer by layer, the edifice of western literature that I had only glimpsed during my vagabond childhood and my adolescence in Jerusalem. I searched the voluminous catalogues for works on history and literature, to immerse myself in the study of Europe's past; and as soon as I was able to I entered into conversation with French students in the court of the Sorbonne. The extent and variety of their knowledge and culture aroused my unfailing admiration, and I realized with a pang the distance between my country and the civilized surroundings in which these young people had been brought up, before coming to this great capital as the most natural thing in the world. It was here, I felt, that universal values were created; the behaviour of this country found a repercussion all over the world. These morose reflections rather wounded my pride as a citizen of Jerusalem, while increasing my nostalgia for my distant home, simple and modest, but my own.

When I tried to draw up a list of lectures to attend, I was faced, as in Italy, with such an *embarras de richesses* that I did not know how to choose. I wanted to grasp everything at once, miss no lecture or conference, read every book and study every subject. I had no inclination to any particular profession that might procure me a livelihood, so I decided to go in for culture in general, as far as I could. The programme of the Sorbonne permitted this, because the number of subjects one might take up was only restricted if one intended teaching in a French secondary school. Months went by before I could make up my mind, but I became chiefly interested in semitic languages, comparative literature and sociology.

When, after all these years, I attempt to draw up the balance-sheet of my years at the Sorbonne, I am forced to confess that the actual knowledge gained has fallen into oblivion, leaving me only a confused recollection and a few manifold copies of notes at the bottom of an old travelling-bag, along with some old postcards and faded photographs. It was probably the method of the French sociological school that left the most lasting impression on me. My professor of sociology was Célestin Bouglé, one of the greatest French sociologists of the day, a disciple of Emile Durkheim. Positivism still reigned supreme at the Sorbonne, and Durkheim had fostered a whole generation of sociologists. I enjoyed his books, written in a clear, precise style, his way of casting doubt on everything, accepting no established concepts, and re-creating a system of definitions by the ruthless analysis of fundamental axioms. Bouglé at the Sorbonne and Lévy-Brühl at the École des Hautes Études inherited his method. The lectures attracted a large audience, whose notes were passed from hand to hand. Later, during my many travels, I tried to apply the fundamentals of the method to the study of Jewish communities whose tendencies and way of life I had occasion to observe. In this way I was often led to conclusions that threw light on the astonishing phenomenon of the Jewish call to unity, founded apparently on nothing beyond the obscure consciousness of belonging to the same stock and sharing the same historical fate.

Adolphe Lods was my professor of Semitic languages. Before attending his lectures I had read his books, luminously clear, if a bit dry, on the Bible and the history of the Jewish people. His pupils, few in number, were mostly Catholic and Protestant seminarists, and a handful of young Semitologists preparing for a scientific career. I once asked him to grant me an interview for the sake of settling my study plan. He was a tall man, dry, a little stooping, with a small pointed beard. On the strength of his name, reminding one of the Polish town of Lodz, I was convinced that he was a Jew, the son of some emigrant from East Europe, and I took care to refer to my origin, my own Palestinian nationality and my Jerusalem citizenship—all without producing the slightest effect on his severe features. I was beginning to feel annoyed at this indifference when he let fall that he was a Frenchman by birth, and a Protestant. We then turned to the object of our interview; the direction my studies were to take, and my preparations for the exams, but I fancied I detected an amused gleam in his eyes that suggested I was not the first Jewish student who had tried to exploit this imaginary common origin.

The programme of my lectures included the study of Syriac, and as this ancient Semitic language was not taught at the Sorbonne, my professor sent me to the Catholic Institute of Paris, and I found myself provided with a certificate—preserved to this day—stating that I was a student of this great Christian institution. My professor of Syriac was a priest with a flourishing beard, full of erudition and easy of approach. Abbé Nau had a kindly welcome for all his new pupils, who were of course not numerous. I was seated one day in his lecture-room beside a young curé, deep in the translation of a chapter of Bar Hebraeus, when the door was opened by a tall youth who bowed to the master, made the sign of the Cross, and seated himself behind me. The Professor, continuing his lecture, explaining and commenting, turned to this new pupil, saying, 'Monsieur M . . . , will you explain this passage?' I pricked up my ears. The name, that of an aristocratic Jewish family of Egypt, was not unknown to me; I had often seen it mentioned in Palestinian newspapers. It seemed extraordinary that this young man should have joined this Catholic seminary and crossed himself piously on entering the room.

After the lesson I said to him, 'Did I hear aright? Is your name M.?'

'Yes, that's my name.'

'Of the Egyptian family?'

'Exactly. Do you know my family?'

'But then you're a Jew?'

'I am of Israelite extraction,' he said, correcting me coldly.

I could not conceal my surprise. We went on with the conversation over a cup of coffee in a local bistro. He told me he was preparing for the entrance exams at the Ecclesiastical Seminary, and studying theology and patrology, hence his interest in Syriac. We had begun by talking French, but unconsciously I slipped in a word of Hebrew now and then, and he replied in very correct Hebrew. As I was congratulating him on this, he told me he had lived in Palestine, and even stayed with Yitshak Epstein, a celebrated pedagogue and linguist, to whom his parents had sent him to improve his knowledge of Hebrew, and bring him in contact with the Jewish atmosphere. He looked back to his stay in Palestine with pleasure. On his return to

Alexandria he had been attracted to the Catholic faith, had ended by being converted and had come to Paris to finish his studies before taking orders.

All this seemed to me obscure and unreal. I had heard many stories of conversion, but this one was not in the same category. Apostasy at a time of persecution, when a man yielded to constraint, was admissible, and I could even have understood a conversion out of love, for the sake of marrying a young Christian. But that a man should renounce Judaism, having once been familiar with its values, simply because he was attracted by another religion, seemed to me incredible.

He went on with his story, telling me how he and a friend had come under the influence of a Catholic preacher in Egypt; that in Christianity he had sought and found an escape from the strict formalism of Judaism, and that Christian mysticism had held a profound attraction for him.

'Did you never realize that you were turning your back on your own people?' I said.

'My people?' he replied. 'What do you mean? Who are they? I was born in Egypt, and have no affinity with the Egyptians. I was educated in France, but don't consider myself French for that reason. I'm not looking for a people, but for a religion.'

I fell silent. I knew the abyss that separated us was beyond discussion.

I never saw him again. For some unknown reason he left off attending Abbé Nau's Syriac lectures. A long while afterwards I read in the paper that two young Catholic priests had been expelled from Egypt because they were doing missionary work among the Jewish youth of Cairo and Alexandria. One of the names was that of this friend of an hour.

The Latin Quarter and Beyond

I

ALL my attempts to find a job had failed. The Jewish community in Paris, which I soon got to know, had little to offer me, with its meagre resources in the way of Jewish education. My funds were getting low, and I was afraid I might have to ask once again for help from home.

Then I happened to meet Shoshana Persits at one of the Zionist meetings at which Palestinian students put in an appearance from time to time. She had just come from Tel-Aviv to see her father, who lived in Paris, and after reproaching me for not having called on them, she invited me to dinner that Friday evening. After this I got into the habit of going every sabbath eve to see Hillel Zlatopolsky at his apartment in the fashionable neighbourhood of Passy, where all the Russian emigrants foregathered who had managed to save some of their fortune.

I had known Hillel Zlatopolsky in Moscow, as an old friend of my father—the one that had given him the job at Omsk. He had lost all his fortune at the time of the Revolution, but on arriving penniless in Paris he had started in business again, and thanks to his relations with the world of finance he had quickly built up a considerable fortune. With a powerful imagination and great intrepidity—in private as well as public affairs—he loved risk, and went in for transactions of uncertain profit, manœuvring skilfully, winning on the swings what he lost on the roundabouts. He had extended the network of his affairs so skillfully that he sometimes hardly knew his way about it himself; but he really enjoyed the financial gambling; the game attracted him more than the winnings.

Seated in his arm-chair after the Friday evening meal, he liked displaying his learning, quoting and commenting on some thought of the Sages, entering into a profound discussion on the Talmud as he had learnt to do in the rabbinical schools in which he had spent his youth. He also had a penchant for

235

literature, and wrote articles published in the weekly *Haolam*, somewhat old-fashioned, but popular with the elderly readers of that conservative, stylish magazine.

His daughter, Shoshana Persits, had settled in Palestine many years earlier, transferring thither her publishing firm, Omanuth, founded in Germany after the war. She came to see her father in Paris on occasion with her children, the eldest of whom, Akiva, was about to take his baccalaureate examination in Paris. Like her father, she was always bubbling over with ideas and plans, and in the Tel-Aviv of that day she had a reputation for immense vitality. She was greatly interested in public affairs, and the books she published were devoured by children and teenagers eager for good literature in Hebrew.

The atmosphere of the house in the Avenue de la Muette was not unlike that of Tel-Aviv and my own home. I enjoyed listening to the adult conversation and the grandchildren's racket, the digressions of the writers and militant Zionists passing through Paris; and on Friday evenings there was the blessing of the wine —the *Kiddush*—besides the eloquent, learned talk of our old friend.

I confided my worries to Shoshana Persits, and she laid the matter to heart, assuring me that there would be a way out of the difficulty. Then, as usual, she began thinking up plans: I could do translations for her publishing house, or, for that matter for the *Encyclopedia Judaica* then published in Berlin. I was not to worry, anyway, there was sure to be a solution. This was very comforting, and I thought myself free of my troubles, but the weeks went by, and I began to wonder if all these promises had not been empty talk.

Then one day my landlady called me to the telephone, which hung in the passage of the hotel. I raced down the four flights: the Zlatopolskys were expecting me on Friday evening. Among the guests I found Moshé Kleinman, editor-in-chief of the *Haolam*, the organ of the World Zionist Organization, published at that time in London. He looked me over in a scrutinizing way, and began a conversation with the obvious object of sizing me up. He clearly thought I looked very young, which was bound to make him distrust me, for the young generation brought up in Palestine was known to be little versed in Hebrew, and without any good basic education. Shoshana then broke into the conversation, singing my praises and declaring that I wrote Hebrew very well, and had even had a certain amount of experience in journalism, having edited the bulletin of the Town Hall of Tel-Aviv, and even contributed to the *Haarets*. I sat there, on the edge of my chair, blushing and awkward, praying Heaven that my catechizer would not probe too deeply into my scanty career. Kleinman, who had worked with my father, yielded at last to Shoshana's arguments and told me of his plan. Printing costs being very high in London, while life in Paris was cheap, the officials in charge of the Zionist Organization had decided to try the experiment of printing their weekly organ in the French capital. They had even signed a contract with a Jewish printer who had set up a press there.

As the editor himself lived in London, he needed a part-time assistant here, knowing Hebrew and capable of doing the make-up of pages and proof-reading, and even editing reports, especially news of Palestine and the Jewish world. The final proofs must be sent to London at the week-end. And as the paper appeared on Tuesdays, make-up must be finished on Sunday, and the copy taken to the night train at the Gare St Lazare, to reach the editor in London next morning.

Kleinman warned me that all this was only an experiment. Even the contract with the printer was only provisional. He fixed my salary at a pound a number, quite a respectable sum for two days' work a week. Mentally converting this into French currency, I found it would give me a decent income of five hundred francs a month, and I accepted it on the spot.

II

This job 'on approval' lasted the whole of my stay in Paris, to the detriment of my studies. My attendance at the press was required three days a week, without counting that on Sunday; instead of resting like my friends, I was busy on my paper from the morning until far into the night. My pay allowed me to live only very thriftily, but my complaints to the officials in charge of the funds, although supported by my chief, had no effect. 'A young student who has had the good luck to pick up a job like this should be content with his lot,' replied the treasurer, and there was no appeal from his decisions. Later on, however, summing up those years in Paris, I did not regret the long hours spent on the *Haolam*, which confirmed the taste for journalism I had had from childhood. It was an old-fashioned publication, with long, rather boring articles, all of it exhaling official conformity. But I was rather proud of my independence: the editor being in London, the editorial staff consisted of myself alone.

Our press had been set up in a decrepit old house at the heart of a grim workmen's quarter. It was a long way from the Latin Quarter, transport was poor, and I had to get up at an hour when my friends were still fast asleep, to catch the motor bus that took me by narrow streets to the Place Voltaire or the Roquette Quarter.

The building stood at the end of a cul-de-sac, and was entered by narrow wooden stairs leading into a dark room with presses on one side and clicking linotype machines on the other. The text of the *Haolam* was set up by a linotypist who could just read Hebrew. As a former working printer on a Jewish paper in Poland, he really only knew Yiddish well, but having got used to reading Hebrew manuscripts without understanding them, he had become so expert that he could decipher whole pages covered with intricate texts. Beside him, at other linotype machines, Russian compositors worked, for the press specialized in Slavic languages. I took my usual seat at a dusty table stained with printing ink, and adjusted the electric bulb that burnt all day, winter and summer, because the only window gave on to the sooty wall of a neighbouring building. I took the roll of galley proofs, pulled on a hand press by an old printer, and began attentively reading long articles, correcting the numerous misprints and taking particular care with the articles by the editor himself, knowing that he was very sensitive about any mistake left uncorrected in his copy. I then went carefully through the reports from the Jewish Telegraphic Agency, sent me in French and English, selected the news to translate, and went back again to the bundle of manuscripts sent from London with the editor's memorandum and detailed instructions, telling me to be sure not to overlook the article by X, to print Y's prose only if I had room for it, the author being a deadly bore who was always badgering him. As for Z, although a writer of repute, his style could be improved on, and if I thought I could abridge his interminable article, so much the better!

At the end of the week, when the time for make-up approached, I took the roll of galley proofs out of my drawer, cut them up with a big pair of scissors, pasted them and gave them a heading, following the advice of a compositor who came from Palestine like myself, and was an expert at the job. He had come to Paris originally to study, but had returned to his old trade for reasons that were not clear. He was a good fellow, loyal and obliging, always ready to lend a hand in case of need. To our mind he was almost rich. His salary allowed him to be generous, and he would always lend ten francs to a mate. We set the headlines in place and arranged the paragraphs, and when the type matter was finally locked up in the chases, with a sigh of relief I allowed myself a cigarette while I chatted with him, or with other employees come to keep me company.

At lunchtime I went alone, or with one of the printers, to have a snack at a local bistro, the proprietor of which might have come out of a lithograph by Daumier, with his red face and blue nose, a blue apron stretched over his great paunch, busying himself with the cooking in his smoky kitchen. From time to time he would leave the cutlet frying in the pan, and go to the counter to pour an *aperitif* for a customer, the driver of a lorry discharging rolls of newsprint in the storeroom of the press, the driver of a wagon drawn by a pair of powerful Brabants, or a white-haired female employee from the press, red-faced, with wide hips, who used to wipe her dirty hands on a piece of paper while she confided her heart sorrows to me. She spared me no detail, including the intimacies of her married life and the habits of her fickle husband, always running after the girls of the quarter, while she toiled here at the printing press to earn enough to support him.

On Sundays in summer, when the heat lay heavy on the city, the sun scorched, and one's shoes sank into the softened asphalt on the pavements, I sometimes asked my friends to an Italian restaurant I had discovered near the press, whose proprietor was a past master at preparing a deliciously tender *escalope milanaise*, covering the whole plate, with a generous helping of *pasta asciutta* and a bottle of Chianti in its wicker sheath. After a long, pleasant break there, I returned to my dark printing office, while my friends went off to Fontainebleau Forest or Versailles to enjoy themselves in the sun.

Except for the *Haolam*, which was printed in Hebrew, our press dealt almost exclusively with Russian work. The *Poslednye Novosty* ('Latest News'), read by Russian emigrants all over western Europe, was printed there, and I sometimes ran across its editor-in-chief, Paul Miliukov, coming to see the manager or to revise an article. He was a cold, slow-moving man with a small, pointed white beard and piercing, short-sighted eyes. I thought of the days when he represented powerful Russia as Foreign Minister in the Provisional Government, and wondered how he had succeeded in adapting himself to the climate of exile, busying himself with trifles in a miserable printing press at the bottom of a muddy cul-de-sac, after holding the destiny of an empire in his hands and hobnobbing with the mighty ones of the world. Once or twice a week I saw Alexander Kerensky come in, the former head of the Provisional Government, who published a rival paper printed here too. I knew him at once from his portraits, seen everywhere in the streets in the days of his glory—hair *en brosse*, a square head, piercing eyes deep in their sockets. But the years had left their mark: his hair was turning white, his face had narrowed and was seamed with wrinkles, and his figure was bent, as though he had grown old before his time. Even in exile the former leaders of the Revolution still carried on their quarrels, their newspapers recalled old disputes, harking back to the past, widening every crack in the Soviet régime. They went on living after the fashion of yesterday, torn by ambitions and regrets, but they knew they were condemned to perpetual exile, without appeal.

At the table next to mine M. Berchine, a distinguished journalist, prepared the weekly *Rassviett*, the Russian language organ of the Zionist Revisionist Party, and Jabotinsky himself looked in at times, on his return to Paris between two journeys, to take a look at proofs and add a leading article before the 'locking' of the paper. I often had long conversations with Berchine as I went over my galley proofs. Although he knew no

Hebrew, he gave me useful advice, initiating me into the mysteries of page make-up, and cheering me by tales of his own blunders as a novice, and how he got out of it when he was caught. All this was of great use to me, struggling alone with my job and often at a loss to find a way out of difficulty. Jabotinsky used to say a few kind words to me, in his precise, clear Hebrew, so relaxed and cordial that it was difficult to recognize him as the fiery orator whose virulent speeches I had often heard at students' meetings and at the conferences of his new Party, which violently attacked the Zionist leaders, and had its nerve-centre in Paris, where there were many faithful Russian leaders of the *Rassviett*.

The conflict between the Zionist Executive and the Revisionists increased in bitterness. The crisis through which Palestine was passing, and the resulting unease in the Zionist ranks, furnished arguments to the Opposition, which attacked Weizmann and his colleagues without respite, making him responsible for every calamity: the perfidious conduct of the Mandatory Government, the failure of the fourth *Aliya* and the economic depression overtaking Tel-Aviv. But this vicious struggle found little echo in the peaceful rivalry of the Paris printing works, where the proofs of violent articles in the *Rassviett* lay side by side with a speech by Weizmann censuring the Opposition in the *Haolam*, separated only by the barrier of language.

III

Moshé Kleinman arrived one day from London, and began as usual by extracting a sheaf of manuscripts from the deep pockets of his voluminous overcoat.

'In one of the issues of the *Haolam*,' he said to me, 'you'll have to print an article by Nahum Sokolov on Spinoza, on the occasion of the two hundred and fiftieth anniversary of his death. He's promised me the article, and Sokolov's a man of his word. He'll be in Paris on Tuesday. I've told him you'll call on him at his hotel to fetch the manuscript.'

On the appointed day I went to the hotel, whose customers included none but Ministers, and members of reigning families, and whose threshold had probably never been crossed by a poor student. I was not a little excited at the idea of this interview.

Sokolov's name had been familiar to me from childhood, when he was editor of the *Hatsefira* and my father's 'big chief'. He was now one of the foremost leaders of the Zionist Organization, Chairman of the London Executive, and every one of his speeches, in Tel-Aviv, Paris or Rome, was published in our papers and commented upon in the world press. My emotion increased as I approached the hotel, especially when the uniformed hall porter demanded to know my reason for coming to disturb the repose of M. le Président.

After a brief wait I found myself in Sokolov's presence, in a luxuriously carpeted Louis XV salon. Sokolov resembled his photographs, which adorned every office in Jerusalem, and answered the descriptions I had so often heard: very carefully dressed, his little yellow beard sprinkled with grey, speaking slowly with the marked accent of a Polish Jew. He asked me about my studies in Paris, and for news of my father, but when at last, with some hesitation, I delivered Kleinman's request, he looked worried and annoyed.

'Yes, of course,' he said, 'I promised Kleinman. Spinoza—it's a big subject. I've taken it up more than once, and I should have liked to write the article. But ... with this ungrateful task on my shoulders. ... For instance, I've now got to go to Rome, and I think after that I'll have to run over to South Africa. And then, to write this article I ought to have a few quiet days at the British Museum, and I've got to go to Amsterdam too. When shall I have time for it?'

Seeing that the plan was destined to fail and I had nothing more to lose, I allowed myself to persist. Perhaps ... all the same ... just a short article. ... It really was not possible for a weekly like the *Haolam* to take no notice of the anniversary of Spinoza's death—and who was better qualified than he to evoke that great figure? Seeing my perturbation, Sokolov smiled and said reassuringly, 'Well, well, I'll do my best. Perhaps I may send you something from one of the stages of my journey, next week.'

And sure enough next week I received an envelope containing the article in question, on unusually large sheets, twice the size of normal ones, with no margins, written in a minute calligraphic script, the letters all separate from one another, nothing erased or cancelled. Here and there, when a detail had escaped his memory, he had pasted a little strip of paper on the right side or the left, bearing a line minutely written, and connected to the body of the text in red ink. With a practised eye I calculated the length of the article and decided that it would cover eight or ten pages of the *Haolam*. In other words, I should have to publish it in two successive numbers. Pleased with the result I had obtained, I sent in my report to the editor.

But before publishing the second part I received another envelope from Sokolov, containing a text twice as long as the earlier one. In his covering letter he explained that while his article was being published, he had realized that he had left out an important phase in Spinoza's life and work, and he did not want his study to be left incomplete. He begged me therefore to publish this supplement before the second half of the first article. As far as I could see, the manuscript would fill three numbers. I asked Kleinman's advice, and he said we obviously could not refuse a request by Sokolov. And regularly, week after week, I was sent supplement after supplement, and the publication of the article took a whole year. The author added historical documents to it, and sent us books with engravings to be copied by photogravure—all this from every sort of place: Poland, Belgium, Roumania, Italy, proving that he was pursuing his research between political missions, actually to such good effect that by the end of the year he had furnished enough material for a stout volume, which appeared in Paris under the title of *Spinoza and his Contemporaries*.

Countless manuscripts began going through my hands. The *Haolam* had only a limited budget and was always hard up. Its continued existence was deliberated at every Zionist Congress, and anybody wanting to balance the budget of the Zionist Organization began by voting against its publication. But owing to the scarcity of Hebrew publications at that time even a modest weekly such as this offered an outlet to writers who could hardly expect to place their copy elsewhere. Besides which, its contributors included respectable public men, patrons of art and philanthropists who flattered themselves they could write, which gave the *Haolam* the air of a review by men of letters after the old style. It was late in reacting to the politics of the day, and events in Palestine were referred to long after they happened. On the other hand, it contained pages of great literary value, written either by young authors in search of a platform or by well-known writers.

I remember my excitement on entrusting the press with *Pages of the Revolution* by a young writer, Chaim Hazaz, who lived, like myself, in one of the Paris hotels for students. He wore a black beard, had glowing eyes, and was exhausting himself in an attempt to find a new formula for the Hebrew novel. He was destined to leave his mark on a whole period of Hebrew literature. When Zalman Shneour was asked for a contribution to the paper, he invariably replied by an ill-tempered 'No'—which did not prevent him from sending us a poem sometimes at the approach of a festival. And I still have the manuscript of Tchernikhovsky's sonnets, which first saw the light in the *Haolam*, and included the wonderful poem *Ilil*, which I knew by heart and recited with gusto to my friends. He also sent us, occasionally, tales and short articles on his Russian past, and his recollections as an army doctor in the Great War. Reading these, I was always surprised by the great difference between his powerful lyric and the dry, flat prose in which these tales were written.

The chances of publication in Palestine were so small in those years of crisis that even an author like Kabak, whose books were very popular, was obliged to publish his new novel, *Shelomo Molkho*, in Paris, and it fell to me to get this great historical fresco printed. Kleinman informed me of this during one of his visits to Paris, adding that he had promised to serialize the book in his newspaper for one or two years, and preserve the stereo-types for later publication in book form by the *Haolam* press. I was not very happy about this, for I doubted the possibility of distributing a Hebrew book printed in Paris. My uncle had meanwhile written to me from Jerusalem, asking me to keep a close watch on the printing and read the proofs very carefully. Glad of the opportunity of doing him a service, I let no printer's error escape me, and as I read through the book I realized the change that had come over his way of writing. He had de-veloped a more vigorous prose, and a much more subtle and penetrating psychological analysis than before. As I had foreseen, however, when at last the book was printed, it did not reach Palestinian readers, and it was a long while before this great historical trilogy was appreciated at its true worth.

All these years I had borne the burden of editorship alone. Even when I was ill I dragged myself to the press, because there was nobody to take my place, and if I was not there the review could not appear. During the holiday months, when my friends scattered to the four winds, I remained tied to my job, reading manuscripts and proofs in the stifling heat of Paris. Thousands of citizens left the capital throughout July and August, and the papers published photographs of the Place de la Concorde, empty, deserted, without a sign of traffic. Only the workers living near my printing office got up early to work without a day's rest. It was not till ten or more years later that Léon Blum introduced compulsory holidays with pay in France, allowing the workers too to take advantage of their vacations.

Comrades

THE great city lay there in its vastness. The Faculties were scattered all over the *Quartier Latin*. At night the lights of Paris offered all kinds of attractions to the young. But the Palestinian students, of whom there were many in the capital at that time, stuck together in a body, living the isolated life.

In earlier days, in Italy, we had formed a homogeneous group, all young, mostly fresh from school, out for the first time beyond the frontiers of our country. Here, however, the Palestinians were not all of the same breed. Among those living in our hotel rooms there were of course some youngsters who had just taken their *bachot*, but next door to them there were *halutsim* who had spent years breaking stones on the roads or digging their barren soil, and had ended by throwing up the sponge for reasons of health or mere weariness. Many others had yielded to the entreaties of their families, in Poland or Roumania, not to sacrifice their future but acquire a profession worthy of the name. Others again had been driven by a genuine thirst for knowledge, and had saved, bit by bit, enough to pay for their studies in France.

Besides these, in somewhat more comfortable hotels, there were mothers of families who had brought their small daughters to Europe to study music, in the secret hope of seeing them develop into infant prodigies in the capital of the arts; 'perpetual' students grown old in the lecture-rooms of the Sorbonne, telling all who would listen of their mysterious relations with French celebrities, and postponing their exams from term to term. Nobody knew what they lived on, unless it was occasional private lessons, and the few francs they contrived to borrow from their friends. In Montparnasse one met Palestinian artists, who having suddenly discovered their vocation, had come to drink at the well-springs of the Paris School. Few of them were destined to fame. Most of them disappeared at the end of a few months, leaving no trace, to be followed by other budding artists who would spend their nights at the Dôme or the Rotonde with

246

empty stomachs, sipping a *café crème*, or else painting feverishly in their garrets like all painters worthy of the name.

Most of all these knew very little French, and seldom mixed with French students, who stuck together likewise and paid little attention to the foreigners crowding the corridors of the Faculties. The French politics of the time were unlikely to excite the newcomers, especially as the university was dominated by nationalist and royalist groups in which xenophobia was rife. A few among us ended by joining the ranks of the Communist Party, which was just emerging from the lethargy into which it had fallen in Poincaré's day. These, caught in the toils of professional revolutionary circles in France and elsewhere, soon vanished from circulation.

We lived in groups, comrades of the same school lodging in the same neighbourhood, others who had made friends after a chance meeting in a restaurant or a lecture-room. However, a tradition established by our predecessors had made it a rule that all Palestinian students should forgather, one evening a week, in the basement of a café in the Place du Châtelet, at the meeting-place of two worlds: the Latin Quarter where we all lived, and the Right Bank, sparkling with lights, and mysterious.

For the price of a cup of coffee or a glass of grenadine we had the right to hold our meetings there, listening to lectures or spending the whole evening in discussions or choral singing, under the vigilant eye of the waiter, who kept account of our drinks and damped down the fire of altercations. For our uproar must not disturb the peaceable Parisian bourgeois sipping their aperitif or their coffee laced with rum in the room overhead.

Our weekly rendezvous soon developed into a permanent club, under the management of an organized committee. At the beginning of the university year, when the holder of the post had completed his studies and taken ship to Haifa, I was elected president in his stead. My friends at the printing office undertook to print invitation cards headed 'Palestinian Club of Paris', in Hebrew and French. The departing members of the committee gave me a long list of names and addresses, and friends volunteered to write out the invitations and send them off. My presidential responsibilities included ensuring that well-known speakers, Parisians or visiting Palestinians, should lend their assistance.

We talked of everything and nothing during those long evenings round the little tables in the café basement—of literature in general, of course, and the future of the Hebrew language, of Zionism, British policy in the East, contemporary music and the moral decline of Europe, modern art and its problems, the revolutionary changes in the theatre, and jazz, the strange Negro music, the strident sounds of which poured out from the Paris night clubs and cafés. Sometimes we forgathered to listen to a lecturer, at other times we filled our programme ourselves by organizing a spoken newspaper or recitations and readings. The members of the Club were not fond of these improvised entertainments, and the lecturers often bored us too. We swore we would never set foot there again, but next week we were all punctual at the rendezvous. The familiar atmosphere attracted us, and the long hours spent in clouds of cigarette smoke had their charm. We exchanged jokes and gossip, we tried to catch up with what was happening in the world, and exchanged news of incipient pairings, fatal passions and disappointed love, exams passed or failed. We bid farewell to those about to return home, and vilified the deserters who had allowed themselves to be lured away by the attractions of Paris and had deserted our company.

Finding lecturers was no easy task. Through my relations with Zionist circles in Paris I often heard of the arrival of personalities on their way through. Then I remained glued to the telephone at the hotel or the press, trying to persuade them to grant us one of their free evenings.

We succeeded in capturing a young leader of the Palestine Labour Party, Zalman Rubashov—now Zalman Shazar, President of Israel—who was returning from one of the innumerable Conferences of the Labour Movement in Europe. I can still hear his thundering voice in our cramped basement, and see him whirling his arms about to punctuate his enthusiastic phrases. Joseph Sprinzak, destined to become the first Speaker of the Israeli parliament, made a willing response to our appeal, but did not scruple to reproach us vehemently for our apathy towards public affairs. Yehuda Karni, the Jerusalem poet, who had come to Paris for medical treatment, gave us a lecture on modern Hebrew in his cavernous voice, and the great poet Tchernikhovsky came to the Club to give a lecture on rhythm in poetry. The better to illustrate its functions and origins he seized the chairman's hands—mine, as it happened—and tossing his arms in every direction showed us how the rhythm of poetry had sprung from the labour cadence of primitive man.

A violent discussion broke out one evening at the Club, on the subject of the modern dances, fox-trot and charleston, all the rage in Paris, which had drawn many members of our group into the dance halls of Montparnasse and to dance parties. I took upon myself to draw up a formal indictment against these decadent dances, which I considered contrary to the spirit of Palestinian society. I preached in favour of our collective dance, the *hora*, of which every movement expressed communion and fraternity, whereas the modern dances were quite unsuited to an idealistic, pioneering people like ours. With youthful ardour, I launched into a severe diatribe, calling down the fire of Heaven upon these dances, upon jazz, and in general the thirst for temporal enjoyment that was taking possession of Europe. A number of counsels for the defence rose in protest, jeering at my narrow-mindedness and my old-fashioned, fanatical, provincial ideas. These were no longer the days of the second *Aliya*, they said, before the Great War. Everything had changed, ideas, notions, ways of life, and the new world around us was certainly different, but in no way inferior to the old romantic one.

I felt defeated, and was looking round for allies when I saw, seated at a table with a cup of coffee, Myriam Baratz of Degania, one of our earliest *kibbutz* pioneers, on her way through Paris after some party meeting in Europe. When she raised her hand to ask leave to speak, I felt sure of my case. But Myriam tossed her short hair, straightened her plump figure in its sheath of white linen, and took me to task. I had only opposed modern dancing so firmly, she said, because I did not know how to dance. I should really have liked to do as other people did; my theories merely concealed my lack of skill. Young people should be allowed to dance as they liked and as they thought best. Did the pioneers of yesterday neither dance nor enjoy life? She herself, for one, remembered the waltzes and polkas of her youth very vividly. That was dancing, if you like! She could have shown the youth of today a thing or two!

As the tone of her intervention became increasingly passionate, the entire assembly went over to her side, drowning her voice with enthusiastic applause. My indictment collapsed under the banter of the audience.

But our Club was called upon to face more serious questions. Anti-Semitism was raging in the universities of Poland and Roumania. Many Jewish students were fleeing from Eastern Europe to continue their studies in Paris. One day we heard through one of our Jewish friends from Roumania that one of the chief spokesmen of anti-Semitism in that country had been invited to give a lecture at the University of Paris. The French government, which was trying to tighten the bonds of the Little Entente with Eastern Europe, encouraged relations with Roumania and extended a cordial welcome to the political figures of that country. So a warm reception had been prepared for the Balkan politician, and everything suggested that his lecture, which was to be held in one of the lecture-rooms of the Sorbonne, would attract a large audience.

The Jewish students came to us for help in sabotaging the meeting. We immediately assembled a gang of stout lads, calling in the Palestinian students of the Veterinary School at Maisons-Alfort—famous for their strength and fighting spirit—as reinforcements. On the evening of the lecture the Jewish students, led by the Palestinians, dispersed to the four corners of the room. The lecturer had hardly begun his delivery when he was interrupted by a shout: 'Tell us something about the Jewish students in Roumania!'

The speaker attempted to disregard this and pick up the thread of his lecture, but shouts burst out again all over the room. Pandemonium soon developed. The Roumanian students, who had come to applaud their leader, replied by insults and fisticuffs. Then our veterinarians went into action. Seizing their chairs, they flung them at the enemy's heads, punctuating their blows with shouts intended for the Roumanian anti-Semites: 'Take that for a Jew! That for two Jews!'

The mêlée became general, chairs flew across the room, fists waved in the air. Finally the lecture was called off, and the speaker was forced to leave the platform.

This victorious evening established the reputation of the Palestinian students as defenders of Jewish honour. In after days we often sent gangs to break up meetings of French and foreign anti-Semite students, by starting a free fight.

Jewish life in France did not appeal to us very much. We knew that the Paris community was numerically strong, but its social life offered little interest. At the university we sometimes met students with typically Jewish names: Weil, Bloch, Lévy, but when we referred to Jewish subjects in conversation they began talking of something else. There were Jews on the teaching staff, too, including well-known scientists like the sociologist Lévy-Brühl, and Gustave Cohen, the historian of French literature, while the best handbook on the history of religions bore the signature of Salomon Reinach. But they all seemed utterly indifferent to our dilemmas. The tragic days of the Dreyfus Affair were forgotten, and their Jewish extraction meant little to them. They were less interested in what was happening in Palestine than their Catholic colleagues, who might question us about our strange national movement and the complex nature of the little country of the East, so close to Syria, under French Mandate, where Arab and Druse risings were sometimes the subject of reports.

We saw more of the Russian and Polish immigrants who had settled in Paris in their thousands on the morrow of the war. Many of them still felt themselves strangers in their new home. They spoke Russian or Yiddish, and lived apart in special quarters, among their own friends. Even their sons, more acclimatized by now, speaking excellent French and educated at Paris schools, were easier to get on with than their native French friends. We came to know a good many of their hospitable families.

But although these young men were affable, we found them little in sympathy with our ideas. Absorbed in their studies, their only interest in politics was concerned with the expected revolution in Europe that was to solve all their difficulties. There were premonitory signs of anti-Semitism in the air, which they could not help noticing, but few of them took them seriously.

Zionism, to them, was a very abstract notion. The local Zionist Organization was led by a handful of Russian Jews who had been active in the movement in their country of origin, besides a few Alsatians attracted by the idea. It was a hardly perceptible movement on the fringe of reality. Meetings were held now and then in a hotel drawing-room to celebrate some event or welcome a celebrity; Jewish reviews appeared and disappeared, various parties discussed obscure points in their programme, all this almost in secret, without affecting the Jewish masses.

Not many French politicians of that day were interested in the affairs of Palestine. A few had been won over to the cause, either through the efforts of their Jewish friends, or through their contact with Chaim Weizmann and Nahum Sokolov, who often came to France in search of allies against the hostile policy of the British Mandatory authorities. Among these were Radical parliamentarians like Anatole de Monzie, whose blind pacifism was later to lead him to the idea of an alliance with Fascist Italy, and Justin Godard, a faithful friend of Zionism, who had the satisfaction, in his old age, of greeting the creation of the State of Israel. A few socialists, too, like Léon Blum, whose authority in the Party was already great, and who never hesitated to put his prestige at the service of the Zionist cause. Victor Jacobson, a shrewd, courteous man, a forerunner of Zionist diplomacy, kept watch from his modest office over contacts with French politicians, while Léo Motzkin was at the head of the Committee of Jewish Delegations, defending the rights of the Jewish minority in Eastern Europe against the wave of anti-Semitism mounting in the young States of the East that had recently attained independence.

The Palestinian students, accused by the Jewish press of indifference and inaction, were out of touch with these institutions, and any attempt at activity on their part always met with failure, anyhow. For instance, our Club responded one day to the appeal of the publishing firms of Tel-Aviv, who were in straits for lack of readers, by trying to disseminate Hebrew books in France. We started a subscription campaign, after the fashion of the Book Clubs that were later to become so popular. But it was no use: hardly anybody caught on. The number of Hebraists in the Jewish community in France was really very limited.

After this first defeat I suggested we should start some evening classes for the young Jews of Paris, to help to spread the Hebrew tongue. We thought the idea an excellent one, especially as these lessons would have increased the incomes of our colleagues, many of whom needed it badly. A group of teachers was carefully selected, and we had only to find premises for our improvised school.

I approached Joseph Fisher, whom I had known in Jerusalem when he was in charge of the Jewish National Fund in France, and asked him for an introduction to the Director of the Rabbinical seminary, who would surely not refuse to put a few class-rooms at our disposal. Fisher was sceptical, but consented, and telephoned to the Director, a French rabbi of high repute and an erudite Hebraist.

He received our delegation with cold, calculated politeness, taking stock of us with curiosity: it was probably the first time he had met with any young Palestinians. The conversation started in French, but as soon as he noticed our halting speech he changed to Hebrew, using a rather learned, elaborate style, which raised our hopes. Having unfolded our plan, we stressed the importance of teaching the language of the Bible, which would bring the pupils closer to the problems of Judaism and Palestine.

It was here, of course, that we made our greatest blunder. As soon as the name of Palestine was mentioned, our rabbi pricked up his ears. He refused our request with rigid politeness, and by way of justifying himself, said in his pure Hebrew, 'You must realize that I can't consent. I'm not interested in Zionism, and shall never do anything to hinder our young people's adaptation to French life. I am an assimilated Jew.'

We were speechless. I looked at my colleagues, rose from my chair, bowing slightly, and went to the door. The fact that these ideas could be imparted to us in classical Hebrew seemed somewhat unreal.

This put an end to our attempts at disseminating Hebrew culture in the Jewish community in France.

II

We were living in this little world of ours, dividing our time between our studies and our student activities, when we discovered the Kovno group one day.

We were pushing our way into one of the rooms at the Sorbonne, to listen to a popular lecture by a well-known professor. The amphitheatre was crowded, and we had some difficulty in finding seats. I was going down the steps, talking to a friend, when someone called out to me in Hebrew, 'Have you come from Palestine? Come here, there's room.'

Turning my head, I saw a plump, fair girl with laughing eyes, and beside her another one, dark and slender. They were dressed in the fashion of the day, in short skirts that showed their knees, and cloche hats pushed down over their foreheads. We accepted the invitation, and before the professor made his appearance they told us, in rapid, lively Hebrew, that they were natives of Kovno; they had just ended their studies at the secondary school in the Lithuanian capital, had entered the Sorbonne, and were living with other friends in a little boarding-house near the Panthéon.

After the lecture we went with them to their *pension*, and other friends joined us. We were invited into one of the rooms, under the disapproving eye of the old landlady, who disliked seeing young men invading her establishment. We were then introduced to the rest of the band, and by the time the door closed behind us a few hours later we knew them all by their first names: Lisa and Vera, Big Leah and Little Leah, Fania and Polia, besides all the boy friends that had gathered round them. When we went back next day our new friends pulled out from under their beds the parcels sent them from Kovno, packed by their mothers with tins of delicious herrings in oil, smoked sardines from the Baltic, spicy sausages, and cakes. They sang us the Jewish songs of their own country, and we launched into endless tales of Jerusalem. We went to the cinema together that evening, and by the end of a few weeks we had become an inseparable band.

That was the end of the Palestinian pride with which we had treated our comrades of Eastern Europe. The Lithuanian girls were studying at the Sorbonne, and their boy friends either at the Faculty of Law, or working at science. We soon made the acquaintance of other Kovno students, who came over now and then from Nancy or Grenoble. They all talked Hebrew fluently and were familiar with life in Palestine; their Judaism was integral, like ours, without hesitation or question. There were some active communists among the young men, and our discussions at the Club became more lively than ever. But most of them felt a great affinity with the Land of Israel, where they were all preparing to go and live sooner or later. The girls knew all our songs, our old saws and our idiomatic expressions, and apparently their study programme had been copied from ours.

But the Palestine of their dreams was very different from the reality. In the romantic prism, coloured by the sentimental idealism inculcated by their teachers, we found it difficult to recognize our country. They often stared in astonishment when we described the hot winds of summer, the rain-storms of a Jerusalem winter and the dreary grey rocks of Judea.

They were very young, and still felt the distance from their home very acutely. Homesickness overtook them especially of a sabbath eve and on feast days, or when the parcels from home arrived. And yet one could feel an obstinate spirit of revolt in them against their native town and their monotonous, provincial home surroundings.

They soon began attending the Palestinian Club and taking part in our most active meetings. The group snowballed: other friends joined it, including Sam, the painter from Chicago, the son of Nadia from Nahalal, who shared my room at the hotel; a young American employed on the Paris edition of the *Chicago Tribune*, a Bulgarian who fell in love at once with one of our girl friends, and students from Roumania and Poland. For the festival of Purim we organized a carnival evening in our basement, and I was covertly chaffed by my friends about the irresistible attraction Lithuania appeared to have for me.

After this we spent all our free time together, roaming the streets of Paris, visiting museums and exhibitions, or going to a popular play. On public holidays we went for excursions along the banks of the Seine or the Marne, where the Parisians celebrate their Sunday rest by fishing, and spent our evenings on the terraces of the Montparnasse cafés, or on the Butte Montmartre. Some of the painters we knew would join us, among them Mané Katz. Small and restless, with a mane of hair that was beginning to go grey, he was nearly always as penniless as the rest of us, but when he sold a painting he liked to display his wealth and invite us to an expensive restaurant or a popular night club. He was very keen on new inventions, and it was thanks to him that, towards the end of our stay, we saw the first talking film, *The Jazz Singer*, with Al Jolson, the great sensation of that year.

Before the end of our second semester, however, the group had begun to split up into couples. I wrote enthusiastic letters home about my girl friends, with photographs taken near Notre-Dame and in Versailles. Father, who had known Kovno in his youth, was delighted, and approved of my choice. The young Lithuanians certainly looked beautiful, in spite of their fashionable get-up. Mother was more straightforward. Which one was it? The tall dark one beside me in the photos?

The Paris winter was coming to an end; the snow was melting on the roofs, the cold rain was leaving off, and the spring sunshine breaking through the clouds. Citroën's gigantic illuminated signs on the Eiffel Tower shone with fresh brilliance, and the horse-chestnuts along the boulevards burst into flower. Soon we should be going for long walks beside the Seine, where the barges slowly made their way down to the mouth of the river. The scent of lilacs filled the suburbs, and at night the horns of the endless line of cars coming down the Champs-Elysées followed as far as the Place de la Concorde and the Grands Boulevards.

Little by little we broke away from the group, Vera and I. Together we discovered remote corners that only young eyes could find attractive, discussing the beauties of nature, the theatre, a book of poems that delighted us both.

Then, of course, we discovered that all this was only a pretext. I wrote to the family saying, 'Yes, it's the second from the left in the photo, and don't forget that her accursed cloche hat covers half her face.' I summoned up my courage and added a few words to Vera's letter home. A fortnight later came an answer from Tel-Aviv. Father was impatient to see his future daughter-in-law, as well as his own son after all these months. Anything might happen. It was quite on the cards that he would be coming to see us soon, for a trip to Europe was under consideration. Who knows? It might not be long.

The Evening of a Life

I

I WAS standing in the telephone call box at the Bourse post office, hanging on excitedly to the receiver, from which a familiar voice was issuing. 'How are you, son?'

Always on the track of novelties, my father had had the bold idea of using the telephone to talk to me from Vienna. I had had a wire from him about it that morning, and as at that time all international calls were made from post offices, I had been waiting there to hear him talking to me across the Alps. His voice was clear and intelligible, I could hear every word. Forgetting everything I wanted to say to him after our long separation, all I could think of was 'What is the time at your end?' 'Half-past ten,' he replied. My watch said only half-past nine, Paris time, yet there we were, having a real conversation with questions and answers. Next day my father wrote to Tel-Aviv, 'The conversation was more distinct and audible than between the Zionist Executive and the Jewish National Council in Jerusalem.'

The cycle of separations and reunions had begun afresh. In the 'Falling House' in Tel-Aviv the luggage had been strapped up, and friends had come to bid farewell to the head of the family, who was leaving for Poland on a special mission for the *Keren Hagesod*, the Zionist Reconstruction Fund.

A few weeks earlier my father had been invited to Jerusalem by Leib Jaffé, who had suggested his joining a mission that was leaving for Warsaw under the leadership of Shemariahu Levin, one of the best speakers of the day, a popular and influential Zionist leader. He had hesitated at first. How could he leave home, with his wife ill, and the children hardly yet acclimatized to their new surroundings in Tel-Aviv? But the mission attracted him: its object was no less than to restore the ruins of Polish Zionism, affected by the crisis in Palestine. It would be an opportunity, too, of meeting old friends of his youth. He would be going to them as an emissary of the new Palestine to which he now belonged, to open their eyes and show them the truth about

257

the country—his truth, vibrant, without a shadow, full of love for Israel and faith in its future.

The mission attracted him all the more, in that the crisis was not yet over. He was convinced that the Jews of Poland would recover their faith in Zion, if only one could show them that this wound, deadly in appearance, was only a form of growing pains, the birth pangs of the great work being achieved in Palestine. Could one not make them realize the living beauty of the land? Could Polish Jewry have really given in to despair? Was it not merely the effect of some terrible misapprehension, some mysterious aberration, preventing them from seeing things in their true light? Their newspapers, with their superficial, frivolous tone, could give no idea of the strength of the popular will that had accumulated in the Jewish community in Palestine, which must triumph visibly one of these days and show what these men were capable of. As for their Zionist leaders, they were enslaved by hollow formulas, outmoded phrases, incapable of telling their followers the simple truth. He spent a long time preparing for his mission, visiting *kibbutsim* and farming cooperatives, jotting down facts and figures, going about with workers in the towns and young peasants in the fields. Everything he saw and heard confirmed his faith. His doubts vanished. He would be able to restore their old enthusiasm to the Jews of Poland.

In any case, he said, to reassure himself and console his family, it would only be a short trip of a few months. Once his mission was accomplished, he would be coming back to them and to his work in Tel-Aviv. He little knew that his fate was sealed and he would be condemned to spend the last days of his short life out of his country, and the home he had built up with so much effort would never rise again.

Relations and friends were waiting for him at the station in Warsaw, in a state of great excitement, as though he were reappearing after all these years in a world he was supposed to have left forever. They assured him he was bound to be successful, and showed him the Jewish newspapers, in which his arrival was warmly welcomed. But next day, when he got in touch with the local notables, he found himself faced by an unfathomable abyss. Polish Zionism had definitely collapsed, and forever, as it seemed. The movement was visibly subsiding, and even the most faithful were turning their backs on it. The leaders were absorbed in party quarrels, elections to the Polish Diet and the rivalries of politicians. What of Palestine and its future in all this? The Zionists were not sparing in their criticism of the Palestinians and their leaders, holding them responsible for the failure of the Polish Jews who had sunk all their fortune in building huge blocks of flats and speculating in the funds. They accused them of all the sins of the country that, only yesterday, they had considered ideal—its unhealthy climate, its orange plantations so tardy in bearing fruit, desert winds drying everything up, price of land falling. Who could ever seek their fortune in such a country again? We were the culprits, we the hundred and fifty thousand pioneers living out there. Every sort of calumny was listened to, with no one to shout, 'Halt! That's enough!' The Zionist Organization was at loggerheads, the Parties were at daggers drawn, and no firm hand was raised to arrest the decline.

This was the moral climate in which my father started his campaign, going from town to town, preaching, describing, trying to open people's eyes. He had never found it difficult to express himself in writing. When his pen was running over the paper, he excelled at depicting, relating, tracing with a fine graver every vibration, every shade in the effort to communicate what he felt to be the truth. The colours on his palette were bright, as though shadows existed only to show up the luminous reality. As he was in his private life, so he showed himself in public affairs. And it was his faith, so pure and entire in its simplicity, that had won him the sympathy and confidence of his readers.

But now he had to deliver his message verbally, and conquer his audience in synagogues and public halls, in the towns and villages of Poland, Galicia and Lithuania, and stage fright seized him every time he mounted the platform. Might not his tongue play him false? He was afraid of not being able to interpret the radiant truth of which he was the mouthpiece, which he felt to be so evident, so palpable. Silently he repeated the ancient prayer: 'Almighty God, turn not away Thy face from the emissaries of Thy people!'

I could detect this anxiety between the lines of the letters I was getting from Warsaw, Lodz, Bendzin, Lublin, Lvov, and many places I had never heard of. I could see him in his long overcoat, a fur cap on his head, floundering through the snows of that distant world, pleading his cause before simple Jews of the people, before adolescents dressed in sheepskins, spending hours with boys and girls in the farm schools of the *Hehaluts*, talking and explaining, bringing the good word from Zion. As he talked to them he forgot the miseries and trials of his country, the poverty and distress, the party quarrels and the bitter struggle for the right to work, the long queues of the unemployed, the strikes, the quarrels in the Municipal Council of Tel-Aviv. The picture he painted them was the one that sang in his heart. Blossoming orange-trees, green pastures, little white houses springing up on the dunes, and the moon lighting up the rocks of Jerusalem; the imponderable sense of freedom, of space unfolding through the valleys, fiery dawns—all the visions peopling his soul since that far-off day when he first set foot on the soil of Palestine.

It was only much later, when I discovered for myself what missions abroad were like, that I realized to the full what he must have gone through, and was trying to express in his letters. At that time, those letters, which I have kept, seemed to me sentimental, even a little naïve. There he was, in those great cities of Warsaw or Lvov, disappointed by his encounters with their notables, returning alone to his hotel room depressed and uncertain. The indifference of these men, sated with honours, self-assured, was intolerable to him. They were all recognized leaders in their towns and communities; they knew everything, understood everything, there was nothing left to tell them about Palestine. They were versed in high politics, and knew all about the rivalries between leaders and clan intrigues in Congress lobbies. When my father poured out all this in his letters at night, despair showed through. In spite of the often humorous style one could sense the gnawing doubt, and often a melancholy bitterness at having engaged in a hopeless venture.

But he occasionally stopped at some little, remote place that the notables of the great cities never visited. This was another world: here he found what he was seeking—a genuine yearning for Palestine, an emotional welcome and profound gratitude to the man bringing them a message from their beloved land. The whole community awaited him at the station, and accompanied him in procession to the hall of the synagogue where he was to speak. He mounted the platform and addressed them in his Yiddish, feeling shining eyes fixed on him, and warming himself at their glow. He talked for an hour and more, without wearying his audience. At night, when the meeting and the banquet were over, the Youth Movements would send a delegation to fetch him, boys and girls forming a circle round him, gazing at him in veneration as he talked to them of the *kibbutsim*, the Emek settlements and the landscape of Galilee. Questions and answers went on till after midnight, as they drank in his words. Then the young people sang in chorus, and he taught them the new Palestinian songs and the Hassidic tunes of his childhood. Wherever he spoke, young people followed him with their ardent eyes, and never left his side. When he took a short rest in his room, he was visited by delegations of artisans or simple Jews wanting to know when and how they too could come to Palestine, what work they would find there; and a mute prayer could be read in their eyes: anything, anything, so long as they could set off for Palestine! They were weary of waiting in their village, or their little town, burning with desire for the new life they dreamed of. Sometimes a visitor would take a worn copy of one of my father's books from his pocket, or newspaper articles cut out long ago, before the war, and start a long conversation, full of respect for the author whose writings had given him such pleasure in his youth, and whom it was now granted him to see in flesh and blood.

When it was time for him to leave, the young people went with him to the train and gathered round him in the station yard, where he made them a farewell speech. Their eyes filled with tears, they flung their arms round him for the last time and led him to his carriage. On his return to the city, enraptured by this revelation of Jewish unity and fidelity, he wrote me excited, happy letters, saying repeatedly that it was all worth while— worries, vexations and disappointments—because of this wonderful moment of spiritual exaltation.

Little could they foresee, he and his colleagues who were

perambulating the towns and villages of Poland, Galicia and Lithuania, that these communities were destined to vanish in the gas chambers and crematoriums, and that hardly any of their listeners would escape the holocaust. A few of them reached other centres of the Dispersion, and formed fresh communities in America and elsewhere; and even today, on my way through a foreign town, I may be approached by an old Jew, saying with a wistful look, 'I was a great friend of your father's, you know. Ever since his visit to the little town I lived in then.' Or one of the young men who had welcomed him in Poland at that time may approach me after a meeting of some kind in Israel—bent, greying—and take me aside to say, 'If it hadn't been for your father I might never have come here. It was he that lighted the pioneering fire in me, when I was only a young man, at home.'

My father might have seen things in a happier light if he had known how some of the seed sown by him would germinate. But besides his disappointment at the way things were tending, he was becoming anxious about being so far from home, not knowing when he would be able to get back to work; anxious, too, as to what would happen to his family if they were scattered, with no haven in which to drop anchor. For while he was devoting himself to his mission, the state of Mother's health was steadily worsening, and the doctors had declared that her only hope of a cure was to go abroad to consult the great specialists of Europe.

II

The fifteenth Zionist Congress, which was held at Basle that year, opened in the depressing atmosphere of a movement stamped with defeat. Ever since my childhood these Congresses had formed landmarks in our existence, each of them standing for a period. An aureole of respect and admiration surrounded the famous leaders who planned our future in Palestine and solved the difficult problems of the Jewish world from the platform. They were the supreme chamber of our parliamentary life, and my heart beat wildly when my father told me he was to attend the Congress as correspondent of Jewish newspapers in Poland, and had obtained a ticket for me as well.

Thoroughly excited, I could not sleep a wink in the train from Paris to Basle. My father was waiting for me at the station, radiant, excited himself at the approach of the great event. A streamer in big letters welcomed the delegates arriving from every part of the world—Poland, Roumania, Hungary, and even France, England and the United States, besides Palestine, of course. We had taken a room in the house of an old Swiss lady, long used to housing participants and visitors to fairs and congresses. The delegates were dispersed among the many hotels of the town, and the most eminent, with Weizmann at their head, had booked rooms at the old, traditional 'Drei Koenige' Hotel, overlooking the Rhine—the one at which Herzl had stayed at the time of the first Congress, in 1897, as witness the famous photograph showing him leaning on the rail of the balcony, watching the river. We met some of the delegates in the street, on their way from their hotels, to the Congress Hall, or from there to the rooms and cafés booked by the political groups, parties and federations for their preliminary meetings. The whole town seemed just a great hive buzzing round the Congress.

I wandered in a dream in the midst of all this activity, led by my father, who told me the names of the V.I.P.s we passed on our way. We greeted old friends, notables of the communities of Poland and Lithuania, whose names had been familiar to me from childhood. Father introduced me with obvious pride, and they exclaimed at finding me grown into a man. On the opening evening I sat in a corner of the hall, lost in the crowd of delegates and guests filling it to the far end of the gallery, the first rows being reserved for the diplomatic representatives of the Great Powers. When I heard the opening speech delivered by Sokolov, and the message from the President of the Canton of Basle, I was thrilled to feel I was witnessing a solemn occasion that would one day be written into the history of the Jewish people.

But when the Congress became involved in the drabness of practical debate, I realized the difficulties with which the Zionist Movement was struggling. The brilliant staging and solemn decorum could not conceal the prevailing atmosphere of insoluble crisis. The balance-sheet of the last two years was disastrous, one long series of failures without a gleam of light. The confidence of the Diaspora Zionists was shaken, the friends who had supported Zionism in the days of its success were closing their purses, and the treasury was empty. It was rumoured about that Weizmann himself had been obliged to call a group of wealthy delegates together and ask them to advance a few hundred pounds sterling for the rent of the hall. All the branch officials of committees were complaining that they could not carry on their work for lack of money. I saw my father taking counsel with Palestinian leaders, and trying to approach the President of the Zionist Organization between two sessions to obtain a loan of a thousand pounds to the Jewish National Council, which was on the verge of bankruptcy.

What a sad, depressing Congress, I thought, as I sat in the gallery listening to the speeches. I watched the heads of the Movement seated on the platform: they were finding nothing better to do than hurl accusations at one another, while the Movement itself crumbled before their eyes. They were powerless to surmount the crisis, but determined to settle personal accounts, absorbed in their quarrels all through the daytime sessions and the evening confabulations.

Weizmann appeared isolated, bearing the burden of the Movement alone. His successes of yesterday were forgotten, but the failures of today were attributed to him. He knew where he was going, he knew the path he had to follow, slow and strewn with obstacles—but which would lead him to his goal. But the body of the Movement had lost patience, all was rancour and bitterness. Throwing his prestige into the scales, he threatened more than once to resign. This cast a gloom over everybody, even his adversaries, accustomed for so many years to being led by him, and wondering what would become of them without him. Sitting beside him, Sokolov, whose serenity never deserted him, looked to me even more placid and aristocratic on the platform than at our brief meeting at his hotel in Paris. His opening speech had been long, too long, rather boring, delivered in a calm, monotonous voice as though he were reading aloud from one of those wide sheets covered with minute characters that I so often deciphered.

Facing them sat the leaders of the Opposition, violently attack-

ing them and their way of doing things, making them responsible for every failure. As soon as it was rumoured that Jabotinsky
was about to speak, the lobbies emptied and the audience flowed
back into the hall. His speeches were always brilliant and sharp-
edged; he saw Weizmann as the source of all our ills, responsible
for the crisis because he bowed in blind obedience to the British
Government's injunctions, and because he lacked conviction and
imagination. No less virulent in their way were the attacks made
by Stephen Wise, the spokesman of the American Zionists,
delivered in a scolding voice, with the intonations of a preacher.
He shouted, and pounded the desk with his fists, criticizing the
Executive on behalf of his fellow Zionists in the United States,
demanding a fresh approach and the relief of the Old Guard,
exhausted by their battles, vacillating, incapable of departing
from the beaten track.

The Americans, who were still living in a period of full
prosperity, refused to understand how the Palestinian economy
could have fallen so low. They put it down to the ignorance and
apathy of the leaders, their own outlook being that of business-
men. They demanded a balanced budget: if the Zionist Organization had insufficient means they must reduce their outgoings,
put the screw on, cut everything down—political expenses,
immigration, the training of immigrants. It was absurd to go on
supporting *kibbutsim* and co-operative villages that were devouring all their resources. The present crisis was due to the policy of
the Executive, which had given all its attention to the Emek
villages instead of encouraging private capital, which alone
could work miracles without recourse to public funds. And what
was true of settlement was equally true of education, for which
the Palestinians themselves must be made responsible, relieving
the Organization of it once for all. In short, economy and reduc-
tion all round, a cool and penetrating outlook on things, and
above all no more ideological enthusiasm of the old kind, which
had brought Zionism to its present terrible situation.

In addition, Stephen Wise submitted Weizmann's attitude towards Great Britain to bitter criticism, insisting that he should
make a firmer, more independent stand. Upon which Jabotinsky
declared himself ready to support Wise's candidature to the
presidency of the Organization, provided power was removed

from Weizmann's hands. Between them, they appeared to have secured the majority, only the Labour delegates fought to the end for colonization and immigration and the extension of plans for development and building. Weizmann, slamming the door, left Basle for Lucerne, with peacemakers in pursuit to persuade him to return. Stephen Wise followed suit, and after a violent dispute with the President, vanished from the Congress Hall, while well-informed persons broadcast the information that he was on his way to Paris and would not be seen again. Emissaries dashed in pursuit of him too, to tone down the differences and bring him back. In the end a 'technical' Executive was elected, with headquarters at Jerusalem: Harry Sacher, Colonel Frederic Kisch, Van Vriesland. The keynote of policy was to be reductions, economies, liquidation. The Palestine delegates left for home with heavy hearts.

III

We were well aware that Mother's days were numbered. She was now forty-six, and twelve years of her life had been darkened by disease. Her condition suddenly took a turn for the worse, the coughing fits became incessant, and the slightest effort exhausted her. She had been unable to leave the house for weeks, and the doctors were explicit that her heart was failing, after resisting for so many years. But even in these difficult days, with her husband absent, she went on fighting, without despairing, although thoroughly aware of the seriousness of her condition. On her own initiative she decided to try a final experiment and consult some European doctors. She gave up the big apartment in Nahmani Street—there was no sense, anyway, in keeping it on, she said, with Father away, her son studying in Paris, and nobody ringing the door-bell any more. She arranged for her mother and the younger boy to live with an old friend of hers, and got ready to start. My sister was to accompany her, as many years before, when they had gone to the Crimea together. As I was living in Paris, famous for its medical authorities, she would go there, in the hope of finding relief in one of the many spas of Europe. The family Ark was once more afloat on an adventurous cruise.

I went down to Marseilles to meet Mother at the port, but

arrived too late. The liner had docked before time, and my sister
had decided to go straight on, to avoid the night train. I spent
the whole day in Marseilles, wandering about the streets, trying
to relax on a seat on a boulevard, racked by anxiety. How
would my sister manage, who would take care of them, and who
would meet them in Paris? All that night I reproached myself
for my impulsiveness, but when my train drew into the station, I
saw Vera waiting for me on the platform, smiling at my discom-
fiture. She and her friends had gone to meet Mother, whom they
recognized at once from her photograph and her big Palestinian
hat. They had taken the two of them to their hotel, and done all
they could to make them comfortable. It was there that I found
them, Mother white-haired, exhausted, struggling for breath, my
sister grown taller, more mature over the years. But my mother's
eyes were still smiling, and though she found speech difficult,
she was still in command, making plans and carrying them out.

When a few days later she went to consult a renowned
specialist, recommended by a young doctor we knew at home,
she obstinately refused to take me with her, and asked one of
Vera's girl friends to go with her instead as interpreter. At that
time I did not understand why she wanted me to stay out of
the consultation. But many years later I found a paper among
her correspondence, which she had prepared in Russian and given
the girl to translate for the doctor. She told him she was aware of
the seriousness of her condition, and all she asked of him was
to try and slow up the progress of her disease, perhaps by sending her to spend some time at a spa. She could not afford to die
so soon; she was not afraid of suffering if she could manage to
live another few years, until her children were old enough to
fend for themselves. She had looked after them and run her
household up to now, in spite of her frequent attacks. She also
begged him not to tell her son how ill she was, lest it should
distract him from his studies.

So when I went to get a report from him next day, he told me
that although her heart was seriously affected, he was sure she
could be cured, and he advised us to send her to Cambo-les-
Bains, in the Pyrenees, near the Spanish frontier, famous for its
pure, health-giving air. She might regain some strength there
after a few months' stay.

So a remote French watering-place in the Basses-Pyrénées became the scene of the last few weeks of our family life. It was then a little tree-shaded town surrounded by mountains, in the Basque country, an hour's journey from Biarritz. In winter it was deep in snow, but in summer it was invaded by visitors from every part of France, heart patients and consumptives coming for a cure, or Parisians on a mountain holiday. The Spanish frontier was not far off, and on both sides of it lay villages with unpronounceable names, whose inhabitants, whether French or Spanish, talked a strange language, a legacy of the Basque race and a symbol of its freedom.

Carts drawn by oxen drove slowly between the ploughed fields on the mountain slopes, along green valleys and rocky paths. White churches raised their belfries in the village square, and the picturesquely clad villagers went in a crowd to mass when the bell sounded. Not a village in the Basque country but devoted its feast days to the game of pelota, and the results of the matches were printed in large type in the Bayonne newspapers, and even those of Pau, the chief town of the department, as well as in the local ones, printed in their mysterious tongue.

The villa in which we lodged, surrounded by a flowery garden, had three or four rooms to let. Our landlady cooked the local dishes while her husband busied himself the whole day with a wireless set, all tangled wires, which he had built himself, and which, to our great joy, occasionally produced, amid accompanying whistlings, sounds that resembled music, emitted by the stations at Bordeaux or Toulouse.

It was holiday time, and so that my sister should not feel too lonely my mother had invited my great friends, Vera and Lisa. Taking advantage of a free week, I joined them, and my father, who had interrupted his work in Poland for the summer, came to Cambo too, after the Basle Congress. We spent some wonderful days in this little corner of paradise, a happy company, climbing the mountains, running down at times by motor bus to the sea at Biarritz to admire the smart hotels and the millionaires' villas and walk along the blackish sand, and then gather in the evening round Mother's bed.

The lively company around her seemed to have revived my mother, and we were beginning to think the old professor was right. Father, as usual, had gone from despair to optimism. He was laying plans already for Mother's return to Tel-Aviv after her recovery, and for my homecoming after completing my studies and getting married. He would rent a big house again, and we would all live there together; the house would be open to all comers, and he would put an end to his travels and find an occupation that would afford him more satisfaction and fewer worries than the one he had been engaged in for so many years. We allowed ourselves to be dragged in the wake of his dreams, and even Mother, the most lucid of us all, smiled discreetly, nodding approval.

But when the rain set in, the dreams were quickly dissipated. I had hardly returned to Paris, my studies and my job, when anxious letters began arriving from Cambo. The autumn wind was blowing, the sky was covered with clouds, and violent rain-storms were whipping the bushes in the garden. This had gone on all day, for two days, a whole week. The cold found its way in through the chinks in the window-frames, and paraffin stoves had to be lighted in the rooms. Thick fog was creeping over the valleys, like the winter clouds that got caught in the Jerusalem hills. The holidays were over, my father left, the girls went back to Paris, and Mother remained alone with her daughter in the little town battered by the wind and drenched by the rain.

My mother caught cold, and my sister wrote that there was no longer any point in their remaining in Cambo. Mother's health was worsening all the time. When I went to see her doctor, he muttered, 'A pity it has rained. That rain is unfortunate.' But I gathered that Mother's case was a hopeless one, and it was doubtful if her heart would stand up to this fresh trial. He advised me to take her home. But as it was autumn, and we feared the winter rains of Tel-Aviv, the family decided it would bo bottor for hor to spend the winter at Helwan, in Egypt, not far from home, but where the sun shines all the year round and there is neither cold nor rain to fear.

We parted at the Gare de Lyon, where my mother and sister took the train to Genoa, whence they were to embark for Egypt. All our little company was there, and Mother, so clever as a rule at concealing her grief and showing a smiling face, was crying silently in a corner of the compartment. We felt certain we should never see her again. 'I apologize to you all,' she wrote from the boat, 'for the scene I made when we separated; but I couldn't help it. I had so much to say to you, and it all seemed tied up in my throat.'

Her last letters reached me from Helwan, the final stage of her life. She lived alone there, tied to her chair, her heart weakening from day to day. She spent her time reading, and writing letters for hours at a time—to her husband in Poland, to me and my fiancée in Paris, to her mother and her two younger children in Tel-Aviv. But she still had the strength to suggest and encourage family plans. When my father wrote that he had been offered a mission in America, she urged him to accept, telling him not to worry about her, she would be all right; begging him not to miss this opportunity of seeing Jewish life in the New World, which would widen his horizon and his knowledge. Her last letters had a twilight luminousness, as if a sublime peace had descended on her. Knowing her end was near, she had balanced accounts with the life of suffering she had known on earth, and the road she had travelled appeared to her as a long sequence of love and happiness. Her sorrows were forgotten, effaced, her sadness dissolved in the mists of the past. All that remained was the feeling of having accomplished her destiny. She had brought her bark safely into harbour, her children would live among her people, and the home she had built up would rise again from its ruins, even when she was no longer there.

All that winter of 1928 my heart was heavy with presentiment. One day when I was in my attic room, the door opened, and two of my Paris friends came in, dressed in black, with mournful faces. Before they spoke, I knew what they had come to tell me. My youth in my mother's protective shadow was at an end.

IV

When the thirty days of mourning were over we were married in a little synagogue in the presence of a circle of friends, and a few days later we started for Kovno, on a visit to my wife's family. My father, whose official duties had brought him to

Lithuania, was there too, and we spent the Passover holidays together in the easy atmosphere of the Jewish town my father knew so well from having lived there in his youth, when he was studying at the Slobodka *yeshiva*.

Before going to Palestine I had never known a typically Jewish town such as Kovno was at that time. In Kiev, Moscow and even Warsaw, we had lived in Jewish quarters, whose streets were entirely peopled by Jews; but they were never more than an enclave in a foreign territory. In Kovno there were of course thousands of non-Jews, and their numbers were increasing with the consolidation of the Lithuanian State, of which Kovno was the capital and metropolis. The shop signs were written in Lithuanian, and the telephone and postal services employed the language of the country. But here, somewhat as in Palestine, one felt it was the *others* who were living on the fringe of Jewish life. Nothing but Yiddish was heard in the street, except when young people hailed one another in the rich, lively Hebrew the Lithuanian students had so delighted me with in Paris. Boys and girls at the secondary schools were engaged, like myself at their age, in writing essays, studying chapters of the Bible and the philosophical tales of the Talmud. They wore a blue-and-white ribbon on their uniform caps. Even shop assistants might address you in Hebrew.

Although it had grown larger and undergone certain changes, Kovno still looked the Russian provincial capital it was before the war. The streets were paved with cobbles, the sidewalks were narrow, and in the by-streets of the suburbs one still walked on boards laid along the side of the road. Asphalt had been laid only on a short sector of the principal street, which the wits called 'the fifty yards of Europe'. Tired horses dragged the slow coaches of the tramway that made a long halt at every street corner. In the centre of the town stood the imposing building of the Orthodox Church, while the Catholic Church was relegated to a remote corner. The best hotels were all in the main street, the Avenue of Liberty (Laisves aleia), where the young people of Kovno paraded up and down on Saturday evenings and public holidays.

Kovno's Jewish newspaper, *Yiddische Schtimme*, had announced my father's arrival with great publicity, and even mine had been generally talked about, partly on account of my family connections, but chiefly out of curiosity concerning the young Palestinian who had married a Kovno girl. I was invited to give a lecture in the hall of the Library, before an audience composed of young men and women, pupils of the secondary school, and friends of Vera and her younger sister, who was in the middle of her school-leaving exams. My parents-in-law were present too, and my father, with a party of his old friends; and the honourable lecturer felt as nervous and shy as a young bridegroom of the old days preaching his sermon on his wedding day.

The Jewish population of Kovno had suffered badly during the war, for the town was near the German frontier, and the Jews had been evacuated eastwards towards the interior of Russia. They had returned at the time of the Lithuanian Independence, and lived through a brief idyll, in which every dream seemed permissible: Jewish cultural autonomy, a Ministry of Jewish affairs, establishment of a Schools System, and even recognition of Yiddish as an official language. Now, however, both the misfortunes of war and the brief post-war period of hope were forgotten. Kovno was once more merely a corner of the Diaspora like the rest. The course of history seemed to have passed it by; its sufferings belonged to the past, its future was without hope. The Jews earned their living quite satisfactorily, and their tables groaned with food. Hydromel fermented in their cellars, melted goose-grease filled great jars, tables bent under dishes of meat, and the spacious houses passed from father to son. The double windows protected apartments from the rigours of winter, though frost-flowers still showed on the panes when the ice on the river had started cracking in the thaw. On feast days the synagogues overflowed, and children's laughter echoed in the schools. Poverty appeared to have taken refuge in Slobodka, in the Lower Town, where bands of restive young men had forgathered, some of whom had been attracted by the communism that reigned across the frontier, while others had drifted to the training centres in the hope of obtaining an immigration certificate for Palestine. Their conversation betrayed the feeling of emptiness and impotence that was weighing them down. Their one desire was to escape as soon as possible from this peaceful boredom to the great cities of Europe, or to the Palestine that looked so attractive, lively and bathed in sunlight, and all the more luminous because of the greyness and gloom of the scene around them, the heaps of dirty snow melting in the streets.

I returned to Kovno not many years later, and again felt divided between affection and anxiety: on the one hand there was the pleasing atmosphere of a deeply rooted Jewish life, on the other the constant fear of an uncertain future, a sense of living in a blind alley. I had often discussed this with my Kovno friends in Paris, students on the point of completing their studies, and tried to prove to them, with my Zionist enthusiasm, that there was no way out for them, nor any way back. But even in my worst premonitions I could not have foreseen how near its end was this Jewish world in the Lithuanian snows, nor the hellish scenes that were to be enacted among the tumble-down wooden huts, blackened by time, of Slobodka, the miserable purlieu that was to become the ghetto and the tomb of the Jews of Lithuania.

In my first few weeks in Kovno all that was still far away. I felt immersed once more in the warmth of a home, and I was still lapped in it when I got into the train that was to take me back to Paris after a long journey through the Polish Corridor. The specific Russian smell—a condensate of sweat, sauerkraut, cheap tobacco and frozen apples—vanished as if by magic when the Lithuanian customs officers left the train at the frontier station of Eydkunen, to be replaced by German railway officials, well-groomed and affable. A few hours later we left German soil again for Polish territory. The compartment doors were closed, and the shutters pulled down, while Polish soldiers with fixed bayonets, commanded by young officers wearing the *shapska*, peered suspiciously into the compartment to make sure nobody escaped from it into the Danzig Corridor. Then, in Germany again, through Berlin—all lighted up—the long night journey towards the Rhine, then more frontiers, checking of luggage and passports in the compartmented Europe of the inter-war period.

In Paris we were back in our own climate again and we started our life as a young student couple.

V

We made our home in a hotel in a street near the Latin Quarter, and divided our time between study and work. But our hearts were heavy at the thought of our scattered family: Father still travelling about Eastern Europe, my younger brother and sister in their little apartment in Tel-Aviv, Grandmother dead only a few months later than Mother and buried in the little cemetery at Beth-Gan. And there were we, feeling responsible as the elders of the family, longing to have finished our studies and be able to return to Palestine and rebuild our home.

Meanwhile, even our daily personal anxieties could not blind us to the signs of the approaching storm. A deep distress was gnawing at the heart of European society, and future catastrophes were casting their shadows before. The Poincaré era was over. Governments were succeeding one another at ever shorter intervals, and the *Canard enchaîné*, which always hit on the right phrase, sported the headline 'Spring is singing, governments are dancing'. A series of financial scandals had shaken the confidence of France in her leading men, especially after the revelation of the malpractices of Marthe Hanau, a clever, unscrupulous business woman who had succeeded in abusing the trust of several leaders of the Radical Party. Her trial, which covered the front page of all the newspapers for weeks, revealed her connection with *Le Quotidien*, considered a liberal, progressive paper, to the final discredit of political circles. A young writer of Marseilles, Marcel Pagnol, had just produced his play *Topaze*, in which a simple-minded schoolmaster from the provinces is thrust into the world of politics by feminine intrigues, and ends up in a picked position among the profiteers of the State, and the name Topaze had become the synonym for a shady politician working the levers in the control room.

In the printing-works quarter when I spent half the week, I could feel the mounting hatred of the thousands of workers hit by the exaggeratedly deflationist policy of the governments of the day. Wages were low, dismissals a daily occurrence, and France was submerged by a flood of strikes. Conversation in the cafés was no longer peaceable and smiling. Drivers and porters, all communist or socialist, appeared to be preparing for the struggle.

Summer was with us again; my friends had gone off on holiday and I was alone in Paris. It was Sunday, and I had gone to work as usual. Everybody was talking about the death sentence on Sacco and Vanzetti, two Italian anarchists considered innocent by the greater part of public opinion. A torrent of protest was reaching Washington from every country in Europe. Writers and scientists were addressing petitions, Labour leaders in Paris were organizing protest meetings, and the police were tired out. The city lived in an atmosphere of barricades.

I had worked till after midnight, and was going to the railway station as usual to send the proofs to London. Walking in a little dark street with one of my mates at the printing works, I suddenly noticed that the street was barred and we were surrounded by policemen. One of these, with a revolver in his belt and a white truncheon in his hand, called out, 'Halt!' I stood still, and by the uncertain light of the street lamps I discerned a number of pedestrians who had been caught like myself in the round-up.

'What are you doing at this time of night?' he asked.

'Coming back from my work.'

'At one in the morning? Identity card!' His tone was imperious. I put my hand in my jacket pocket, and my blood froze. The pocket was empty. I had changed my jacket that morning, and my yellow identity card was still in my old suit. I had nothing on me, no document to identify me except a cheque that had come from London that morning. I tried to explain what had happened, but the policeman paid no attention. I was seized and pushed into the prison van, crushed against a mass of sweating, groaning men, trampling on their feet and having my own trampled on. The crowded van started off.

At the police station I was flung into a crowd of other detainees. Black delivery vans brought in their human loads one after another: workers in dirty caps, prostitutes tearing their hair and howling to the echo, tramps picked up from the seats along the boulevards, and mere frightened pedestrians. The room was too small to hold all this humanity, but I elbowed my way to the table where a sergeant was entering our names in a file. I tried to explain that I was the victim of a mistake. I was a student, and a British subject, and my identity card was in a drawer at my hotel. I demanded to be allowed to ring up my friends. He tossed me an indifferent glance and said, 'Shut up!' I protested all the more. He shouted furiously, 'Hold your jaw!' and added an oath. As I still persisted, I suddenly found myself being lifted towards the ceiling and let fall again, with my breath stopped. On recovering it I drew in the reek of the crowd around me—sweat, dirt, cheap scent. Black rings danced before my eyes. I tried to sit down, but there was no room; we were now standing shoulder to shoulder, foot to foot.

At daybreak we were removed from our police station and driven through the empty streets. An old tart dozed on the seat opposite me, a workman with a drooping moustache stuck the fag end of a cigarette in the corner of his mouth, muttering, 'Ah, the swine! The swine!' A bored policeman kept an eye on us, while the van drove a long way through the streets. Between the window bars I caught sight of a bridge over the Seine. An enormous gate opened and shut: the Palais de Justice.

I spent the whole day in a big room with barred windows, in the company of suspects of every kind: thieves, vagabonds and innocent pedestrians fallen into the nets of the round-up. I had nothing to eat, having no money in my pocket except the wretched cheque from Lloyds Bank, otherwise I could have bought some bread, like my fellow detainees. From time to time I was called upon to state my identity, and my renewed protests produced a volley of abuse. Photographed in profile and full-face, finger-prints taken, I saw myself in for a long spell in jug.

At last a police officer in mufti called out my name, looked at a file he was holding, and told me a copy of my identity card had been found in the files at police headquarters. I started to protest against the treatment I had undergone, but the officer said kindly, 'My young friend, you may thank your stars that you have nothing worse to complain of than these few hours of incarceration. Remember in future that one doesn't go about the streets of Paris these days without one's identity card. Be more careful, and try not to fall into our hands again.'

I was reminded of this episode many years later when I was

Israeli Ambassador in Paris. I was invited to attend the inaugura-
tion of the Place Léon Blum. Guy Mollet, then Prime Minister,
was sitting on the platform, surrounded by his ministers. President Vincent Auriol, likewise an old socialist, delivered his
speech, rolling his Toulouse 'r's. The platform was crowded by
socialist leaders, the Ambassador of Israel being the only diplomat
present. Looking round me, I suddenly felt a sensation of *déjà
vu*. This square surrounded by sooty walls, this massive building looming up before me, when had I seen them before? It was
one of the many town halls of the city, a building of no origin-
ality, in *fin de siècle* style. Near the entrance gate, below the
wide steps, I caught sight of a narrow doorway surmounted by
a blue lamp bearing the word 'Police'. Suddenly I remembered.
This was the police station where I had been shut up after a
round-up, in that far-off summer of my youth.

VI

Having at last completed his mission, my father spent a few
days in Paris with us on his way back to Tel-Aviv. The depression from which he had suffered after Mother's death had
gradually given way to his habitual pleasure in life. He had
recovered his balance, and recovered too from bouts of illness
during the winter that had caused him a great deal of pain, to
which he was very sensitive. He had all sorts of details to give us
of his travels and his meetings with old friends. Speaking hardly
any French, he felt tongue-tied in the streets of Paris, but this
did not prevent him from coming home every day loaded with
presents. He bought everything that caught his fancy, and
opened the parcels with the radiant expression of a child preparing a surprise. We knew he could not really afford such
generosity, and would have great difficulties to face on his
return, and we implored him with the seriousness of young
people beginning to assume responsibility—not to squander his
money. We had at last to confiscate his wallet, leaving him only
enough for his fares.

He was hatching plans for the future once more, and associat-
ing me with his dreams as usual. His book *The Day Dawns* had
just been published in Palestine, a collection of articles published
earlier at various times. He had always had it in mind to do

this, distressed by the ephemeral character of his writings, scattered among old newspapers. Unfortunately the Jerusalem press that had printed the book was so deeply in debt that its whole output had been seized by the creditors. Then in Warsaw he had signed a contract for a new edition of his historical work *The Bné-Moshé and their Times*, and the book was soon due to appear. But for some reason it had not yet been printed, and this was a further source of anxiety. When we were all together he would talk to us of his intention to engage in research on the sources of the Talmud, a considerable undertaking that would entail a great deal of preparation. When would he find time for this? And how would he manage to support his family?

Sometimes when he analysed his situation, or on his return from a disappointing visit to some wealthy man on whose assistance he had counted, he appeared worried and melancholy, but he soon recovered. Most of the time he was cheerful, joking with us and our friends, and going to a café with the lot of us. One evening he even consented to go to a cinema—for the first and last time in his life—but he fell asleep at the beginning of the film and only woke up at the sound of the drum in the little orchestra, marking the end of the performance.

We went with him to the station, where he took the train to Genoa. Nearly all my friends were there, for they all loved him. As the train drew away from the platform we saw his smiling face for the last time at the window, and the hat he was waving in farewell. A week later his first letter reached us from Tel-Aviv, joyful and happy as usual.

The family was installed in a large apartment again. The furniture had been taken out of store and the books out of their packing-cases. The children were deep in their school work; my sister was preparing for her school-leaving exams, and they both spent most of their time with their school friends. Back at last at his desk, my father had started writing again with the passion of a man of letters long separated from his calling. Newspapers in Palestine and abroad were publishing his inspiring reports on the towns and villages he had visited in the course of his official tour, on the people he had met and the communities which he had visited, the problems and education of youth. Even today, as I turn over those articles, cut out and preserved in old files, a lively picture springs to light, full of his love for the communities to which he had given something of his own soul on his brief passage through them.

All that year he had only very minor work to do, and as he felt full of vigour he sought an outlet for his unemployed energies by devoting himself again, body and soul, to the professional interests of the Writers' Association, and to the weekly paper, *Mosznaim*, which had at last begun to appear. He had great hopes of this fresh platform, which was soon to attract the best writers of the country, and even those still resident abroad, inaugurating a new era in the history of Hebrew letters.

Time passed quickly, and once again a burning hot summer fell upon Paris. A Zionist Congress was held again in Basle, and everybody predicted that it would prove a turning-point in the history of the Zionist Movement, because it was going to set up the Jewish Agency from which Weizmann expected such great results, in spite of the obstinate opposition on the part of Itshak Grunbaum and his young disciple Nahum Goldmann. The news from the Jewish Telegraphic Agency that I translated for the *Haolam* announced that the non-Zionist Jewish philanthropists of the United States, headed by the great Louis Marshal, were prepared to assume financial responsibility for the building up of the country, which would put an end, once and for all, to our economic difficulties. Palestine would be able to reopen its gates to massive immigration. Opinions were divided between the prophets of doom and the inveterate optimists, who were forever fighting one another in newspaper articles, while my father wrote enthusiastic letters about the great days awaiting the country and the first signs of recovery that were beginning to make themselves felt.

I stayed in Paris alone again that summer, my wife having gone to spend the vacation with her parents in Kovno. My friends were scattered, and the leading Zionists were in Basle for the Congress. The Bibliothèque Nationale, where I used to study, was closed for the summer, and I stayed almost all day in my hotel room, perspiring in the heat of Paris and trying to concentrate on my university work.

One morning someone knocked at my door. The landlord himself had come up to the third floor to hand me a letter and a telegram. The handwriting on the envelope was my father's, but the telegram, signed by my sister, said 'Return immediately'. I opened the envelope with a trembling hand, hoping to find the explanation of the mystery. It was a long missive, in which my father told me a lot of things about Tel-Aviv, and announced his intention of going abroad for a year's study of European languages, and to make contact with the great press of the world in quest of correspondents in Palestine. Then he could at last devote himself to literature without having to think of his daily bread.

I clung to the slender hope that there might be some mistake. The letter was undoubtedly from my father. How could misfortune have befallen him in the few days since he had posted it?

I ran to the post office to send a telegram expressing my astonishment, and spent a sleepless night trying to convince myself that it was all a mistake. It seemed incredible that a man should end so suddenly, almost before the ink on his notepaper had dried. I got ready to start, still under the senseless conviction that something must happen, that I should suddenly be told it was all a terrible mistake. Nevertheless I went out to look for one of my few friends left in town, ran into one, and asked him to take my place at the newspaper office as he had done once or twice before. For further safety I went to some Paris acquaintances and borrowed some money from them for my travelling expenses. I came back reassured, persuaded that everything was going to be cleared up. But hardly had the hotel door opened when the porter handed me a fresh telegram, in French this time, and in unequivocal terms: 'Expecting your immediate return'.

On the ferry boat crossing the Suez Canal I met a passenger from Palestine with a newspaper in his hand. On the front page, framed in black, was a photograph of my father. I remained alone all that night, beside the window of the train, looking at the white sand of the desert. When dawn appeared, the sun shone on the red roofs and green orange-trees of the first villages of my country.

Index

Index